TRANSACTION PROCESSING SYSTEMS

PRENTICE HALL
ADVANCES IN COMPUTER SCIENCE SERIES
Editor: Richard P. Brent

Gough & Mohay	*Modula-2: A Second Course in Programming*
Hille	*Data Abstraction and Program Development using Pascal*
	Data Abstraction and Program Development using Modula-2
Rankin	*Computer Graphics Software Construction*
Seberry & Pieprzyk	*Cryptography: Introduction to Computer Security*
Maciaszek	*Data Design and Implementation*
Cady & Howarth	*Computer System Performance Management and Capacity Planning*
Newmarch	*Logic Programming: Prolog and Stream Parallel Languages*

TRANSACTION PROCESSING SYSTEMS

E. V. KRISHNAMURTHY

Australian National University
Canberra, Australia

&

V. K. MURTHY

Fujitsu Australia Software Technology Ltd
Sydney, Australia

PRENTICE HALL

New York London Toronto Sydney Tokyo Singapore

1 2 3 4 5 95 94 93 92 91

Typeset in Australia by Adtype Graphics Pty Ltd, North Sydney, NSW
Printed and bound in Australia by Macarthur Press Pty Ltd, Parramatta, NSW

ISBN 0-13-928128-2

National Library of Australia
Cataloguing-in-Publication Data

Krishnamurthy, E. V.
Transaction processing systems.

Bibliography
Includes index.

ISBN 0-13-928128-2

1. Transaction systems (Computer systems). I. Murthy, V. K. II. Title.

005.74

Library of Congress
Cataloguing-in-Publication Data

Krishnamurthy, E. V.
Transaction processing systems / E.V. Krishnamurthy and V.K. Murthy.
Includes bibliographical references and index.
ISBN 0-13-928128-2 : $40.00
1. Transaction systems (Computer systems) I. Murthy, V. K. II. Title.
QA76.545.K75 1991
004' ,3--dc20 91–25217
CIP

Prentice Hall, Inc., *Englewood Cliffs, New Jersey*
Prentice Hall Canada, Inc., *Toronto*
Prentice Hall Hispanoamericana, SA, *Mexico*
Prentice Hall of India Private Ltd, *New Delhi*
Prentice Hall International, Inc., *London*
Prentice Hall of Japan, Inc., *Tokyo*
Prentice Hall of Southeast Asia Pty Ltd, *Singapore*
Editora Prentice Hall do Brasil Ltda, *Rio de Janeiro*

PRENTICE HALL

A division of Simon & Schuster

Contents

Preface

This book introduces the principles and practice of transaction processing. Research and development in this field have been very active in the last decade, as indicated by the enormous variety of technical papers, articles and commercial products. It is a particularly fascinating field, being a blend of operations research, computer, communication, information and database engineering, computer science and formal logic. All the topics covered in this book have been taught at senior undergraduate and graduate level.

The work is intended for serious study by university students in computer, information and management sciences as well as by computer and database professionals. It is not a book of buzzwords but a text requiring close attention. Style and presentation have been kept simple so as to initiate readers unfamiliar with this area and to provide a good background for advanced study and for professional development.

Chapter 1 presents an overview of cooperating computers and user services, which is followed in Chapter 2 by a discussion of the basic aspects of transactions, their properties and representational schema. In Chapter 3 we deal with transactions performing at a central site which give rise to localized schedules. The most important concurrency control mechanisms, such as locks, timestamps and certifiers, are described in great detail in Chapter 4; and the distributed or multisite schedules and methods for dealing with them are discussed in Chapter 5. The important topic of designing resilient or fault-tolerant schedules is the subject of Chapter 6, and is followed in Chapter 7 by a description of some important commercial and prototype operational transaction processing systems. Finally, the use of microcomputers as a platform for transaction processing is outlined in Chapter 8. Exercises are provided at the end of each chapter, as is a set of important references for further study.

It is difficult to write a book of this type without deriving many valuable ideas from various sources — published articles, manuals and freely circulating commercial pamphlets. Since some of the proprietary products were not available in a detailed form the readers are advised to contact the vendors (addresses given in Appendix) for further details where the information given in this book is incomplete. The authors do not accept responsibility for any inaccurate information about these products.

The authors wish to state that the material contained in this book is entirely scientific in nature and is presented with a view to disseminating knowledge to all academics and professionals interested in this subject. They also wish to state that the book represents neither the views nor the commercial interests of the organizations in which they are employed.

Finally, the authors express their indebtedness to Richard Brent of the

Australian National University, Andrew Binnie and Gillian Gillett of Prentice Hall Australia, and freelance editor Graham Grayston, for their help and friendly advice throughout this project.

In addition, the second author thanks Zen Loy, Bruce Rankin, Hajime Yoshioka, Masahiko Fujita and other colleagues in Fujitsu for the interest they showed in this work.

1 Cooperating computers: building user services

1.1 INTRODUCTION

Increasing the productivity of a computer system by maximizing speed, efficiency and reliability is the major goal of computer science and technology. Over the last decade great efforts have been made in order to achieve that goal. They have produced greater processor speeds through the development of very large scale integrated circuit technology (VLSI); very large expanding memory capacity with fast access by way of virtual storage and cache techniques; and greater bandwidth in message transmission as a result of developments in communication network technology, for example fibre-optic cables and satellite channels — all at reasonably low cost. On the basis of those new technologies, computer scientists and engineers have developed new fundamental techniques for organizing, coupling and controlling a very large number of cooperating processors for parallel, concurrent and distributed processing.

Although there are numerous taxonomic approaches for classifying parallel, concurrent and distributed processors, it is adequate from a practical standpoint to classify cooperating processing systems into three broad categories:

1. *Parallel processing system.* Typically, the following processors belong to this category: vector-array processors, super computers and systolic processors. They consist of hundreds or even thousands of identical (or homogeneous) processors, each capable of only a few simple instructions, tightly coupled through hardware with a suitable topology (such as a mesh, hypercube, butterfly, shuffle-exchange, cylinder or torus) so that adjacent processors can communicate through shared memory. The sharing of data and processing in these systems are synchronously controlled by a clock to realize massively parallel computations. In these systems the time for communication between processors is less than the time taken for a typical computation step.
2. *Multiprocessing system.* Typically, this system consists of tens of identical (or homogeneous) processors integrated by hardware into one centralized system and sharing a common memory or a virtual address space. The time for communication between processors is less than the time taken for a typical computation step.
3. *Distributed processing system.* This system consists of tens or hundreds of

not necessarily identical (heterogeneous) processors, each capable of performing a task of different size asynchronously, loosely coupled through a network, such as a ring, a bus or a telephone line, satellite channels, fibre-optic cables or microwave links. The time for communication between processors may be greater than the time for carrying out a typical computation task.

Since the above systems and their areas of application are quite well known and are widely discussed in introductory books on parallel processing and distributed processing (Krishnamurthy 1989; Crichlow 1988; Coulouris and Dollimore 1988), we will only discuss them briefly.

The parallel processing system is essentially for scientific computation where number crunching or matrix problems are involved, while the multiprocessing system is well suited to centralized data processing. However, other real-life applications, such as commercial and banking operations and airline reservations, which depend heavily on file and database processing at several centres or sites, require a distributed processing system. In this type of system, not only the computers but also other vital and expensive hardware and software resources are connected through a network for on-line access, thus permitting interaction among many users and computers at different geographic sites.

The computers in the network on which the users run the application programs are called 'hosts'. Usually, two different types of networks are used: local area networks (LANs), which operate within a limited local area, such as a college campus; and wide area networks (WANs), or long-haul networks, which cover a larger geographic region, such as Australasia.

In a LAN each computer is directly connected to another through a specific topology (such as a ring, star, tree or mesh) without requiring any routing. A good example of a LAN is the Ethernet. A WAN, however, needs to use a routing system because of the varying volume of information traffic, the heterogeneous nature of hosts, the presence of multiple possible paths that provide redundancy, and reliability requirements. An example of a WAN is the ARPANET in the United States (see Tanenbaum 1988; Stallings 1988; Halsall 1988).

These networks thus enable interhost data transfer, communication and computation. Hence different processes can be carried out simultaneously at different hosts, thus gaining speed and increasing productivity. Also, if a host fails, another host can take over the work; this provides for fault tolerance and reliability.

1.2 SOFTWARE INTERFACE

In a large network of processors, we need to coordinate and control the user–host and interhost interactions; that is, we need to build a software interface that will control the resources provided by the computers and act as an intermediary between the users and computers. This interface is called the *operating system* (see Deitel 1990; Bach 1986; Maekawa et al. 1987).

Before the operating system was developed for the uniprocessor, there was only a uniprogramming environment in which only one user was permitted at a time. Much of the processor time remained underutilized, since there was a great difference in speed between the processor and input-output devices. The evolution of the concepts of multiprogramming and time-sharing permitted more than one program to run simultaneously from different user terminals; this provided the required interactive environment for the users. The concept of virtual storage provided a means of expanding computer main storage by allowing the computer directly to access outside storage devices as though they formed part of the main storage itself. All these developments necessitated the design of more powerful and complex operating systems with several important supervisory functions: resource management, memory management, processor management, devices management and information/file management, including security and protection of files. The development of operating systems is thus crucial for increasing the productivity of the computer system.

Since an operating system is built around the basic instructions of the bare machine, it provides many more instructions than the basic hardware instructions. The total set of these instructions is called the 'extended machine'. It is convenient to build the operating system around a basic set of services, called a 'kernel', 'core' or 'nucleus'. This set represents a very small portion of the code of the entire operating system, but it is among the most intensively used. Usually it has the following functions:

1. interrupt handling;
2. process creation and destruction;
3. state transitions of processes;
4. process suspension and resumption;
5. process synchronization;
6. interprocess communication;
7. input-output control;
8. support for storage allocation/deallocation;
9. support for file systems;
10. support for procedure calls.

The higher layers of the operating system are then built around this kernel so that each outer layer can call on the services of all the inner layers.

When processes are created by the operating system so that the parent process and the child process share some or all the variables and address spaces, we call them 'lightweight processes'. A kernel which provides a lightweight process is called a 'lightweight kernel'.

1.3 TRANSPARENCY ISSUES

The operating system is supposed to be transparent to the users; that is, its actions and the hardware actions are to be concealed from the users. When the design of the operating system was extended from the uniprocessor to a multiprocessor, the users' tasks still communicated through shared variables and tables as in the uniprocessor. It was therefore possible to design a centralized multiprocessor operating system so that the users could have the impression that they were still working with a 'virtual uniprocessor'.

However, extending the design of a uniprocessor to a large distributed network of computers, achieving transparency (so that the users see a 'virtual uniprocessor' rather than a collection of distinct processors) is not easy (see Tanenbaum and van Renesse 1985. Eight forms of transparency have been identified by ANSA (1987). These are:

1. access transparency, which permits local and remote files to be accessed by using identical operations;
2. location transparency, which permits objects to be accessed without explicit knowledge of their location;
3. concurrency transparency, which permits several users to access shared files, while at the same time maintaining exclusivity and preserving the consistency of the files;
4. replication transparency, which permits the use of multiple copies or versions of files without the users being aware of them;
5. failure transparency, which tolerates hardware and software faults and operates across them or recovers without the users being aware;
6. migration transparency, which permits data objects to be moved across the network without affecting the performance of the user's program;
7. performance transparency, which permits the system to undergo reconfiguration under varying load conditions in order to achieve load balance;
8. scaling transparency, which permits expansion of the system and applications with no change in the structure of the system and the algorithms used.

Four kinds of models have been suggested for building the distributed systems using a LAN:

1. *Workstation/server model.* Here each user has a single powerful computer (called a 'workstation') in which application programs are executed. Such a system can support a global file system providing location and access transparency for files. A typical example of a practical system based on this model is the Sun Network file system that uses BSD 4.2.UNIX (see Coulouris and Dollimore 1988; Tanenbaum and van Renesse 1985).
2. *Processor pool model.* Here a pool of processors provide a service for the execution of programs. Each user has a terminal and interacts with the pool. The users are allocated additional processors whenever more computing power is needed; otherwise, the additional processors go back to the pool to serve some other waiting process. Hence access, concurrency and failure transparencies are provided. The Cambridge University Distributed File System is an example of this model. It provides for access, concurrency and failure transparencies for file system manipulation.
3. *Hybrid model.* Since this model is a combination of the workstation model

and pool model, it can provide access, location, concurrency and failure transparencies. If files are replicated, replication transparency is also possible. The Amoeba system designed by the Vrije University of Amsterdam is an example of this type. It provides for all transparencies except migration, performance and scaling transparencies.

4. *Integrated model.* This model is suitable for a heterogeneous network of single-user and multiuser computers. Each computer is provided with adequate software to function as a server as well as an application processor. Since file naming is global and programs can be run in any machine, a file can be taken from one computer and loaded into another computer to run using software available from a third computer. Hence all required transparencies are provided. The LOCUS system, developed by the University of California at Los Angeles, is an example of this model. It provides all the transparencies for file system manipulation except the performance and scaling transparencies.

1.4 COMMUNICATION-ORIENTED OPERATING SYSTEMS

Since the distributed operating system needs to communicate between different computers and processes, as well as transfer files, facilities should be provided for passing messages without sharing memory. They can be in the form of send and receive primitives used in the programming language known as Communicating Sequential Processes (CSP) and its derivative occam, or Remote Procedure Call (RPC), used in the programming language Ada. These facilities are described below:

1. Handshake

Here, the send and receive primitives are used for communication. They can, for instance, be used to send a message to a destination and to acknowledge the receipt of a message. This form of two-way communication in which a process passes on a message and the receiver acknowledges it is called a 'handshake'.

2. Remote procedure call

The remote procedure call provides for a stronger form of communication than does the 'handshake'. In the latter the receiver only acknowledges the arrival of the message and the sender then proceeds further. In the remote procedure call, however, the sender waits until the receiver sends a reply after executing a specific task requested by the sender. The remote procedure call can therefore be used to realize a model popularly known as the 'client-server model', in which the client requests a server to perform a task of which it is capable and waits until the server completes the task and returns the required result.

The client-server model splits the information management function of the operating system into two components: a front end (client), where the data is manipulated and displayed; and a back end (server), where data is stored and accessed. The users interact only with the client directly through a program, and not with the server. The client has no direct access to the data; it is the server that provides connections to the data. Thus the client and the server can be different machines; and this makes it possible to handle a heterogeneous network and at the same time provides user transparency to the file transfer and the execution of programs.

A major advantage of using the client-server model concerns concurrent file and database processing. A single server can serve many clients in an interleaved manner, and multiple servers can serve multiple clients in the same manner as long as there are no conflicts in access of data. Thus a high degree of concurrency can be achieved, accompanied by increased productivity.

Another desirable feature is the insulation provided to protect the data from being corrupted by the client, since the server receives the commands, checks the privileges of the user, verifies syntax, checks the availability of objects and executes operations. In addition, fault tolerance is provided more easily in this approach, as a failed server can be replaced by another server without the user being aware of it. Thus in the design of the distributed operating system all the required transparencies can be achieved through the use of the client-server model.

Furthermore, it is important to know that a server can become a client of another server and so on recursively. Also, in general the notion of client-server need not be an asymmetric relation: it can be symmetric or each process can call the other.

A very early, but very important practical intersystem communication tool that exhibits the client-server concept is the widely used special-purpose operating system known as CICS (Customer Information Control System), developed by IBM for uniprocessor systems. Its main function is to control the execution of on-line applications which are requested by the end-users at the terminals. When the user wants to execute an application program, CICS activates it at another site. CICS also provides for 'function shipping', which consists of sending a single data access primitive to a remote site. Thus if one wants to access data at one site from another site, this can be done through function shipping. Hence access transparency is provided by CICS. (We will deal with CICS in Chapter 7.)

1.5 FILE AND TRANSACTION SERVICES

A file is a named collection of data objects, and is usually stored on disk or tape. Important file operations are: open, close, create, destroy, copy, rename, list, read, write, insert, delete, update.

A file service system is a very important component of an operating system. It is generally concerned with methods of storing and accessing data, mechanisms for sharing and referencing data, management of storage space, and maintaining the integrity of files so that they are not corrupted. A file service system consists of three basic services:

1. *Block service.* This service provides for allocation of disk blocks and provides operations for storing and retrieving them.

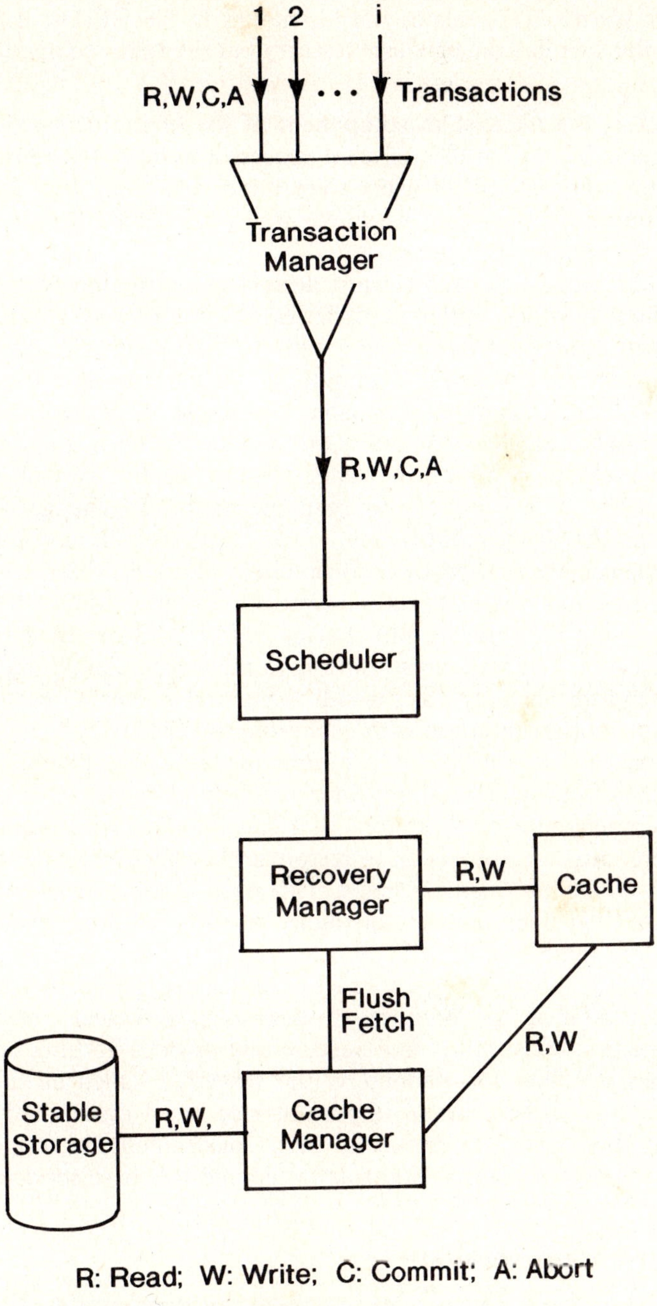

Figure 1.1 Centralized database management system

2. *File service.* Unique file identifiers (UFIDs) are used for referring to files; only client programs with the correct UFID can access, and read or write the file data.
3. *Directory service.* This relates the file names to file UFIDs; it also checks whether the user has the privilege to carry out the required operation on the file.

In the 1970s, the file system component of the operating system generally stored and managed all the files of a uniprocessor system. On multiuser time-sharing systems the files of all users were under the control of a centralized operating system; all these files were essentially 'mutable'; that is, subject to modification by update operations.

Recently, the trend has been toward designing distributed file systems that can handle files in widely different varieties of computer systems at different sites, each with a different operating system and file system. A distributed file system enables the user to access a remote file for performing operations. Consequently, it is more convenient and safer to provide 'immutable' files (that is, ones that cannot be readily corrupted). Once the file has been created, an update creates a new version retaining the older version. Such a system is useful in many cases where it is necessary to keep the history of changes in files and provide for recovery from failures.

When a file service is used by a single client at a site, there is no problem about the reading and writing of data from files. However, when a large number of clients are using file services and sharing data in a distributed system, side effects may arise in their programs resulting in inconsistent or wrong data on the files. It is therefore necessary to provide ways and means to ensure that the client programs do not interfere with each other destructively.

A commonsense approach for avoiding inconsistency due to interaction among clients is to provide facilities for each client to have exclusivity (mutual exclusion) of a sequence of operations that can interfere with other clients. In addition, there must be a provision to restore a file whenever a client or a server suddenly fails in the intermediate stages. This means that every client and server should execute their operations either totally or not at all thus ensuring consistency. If they are unable to do this because of their failure or because of some other fault, the file should be restored by another server to its original state before the execution of the failed set of operations. A sequence of actions that runs to completion consistently and successfully or does nothing under failure (since the partial effects are undone by the server) is called an *atomic transaction.* Such transactions play an important role in all distributed computing systems, and they form the backbone of a constrained file service called a *transaction service* that plays a vital role in file and database services.

1.5.1 Transaction service

A transaction service is a file service that supports atomic transactions in some or all the files. In a distributed system where a large number of users are present at different sites, the key issue in the design of a transaction service is to increase the degree of concurrency and at the same time ensure that all file operations are consistent when atomic transactions are completed or that the file is restored when there are failures. The successful completion of an atomic transaction results in a state called 'committed', while the failed transaction results in a state called 'aborted'. These two states are mutually exclusive with respect to any one transaction.

When we deal with a client-server organization, the aborted state can result owing to the client's or the server's failure. It is the server's duty to restore the file to its original state; this complex process is called 'recovery'. It is a time-consuming operation, intensive in its use of hardware, software and communication, when a large number of transactions abort at different sites. This is because it is necessary to record the history of events that have taken place from the beginning. This history, which is called a 'log', is stored in a stable storage (such as a disk which retains its contents when power fails) as the transactions progress.

The log contains the information on the identifier of the transaction, the identifier of the record, the action carried out, the value of the record before and after the action, and a reference to the previous log of the transaction. Thus using this information we can 'undo' all actions done by transactions which failed to commit; and also 'redo' all actions for committed transactions whose values are not yet written in stable storage but are lost from a volatile storage (such as a cache which does not retain its contents when power fails). Obviously, recovery requires facilities that control data transfer among the different types of storages. The recovery actions certainly reduce the degree of concurrency that can be achieved.

A file service provided with recovery facilities is said to be a 'robust' or 'durable' file service; otherwise, it is called a 'traditional file service'. A robust file service ensures that changes made to a file are not lost in the event of a failure. Two interacting modules called a 'recovery manager' and a 'cache manager' play an important role in recovery; together, they are known as a 'data manager'. To the outside world, however, only the recovery manager is visible, since it controls the cache manager (see Figure 1.1).

The recovery manager ensures that the stable storage contains all and only the effects of committed transactions and none from failed transactions. Thus if a failed transaction has written a value in the stable storage, the recovery manager should 'undo' it. Also, if a transaction has committed before writing in the stable storage, and this information is lost from the volatile storage, the recovery manager must 'redo' the actions of the transaction and ensure that they are recorded in the stable storage.

The cache manager, on the other hand, is responsible for fetching an item from the stable storage and transferring it to the cache (an operation called 'fetch'), and it can also transfer a copy of an item from the cache to the stable storage (an operation called 'flush').

Since the log record contains the required information for 'redo' and 'undo', it should be reliable. This means that we must avoid any failure that can happen between the two independent actions: database update and log write-up. For this purpose, two safety rules known as the 'log write-ahead protocol' are used:

1. Before updating the value of a committed transaction by an uncommitted transaction, record the old value in the log.
2. Before committing a transaction, ensure that its value is already written in the log.

To implement a transaction service we need two other modules: a 'transaction manager' and a 'scheduler' (see Figure 1). The transaction manager receives the file operations and forwards them to a scheduler which controls the concurrency of execution of transactions. The scheduler restricts the order in which the data manager performs read, write, commit and abort so that consistency is achieved. It can reject an operation, thus leading to an aborted transaction. Using the terminology of the client-server model, we may compare the transaction to the client (or front end) and the transaction manager, scheduler and data manager to the server (or back end).

The system that supports a transaction service which ensures atomicity, concurrency and recovery is called a transaction management system and can form part of a file system in an operating system or a database system.

1.6 DATABASE TRANSACTION SERVICES

A database is a structured collection of interrelated data stored in the stable storage of a computer system. In file systems each application program maintains its own files, often with considerable redundancy. In a database the different separate files are usually integrated; that is, the files are unified and redundancies are partially or wholly eliminated. Thus a centralized control is imposed over the data, which is an advantage from the point of view of maintaining consistency of files, since data duplicates need not be taken care of. On the other hand, the integration of files results in several users wanting to access the same piece of data concurrently. This must be permitted in such a way that the users' programs do not interact unfavorably, thus causing inconsistency of files.

A database that is located at a single site is called a centralized database. If several centralized databases at a number of sites are linked by a computer network, this collection is called a distributed database. Three kinds of models are used to build a database (see Date 1986; Hughes 1988):

1. a hierarchical model;
2. a network model;
3. a relational model.

The hierarchical model represents the information in a hierarchy with logical records of information having subrecords which themselves may have subrecords, and so on, thus resembling a rooted tree.The network model uses a graph (connected or disconnected) to represent the inherent relations among the different data entities, while the relational model uses tables to represent the relations among those entities.

Very early commercial systems used the hierarchical model (e.g. the IMS System, System 2000) or the network model (e.g. CODASYL). Currently, however, the relational model (e.g. INGRES, ORACLE, DATABASE 2 (DB2), RDB II) is gaining importance, since it supports the distribution of the database at different sites through fragmentation of relations and provides for 'fragmentation transparency' and, as a consequence, can support distributed query and transaction services (see Date 1986; Valduriez and Gardarin 1989).

For a given model, the language of the high-level operations of the database model is called the query language. Employing this language, users can access and manipulate the database directly. Usually, conventional programming languages can be used to write programs.

The computer program that interfaces between the user and the database is called a database management system (DBMS). Since the DBMS provides all the facilities for file maintenance as well as query facilities for the information stored on the files, it has to use the basic services of the operating systems and build on them.

The building of the file management system and the DBMS have many features in common. In fact, the concurrency feature is absolutely essential in the DBMS whether the database is centralized or distributed. This is a consequence of the integration of all the files while the database is being created. As a result, the data is shared among different users, who may thus have to access concurrently the same data object or sets of data objects having an overlap. We therefore need to build a transaction service on the database. This requires special mechanisms that preserve exclusivity or atomicity of transactions and achieve consistency when logically or hierarchically related files are handled by different clients. Such mechanisms are called 'concurrency control mechanisms', and they provide support for the concurrency transparency. It is easier to design them for a centralized database system than for a distributed database system because in the latter case we need to consider the complexity as well as reliability of communication between several sites.

The DBMS has the following functional components:

1. buffer management;
2. file management;
3. query management;
4. security management;
5. transaction management.

Since all these components except query management are available on the operating system, a DBMS can be conveniently built on the top of a suitable operating system. In the next section we will deal with the basic principles of the design of the operating system.

1.7 DISTRIBUTED OPERATING AND FILE SYSTEMS

To design an operating system for cooperating processors in a network, we use two different approaches: the top-layer network-software approach and the distributed (or kernel-redesign) approach.

1. The top-layer network-software approach

This approach is simpler than the distributed approach and is usually intended for an identical or compatible set of machines. This set usually consists of a collection of identical personal computers or other compatible computers linked by a local area network. As the name indicates, the top-layer network-software operating system is built on the top of an already existing local operating system in each machine. This means that the existing kernel on which the higher layers are dependent remains unchanged. The new top layer takes care of the routing of the system calls — local or remote — through 'handshake' or remote procedure calls.

2. The distributed (or kernel-redesign) approach

Since the top-layer approach is not usually very efficient in providing all the eight required transparencies, it is necessary to design a totally new operating system, with a new distributed kernel, that can provide them. Such a kernel has functions for communication and migration of processes.

1.7.1 Examples of top-layer network software systems

1. *Newcastle Connection*: This system adds network management capabilities and remote procedure call facilities to UNIX through a top-layer on the UNIX kernel. It provides only access transparency for files (Shrivastava 1985).
2. *Sun Network File System*: This system, which evolved from the Newcastle Connection, uses BSD 4.2 UNIX and is a workstation model (Coulouris and Dollimore 1988). It provides for location and access transparencies of files.

1.7.2 Examples of distributed operating and file systems

1. *Cambridge University Distributed File System*. As already mentioned, this system is a pool model consisting of processors and servers. It provides for access, concurrency and failure transparencies.
2. *Accent Distributed Operating System*. This system was developed by Carnegie-Mellon University; it has a message-passing kernel.
3. *V-kernel*. This system was developed by Stanford University. It belongs to the workstation model, since the kernel supports a client–server model.
4. *Amoeba*. This system, which was developed by the Vrije University and CWI, both of Amsterdam, uses a message-passing kernel and provides for all transparencies except migration, performance and scaling. It belongs to the hybrid pool-workstation model.

5. *LOCUS*. This system was developed by the University of California at Los Angeles. It is closely related to UNIX, and provides for all transparencies except performance and scaling. It belongs to the integrated model.
6. *Apollo Domain*. This system, which was designed by Apollo Computer Incorporated, provides for all transparencies other than replication, failure, performance and scaling. It belongs to the integrated model.
7. *Xerox Distributed File System*. This system, which was developed by the Xerox Corporation, provides for transparencies other than replication, migration, performance and scaling. It belongs to the workstation model.

1.7.3 Client-server DBMS systems

Some of the recent database systems, such as Sybase, INGRES and ORACLE, use different forms of client-server models and different kinds of mechanisms to achieve concurrency transparency.

Sybase uses a multiclient single-server model in which the actions of the clients are interleaved; that is, the control used by the single server is multithreaded.

Ingres uses a multiclient multiserver model in which each server has multiple clients and has a multithread control. It is designed to operate on both LANs (Ethernet) and WANs (ARPANET). It provides for location transparency (so that the total database, though physically dispersed, appears as a set of local relational tables), as well as for replication and concurrency transparency. Thus it is suitable for distributed transaction processing.

ORACLE uses multiple client-server pairs in which each server has a single client and a single thread of control.

The design of a transaction management system that achieves consistency by eliminating side effects, ensures atomicity of actions on data items and provides a robust service for recovery from failures is a very complex and interesting area of study. How such a system can be designed for a centralized or a distributed database system in order to achieve maximal productivity is the main subject matter we will be studying in this book.

EXERCISES

These exercises are intended to widen the reader's background knowledge of transaction processing in hardware, software and database systems. References are provided to assist the reader with topics not covered by this book.

1. Explain the difference between tight and loose coupling of computers (Krishnamurthy 1989).
2. Why is tight coupling needed for a large parallel processing system with thousands of interconnected processors (Krishnamurthy 1989)?
3. What are the commonly used topologies for LAN? Study the transmission speed, number of devices supported and the medium used (Stallings 1988).

4. What is a kernel of an operating system? Study the kernel of the UNIX operating system. Study how the Newcastle Connection extends a uniprocessor UNIX system to distributed processing (Shrivastava 1985; Bach 1986).
5. Explain the difference between ordinary non-database file systems and database systems (Date 1986).
6. What is a monitor? How is it useful for operating system design? (Krishnamurthy, 1989; Maekawa et al. 1987).
7. What is meant by 'atomicity of actions'? Explain this concept with respect to the semaphore mechanism. How does this notion of atomicity extend to a transaction (Krishnamurthy 1989)?
8. What are the basic differences between message passing and shared memory synchronization schemes (Krishnamurthy 1989)?
9. Study how the remote procedure call works in Ada to realize the client–server model (Krishnamurthy 1989).
10. Study how occam handles a 'handshake' synchronization. How can it be used to realize a producer–consumer model (Krishnamurthy 1989)?
11. Study the different architecture models for distributed systems (Coulouris and Dollimore 1988).
12. Explain the different forms of transparencies in the design of a distributed operating system and their significance (Coulouris and Dollimore 1988).
13. What are stable, volatile and nonvolatile storages? Why are they all needed to build a fast, reliable computing system (Shrivastava 1985)?
14. Study the memory hierarchy in a computer system. Prepare a table that describes the technology used, the capacity, the size of transfer of information in bits, and access speed of modules such as register, cache, random access memory (RAM), fixed head disk, moving head disk and tapes (Stone 1988).
15. What is a virtual memory? Explain its function (Stone 1988).
16. What is a cache memory? Explain its function (Stone 1988).

REFERENCES

ANSA. 1987. *ANSA Reference Manual Release 0.03.* Alvey Advanced Network Systems Architecture Project, Cambridge, UK.

Bach, M. 1986. *The Design of UNIX Operating System*, Addison-Wesley, USA.

Coulouris, G.F and Dollimore, J. 1988. *Distributed Systems*, Addison-Wesley, UK.

Crichlow, J.M. 1988. *An Introduction to Parallel and Distributed Computing.* Prentice Hall, UK.

Date, C.J. 1986. *An Introduction to Database Systems.* Addison-Wesley, USA.

Deitel, H.M. 1990. *An Introduction to Operating Systems.* Addison-Wesley, USA.

Halsall, F. 1988. *Introduction to Data Communication and Computer Networks.* Addison-Wesley, USA.

Hughes, J.G. 1988. *Database Technology*. Prentice Hall, UK.

Krishnamurthy, E.V. 1989. *Parallel Processing: Principles and Practice*, Addison-Wesley, UK.

Maekawa, M., Oldehoeft, A.E., and Oldehoeft, R.R. 1987. *Operating Systems.* Benjamin Cummings, Reading, Mass.

Shrivastava, S.K. 1985. *Reliable Computer Systems,* Springer-Verlag, USA.

Stallings, W. 1988. *Data and Computer Communications.* Collier-Macmillan, UK.

Stone, H.S. 1988. *High Performance Computer Architecture.* Addison-Wesley, USA.

Tanenbaum, A.S. and van Renesse, R. 1985. 'Distributed operating systems'. *ACM Computing Surveys*, 17,419–70.

Tanenbaum, A.S. 1988. *Computer Networks,* Prentice Hall, USA.

Valduriez, P. and Gardarin, G. 1989. *Analysis and Comparison of relational database systems.* Addison-Wesley, USA.

2 Transactions: structure and representation

2.1 BASIC TERMINOLOGY

A database management system (DBMS) is a collection of interrelated files and a set of programs that allow several users to access and modify those files. Thus it provides the interface between the data stored in the database and the application programs and queries submitted to the system. Its primary functions are:

1. to interact with the file system of the operating system, and store, retrieve and modify data;
2. to ensure that the data satisfies certain conditions (called integrity constraints) specified by the database designer;
3. to maintain security of access to files ;
4. to provide for recovery from failure; and
5. to provide concurrency control for multiple users.

In order to describe those functions in greater detail, it is necessary to introduce certain basic definitions and terminology:

1. *Database*
   A database is defined as a finite set of named objects: x, y, z, . . .
2. *Values, states and transitions*
   Each object may be addressed either directly or indirectly and assigned values. A set of values assigned to all the objects defines a particular state of the database. Hence, depending on the values assigned during the progress of a computation, the database can undergo transitions to different states.
3. *Consistency*
   The database designer can define some of the possible states assumed by a database as consistent and others as inconsistent. 'Consistent' means that a particular property is satisfied; 'inconsistent' means that a particular property is not satisfied. For example, in an airline reservation system two consistency conditions can be imposed:
   (a) No two passengers are given the same seat number.
   (b) The total number of seats reserved is less than or equal to the capacity of the aircraft used.

If either of those conditions is violated during the operations on a database, we say that the database goes to an inconsistent state. Such conditions are usually formulated as statements in two-valued logic (called 'predicates') that are either true or false. Thus a database is said to be consistent if and only if all such predicates are true when the processing begins and ends. In that case, we say that the database preserves consistency.

4. *Granularity*
Since every object is a stored memory item, its size can vary widely; that is, an object may be occupying a word, a page, a record of a file or a field of a record. To indicate the relative sizes we use the term 'Granularity'. Granularity is relevant when we actually deal with the implementation of operations on the objects.

5. *Actions*
At a suitable granularity level, the operations on data objects are called 'actions'. For example, the following are actions:

   Read x: Assigns the current value of x to a program variable.

   Write x: Changes the current value of x to a value previously computed by a program.

   Increment x: Adds an integer **a** to item x.

   Decrement x: Subtracts an integer **a** from item x.

   Lock x: Locks object x for performing exclusive or shared action.

   Unlock x: Unlocks a previously locked object x.

   Await lock x: Waits for a lock on x until signal.

   Share lock x: Locks object x for shared action.

   Mutex lock x: Locks object x for exclusive action.

6. *Open, active and closed states*
A database is considered to be in one of the following states:

   Open: The database is ready for processing.

   Active: The actions are being carried out on the database.

   Closed: No processing is allowed on the database.

7. *Requests*
These are the actions required to be carried out on a database by the user.

8. *Atomicity of actions and transactions*
A finite sequence of requests as defined above is called a *transaction.* The transaction is merely an execution of a program consisting of the different actions. Each action is assumed to be carried out on an object in a mutually exclusive manner without interference from any other action in the same transaction or a different one. When two actions are to be carried out on the same object concurrently, they are sequentially executed one after another mutually exclusively and nondeterministically. That is ensured by a nondeterministic wait action (AWAIT) that awaits the completion of each action before the next action begins on the same object. This is called the 'atomicity' or 'indivisibility' of each action. Devices such as 'monitor' or 'semaphore' can be used for await action, thereby ensuring atomicity of action.

When dealing with a transaction consisting of many actions, we must ensure that all these actions are performed or none at all. This is called *transaction atomicity*. In practice, to achieve transaction atomicity we must ensure the following:

(a) All the actions of a transaction are atomic.

(b) If for some reason a transaction is only partially executed (that is, it is incomplete), all its actions are undone, so that it has no effect on the database or on other transactions.

2.2 SYNTACTIC STRUCTURE OF A TRANSACTION

A transaction begins its life with a START action on an open database. It then carries out one of the earlier mentioned actions on the database objects and finally signals the successful completion of its actions by a COMMIT operation. Such an operation should leave the database in a consistent state.

A transaction, however, may not achieve the desired goal because of possible failures and errors due to conflicts within its own operations or from other transactions. In such a case it has to abort, thus undoing all its actions from the start, so that it does not have any effect on the database (that is, the database is left in a consistent state).

Thus by design commit and abort operations are mutually exclusive. Further, the commit operation guarantees that the normal termination of a transaction has left a permanent and consistent change in the database and will not undergo abort. Similarly, the abort operation guarantees that the transaction is uncommitted to any of the earlier actions carried out and that the database remains consistent. We call a transaction 'active' if it is neither committed nor aborted.

Thus we may look upon the life of a transaction as a finite-state transition system (or a syntax graph), as in Figure 2.1(a).

After a start, each transaction either reads, writes and commits (or aborts); or reads and commits (or aborts); or writes, reads and commits (or aborts); or writes and commits (or aborts).

In order to avoid read-write conflicts, we need to ensure that only one of these actions can take place on a given object; that is, each action is *mutually exclusive* with respect to a specified object. This is achieved by using an await operation, which is like a spinlock (busywaiting), or other devices to ensure atomicity. It is then assumed that these devices are also accessed atomically as indivisible operations with no interference from other actions.

Note that no looping or repetition should occur in this transition graph, in other words, read or write actions on any object in a transaction should not occur more than once in the lifetime of that transaction. Such a transaction is described by a directed acyclic graph in which the actions are totally ordered in time; that is, each action is ordered with respect to any other action as earlier or later in the time axis.

Figure 2.1(a) essentially dictates the syntactic structure of a transaction. Additional states and additional constraints may be introduced into this syntactic structure so as to ensure unambiguous, consistent and recovering transactions. The former lead to different models, known as *restricted models, action models* and *recovery models.*

2.2.1 Restricted and action models

For instance, the restriction that no transaction is allowed to write unless it has previously read a specified data object enables us to select a subgraph of the transition graph in Figure 2.1(a). Such a restriction in the syntax leads to a model (or mode) called a 'restricted transaction model'. If, however, each transaction is made up of a 'read' (R) action followed immediately by a write (W) action on each data object, this is a particular case of a restricted model called an 'action model'.

The description of a transaction as in the above models, using only its syntactic structure without any reference to the actual meaning or interpretation in an application domain, is known as a syntactic model. In this model the meaning of actions such as read or write is simply abstracted away or left uninterpreted. However, since the read action is an assignment statement and the write action is a function computation, together they can perform an enormous variety of computations with objects of different types in any application domain — for example, bank accounts, flight reservations, student grades and remote control. Since the primitive actions in this model are read and write, the syntactic model is also known as a 'read-write model'.

2.2.2 Recovery model

In the previous model we assumed that the transaction can only commit or abort. This is an ideal situation where hardware and software are failure-free. In practice, however, any computation is subject to failures of the following types:

1. logical errors, such as nonavailability of resources or data, overflow and input failure;
2. system errors, such as deadlock and livelock;
3. hardware failures, such as loss of information from volatile storage (cache);
4. nonvolatile and stable memory failures, such as failure of a disk (usually it is assumed to be failure-free).

In order to deal with the failures (other than those in the fourth category), we introduce two extra 'complaining' states after the active state, but before the commit or abort states (Figure 2.1(b)):

1. A state called 'failed' that complains that normal execution is not possible owing to a hardware error. The transaction then has to be aborted, all its actions are undone and it is restarted.
2. A state called 'about to commit' in which the transaction has finished its execution except that it has not written its values in a stable storage from the volatile storage. At this time a failure of the volatile storage is possible.

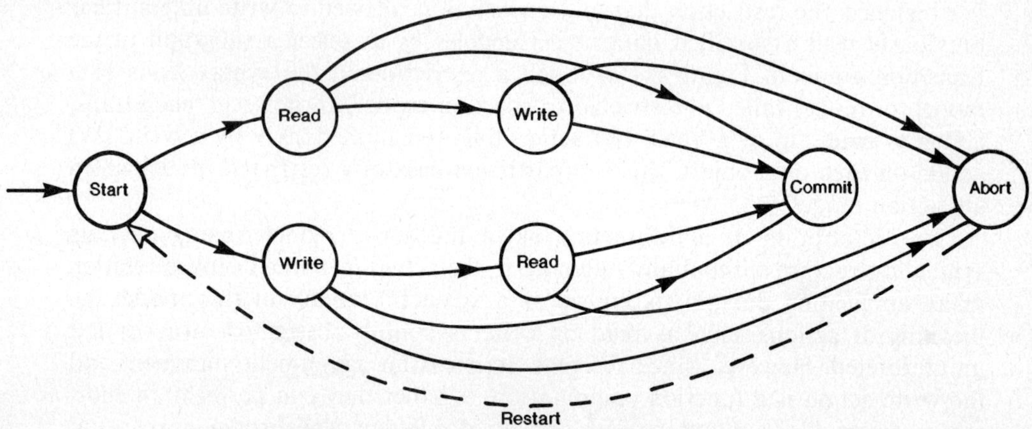

(a) Action model

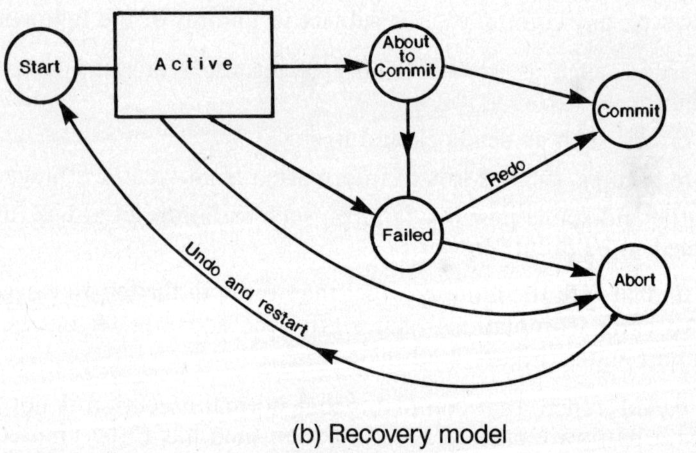

(b) Recovery model

Figure 2.1 Transaction syntax

If it occurs, all the actions of that transaction have to be redone and the transaction is committed, provided that no other failures force it to reach the failed state and eventually abort (and so to be undone and restarted).

Figure 2.1(b) illustrates the recovery model.

2.3 TRANSACTIONS: INTERACTION AND DESCRIPTION

When two or more transactions are performed on one or more objects, two different modes of actions are possible: serial mode and concurrent (or parallel) mode.

In the serial mode each action in a transaction as well as actions in other transactions are totally ordered in time; or these actions flow sequentially. Hence this mode can be represented by an unbranched directed tree, resembling a chain or a single thread passing through several beads, each bead representing an action (see Figures 2.2 and 2.3). Obviously, this mode is slow in speed from the computational point of view.

To increase the speed, we need to introduce a higher degree of concurrency where we can interleave actions of different transactions while still maintaining the consistency conditions of the database.This is achieved by the concurrent (or parallel) mode. In this mode some of the individual conflict-free actions of different transactions on the same object and different actions of the same transaction on different objects may be carried out concurrently, thus exhibiting a partial order with respect to time. This means that not all such actions may be relatively ordered as earlier or later, since some of them may be simultaneous and hence incomparable. A partial order is described by a branched *directed acyclic graph* resembling a multithread or a knit (Figure 2.4).

Both these modes of actions can be visualized by using a matrix called an *access control matrix* or for short *access matrix*. The rows of the access matrix A represent labelled transactions, and each column represents a named data object on which the desired actions are performed. Thus each column denotes a shared variable (memory space) through which communication takes place among the different transactions at different instants of time.

Let us assume that there are t distinct transactions and d distinct data objects. If we index the rows by transaction labels 1, 2, 3, . . . i, . . . t and columns by object labels 1, 2, 3, . . . , j, . . . d, then there are t.d elements in A. Each element Aij is further divided to contain as subelements the different actions — For example, read (R), write (W) — that may be allowed on each data object. It is convenient to assume that there are p such different actions (apart from abort and commit). The last column in each row contains the information as to whether that transaction was committed (C) or aborted (A). Thus the access matrix contains a total of (ptd + 2t) entries.

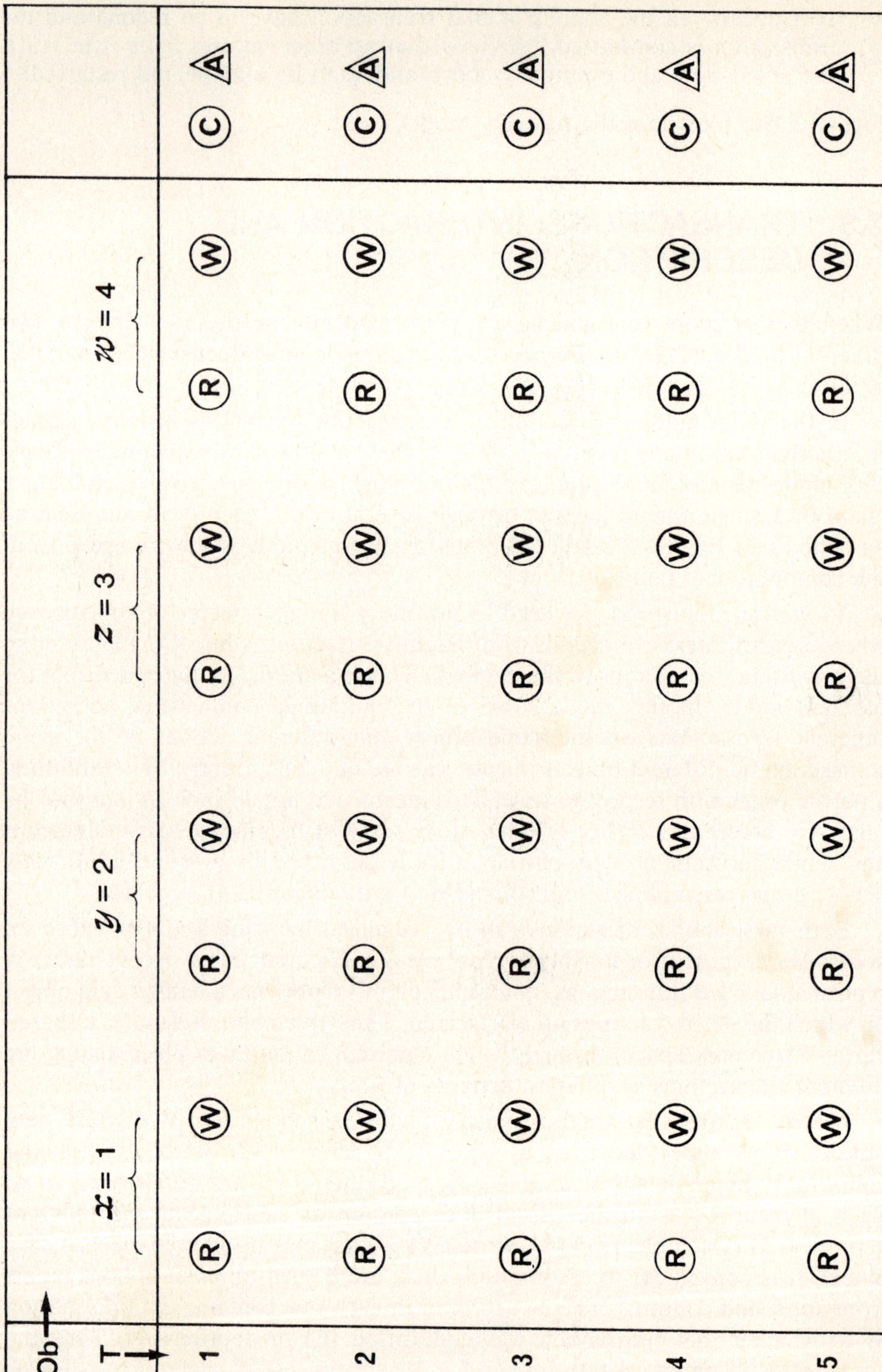

Figure 2.2 Access matrix

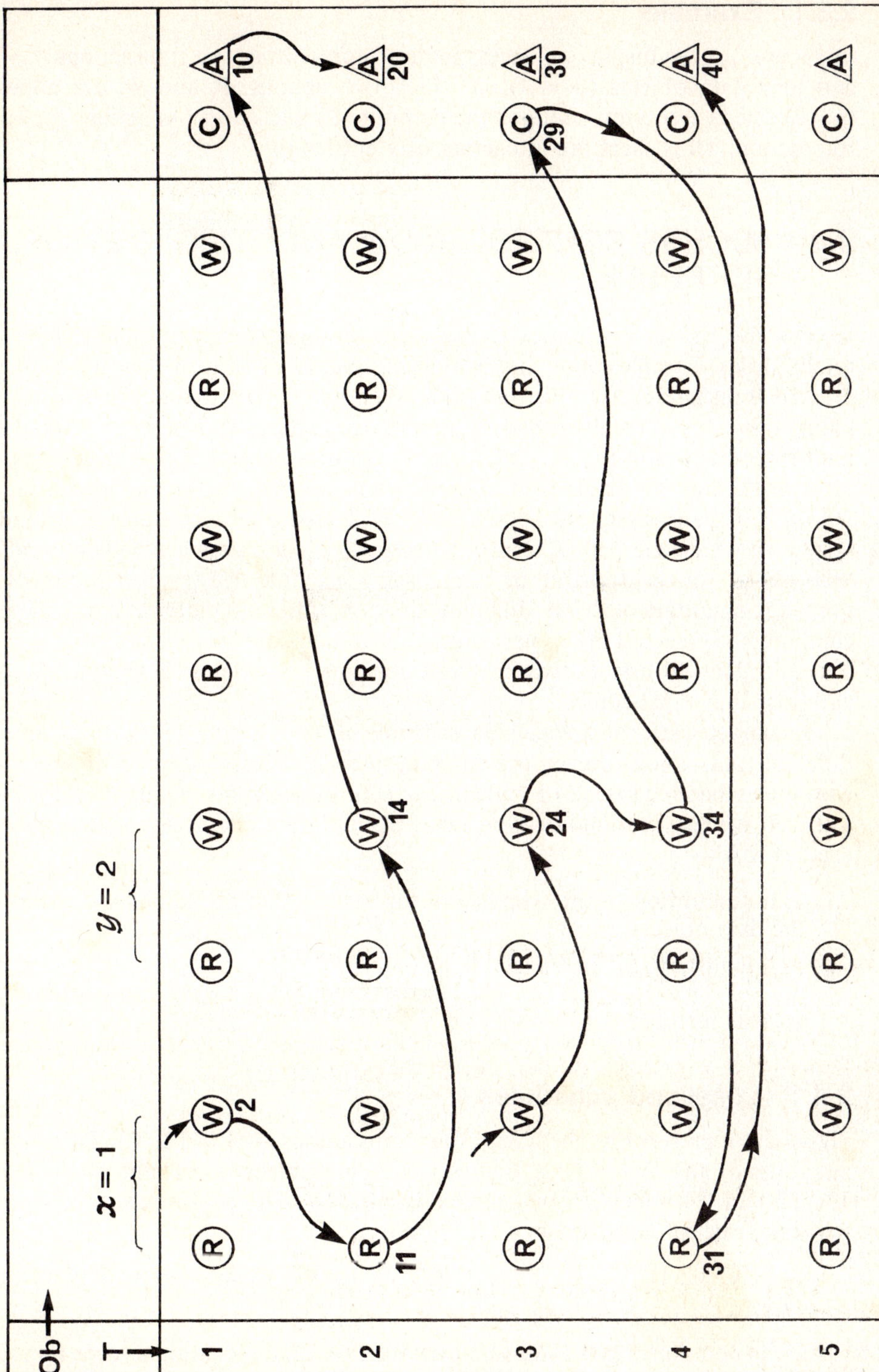

Figure 2.3 Single-thread topology

2.3.1 Example

In Figure 2.2, we display an access matrix representing five transactions (t = 5) and four data objects (d = 4) on which two actions, R and W, are allowed (p = 2); the last column contains the commit (C) and abort (A) actions for each transaction. Thus there are altogether fifty entries in A.

2.4 ACCESS CONTROL FLOW AND TOPOLOGY OF A SCHEDULE

We can use the access matrix to represent a single thread of control flow for totally ordered transactions and a multiple thread of control flow for partially ordered transactions.The directed path taken by a single thread or the directed paths taken by a multithread represent the access topology. A thread or multithread is useful for viewing the progress of a collection of transactions.

A collection of interleaved actions from various transactions is called a *schedule*. If the transactions act on a central database in a centralized computer system in which memory is shared among processors, such a schedule is called 'a localized' (or 'centralized' or 'single site') schedule. However, if the transactions act simultaneously at different sites on different databases in different computers connected by a network, such a schedule is called a 'distributed schedule'. We will first discuss 'localized schedules' and later (in Chapter 5) deal with distributed schedules.

A characteristic of a localized schedule is the sharing of memory among different transactions during the computation.The access matrix representation with the embedded thread or multithread control describes the manner in which a shared memory communication takes place. Hence the access matrix can be used as follows:

1. as a description of the schedule of the actions that are to be carried out on the data objects;
2. as a log (recorded in the stable memory) description of *actions carried* out on the data objects. The log can be used for recovery from failures of volatile memory.

2.4.1 Localized schedules

Figure 2.3 represents a schedule of four transactions — T1, T2, T3, T4 carrying out R (read) and W (write) actions on two data objects x = 1 and y = 2; finally T1, T2 and T4 abort (A), while T3 commits (C). The action sequence (or the schedule) can be described by:

> T1xW, T2xR, T2yW, T1A, T2A and T3xW, T3yW, T4yW, T3C, T4xR, T4A

where the notation T2xR means that transaction T2 on location x reads its value (contents); T3xW means that transaction T3 on location x writes a value for x;

T3C means that transaction T3 commits; and T4A means that transaction T4 aborts. Further, we can omit the prefix T in each element of this sequence if we implicitly assume that the first numeral stands for the transaction label.

Thus we can rewrite the above action sequence as an ordered set of triplets:
Transaction label (T): Data object (D): Action (P)
and doublets:
Transaction label (T): Commit (C) or Abort (A)
as below.

1xW, 2xR, 2yW, 1A, 2A and 3xW, 3yW, 4yW, 3C, 4xR, 4A

Here there is interleaving of actions of T1 and T2 as well as of T3 and T4, but the actions of all four transactions are not interleaved. Thus there are two independent (or disjoint) single threads of action sequences in Figure 2.3. If the action entries are taken as points and the successive actions are connected by directed lines, we get a directed acyclic graph. This graph is unbranched since there is a total order in each interleaving.

2.4.2 Logs

As already mentioned, a log records the history of actions in a stable memory for recovery purposes. Since R actions are not relevant for this application, to save space it suffices to record W, C and A actions only. When W actions are stored, we need to record together with the triplet (such as ixW) the initial value of x before W and the final value after W. The initial value is represented by I_x and the final value by F_x; this will appear in the log as ix(I_x, F_x)W.

2.5 NUMERAL SEQUENCE CODING OF SCHEDULES

Since the access matrix has a predetermined number of rows and columns, and since the number of actions is finite and known, it is convenient to describe the schedule by encoding each triplet in the action sequence into positive integers and to decode this sequence when it is needed. Such a scheme avoids recourse to pictures and enables us to do mechanical analysis of the schedule. Before explaining the encoding and decoding schemes, we will illustrate the basic principle for describing the schedule by using the array addresses in the access matrix.

For the sake of simplicity, consider Example 2.3.1. We assign each entry in the access matrix, starting from the top-row leftmost entry 1xR, a serial number beginning in 1 and ending in (tpd + 2t); the serial numbers are assigned in row-major order top-down and left to right. Each entry then receives a unique numerical label, which essentially assigns unique labels to the points or vertices of the directed acyclic graph (DAG) through which the lines or edges of the DAG would pass. This sequence of edges is the representation of the thread of the schedule.

2.5.1 Example

In Figure 2.3 the thread for the interleaving of T1 and T2 starts at 2 and passes through 11, 14, 10, and 20, while the thread for the interleaving of T3 and T4 starts at 22 and passes through 24, 34, 29, 31 and 40. As already mentioned, these two threads are totally ordered and so there are no branches in the tree.

2.5.2 Row-order and flow-order connectivity list

When branches are encountered, however, the schedule corresponds to a partially ordered multithread flow. In such a case, we need to encode the graph as a connectivity list consisting of a list of a pair of nodes that denote the directed edges. We can do this row by row top-down, left to right (a 'row-order connectivity list') in the access matrix. Also, the connectivity list can simply list the pairs of nodes in the 'flow order', beginning with the starting nodes and keeping up with the successive neighbouring nodes. Such lists are useful as input for graph algorithms.

2.5.3 Example

In Figure 2.4 we have a schedule that has multithread access topology. This schedule is described by the row-order connectivity list thus:

{(1,2), (2,4), (2,21), (4,9)}

{(11,2), (11,14), (14,4), (14,19)}

{(21,22), (22,29)}

Here the pairs of actions (1xR, 2xR), (1yW, 3xR), (1xW, 2yW) and (1yW, 2C) are concurrent; they correspond respectively to pairs of nodes: 1 and 11, 4 and 21, 2 and 14, 4 and 19.

The same schedule can be described by the flow-order connectivity list thus:

{(1,2), (11,2), (11,14), (2,4), (2,21), (4,9), (14,4), (14,19), (21,22), (22,29)}

2.5.4 Encoding triplets and doublets into numerals

We will now describe a simple algorithm to encode each triplet and doublet into a unique number. Note that we have t transactions, d data objects and p actions (apart from commit and abort) in any schedule:

Let a triplet be specified by T D P where

$1 \leq T \leq t;\ 1 \leq D \leq d;\ 1 \leq P \leq p$

Also assume that each data object 1 through d is assigned a unique numeral label: x = 1, y = 2, z = 3, . . . ; and that each action (other than commit (C) and abort (A)) 1 through p is assigned a unique numeral label: R = 1, W = 2, . . . Then each triplet is encoded into a number N using:

$$N = (T - 1)(p.d + 2) + (D - 1).p + P$$

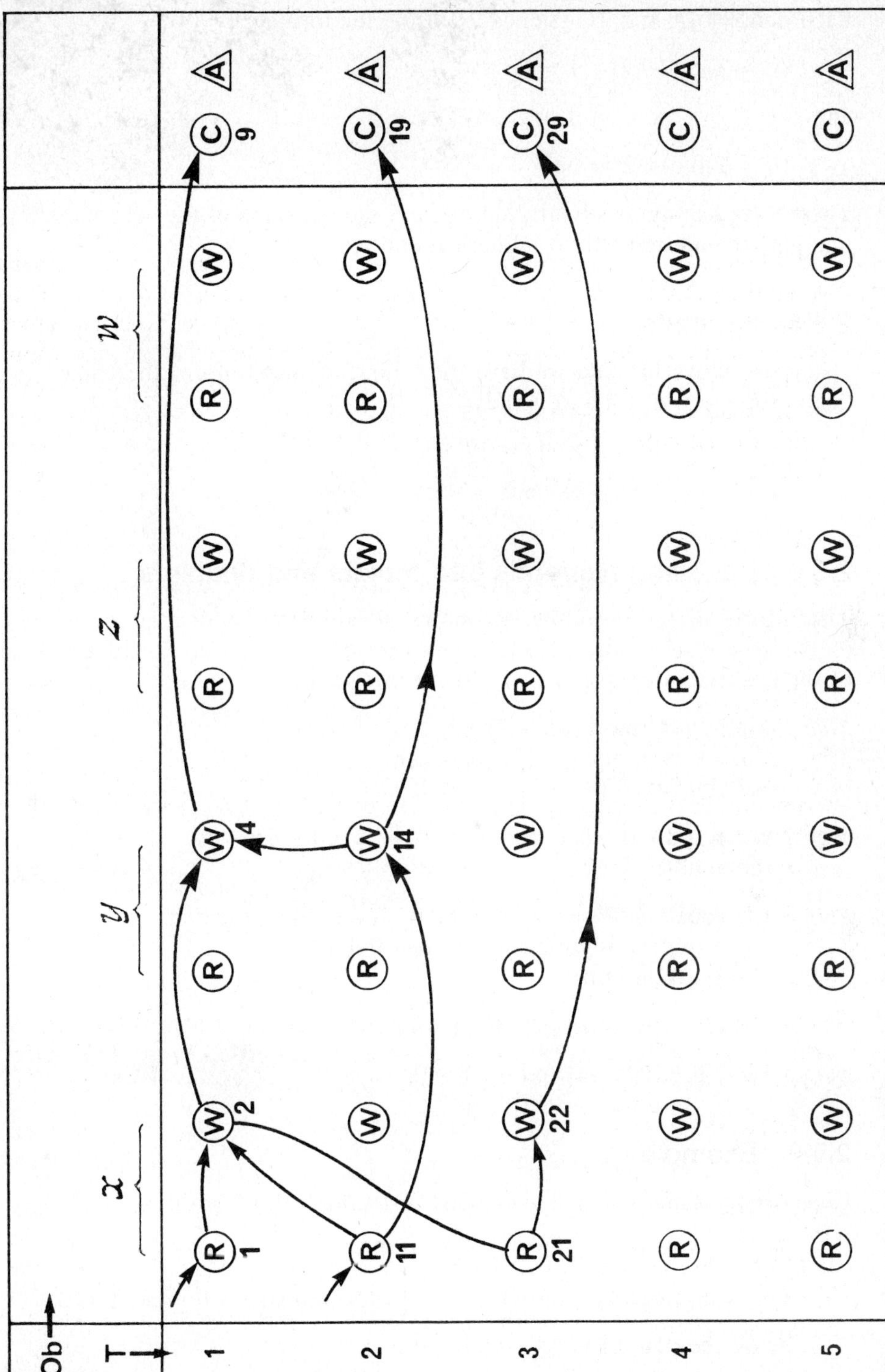

Figure 2.4 Multithread topology

Each doublet TA and TC is encoded using the formula:

$$TC = T(p.d + 2) - 1 = N$$

and

$$TA = T(p.d + 2) = N$$

These formulae are easily arrived at from the structure of the access matrix by mapping the addresses into numerical entities.

2.5.5 Example

Using the above formula we have the following encodings of the triplets given below, for t = 5, d = 4 and p = 2:

3yW = 24; 2C = 19; 3C = 29; 4A = 40

2yW = 14; 3xR = 21; 5zW = 46; 1yW = 4.

2.5.6 Decoding numerals into triplets and doublets

The algorithm for decoding the numeral code into a doublet is as follows (hereafter *a mod b* is the *positive remainder* obtained in the Euclidean division of the positive integer *a* by the positive integer *b*):

Step 1 Find r = N mod (pd + 2);
if r = 0 then find T = N/(pd + 2);
the doublet is TA.

Step 2 If r = (pd + 1) then find T = (N + 1)/(pd + 2);
the doublet is TC.

Step 3 If r equals *neither zero nor* (pd + 1) then it is a triplet;
find r mod p; if r mod p = 0 then P = p;
else P = r mod p.

Step 4 Find (r − P); then D = [(r − P)/p] + 1.

Step 5 Find T = [(N − r)/(pd + 2)] + 1.

2.5.7 Example

Consider the same schedule described in Example 2.5.5 with:

p = 2, t = 5, d = 4 and (pd + 2) = 10

1. If N = 30, then r = N mod (pd + 2) = 30 mod 10 = 0 ; and T = 3;

   hence the doublet is 3A (Step 1).

2. If N = 29, then r = N mod (pd + 2) = 29 mod 10 = 9; so

   T = (N + 1)/(pd + 2) = 3; hence the doublet is 3C (Step 2).

3. If N = 24, then N mod (pd + 2) = r = 4; and r mod p = 4 mod 2 = 0; hence P = 2 (Step 3).

   Hence D = [(r − P)/p] + 1 = [(4 − 2)/2] + 1 = 2 = y (Step 4),

   and T = [(24 − 4)/10] + 1 = 3 (Step 5). Thus the triplet is 3yW.

2.5.8 Uses and limitations of the access matrix

The access matrix has several important functions:

1. It serves as a pedagogical aid for visualization of the concurrent control flow; this is somewhat similar to using a flowchart for sequential control flow.
2. It offers protection capabilities: we can use it to define permissible actions by a transaction or a user on each data object by setting a Boolean flag along with actions such as R or W. For example, a particular user may be allowed only to read, whereas another user may read or write. Such restrictions in access can be easily included.
3. It provides for recovery from failures, if it is stored as a log in the stable memory.

The use of the access matrix, however, has a particular limitation. When a large number of transactions and numerous data objects with different copies or versions are encountered, the explicit use of the access matrix and the related numeral sequence coding of the elements of a schedule can become cumbersome for practical implementation. In such a case, the individual elements of the schedule are to be represented by choosing a composite data structure (for example, records in which one of the fields is of the pointer type) to perform pattern matching of the labels of transactions, names of data objects, labels of versions or copies, and names of actions.

Keeping this limitation in mind, we will use the access matrix and the numeral sequence coding of a schedule because they are good notational aids for understanding the basic concepts of concurrency control problems and related graph algorithms.

2.6 CONFLICTS AMONG ACTIONS AND COMPATIBILITY

In the syntactic model, we used only the read and write actions on the data object. These two actions conflict with each other in the sense that they cannot both be performed concurrently on the same data object in any transaction. Also, for different transactions the read actions on the same object can be carried out concurrently by two or more transactions, but this cannot be done when at least one of them is a write action. Thus when actions from two or more transactions are to be applied to the same data object concurrently, we need to introduce a mode of conduct or protocol among those actions so that they are conflict-free and hence compatible. A compatible protocol can be represented by a matrix known as the 'compatibility matrix'. This matrix is shown in Figure 2.5 for any two transactions Ti and Tj with read (R) and write (W) actions in a schedule.

	Tj	
Ti	read (R)	write (W)
read (R)	Yes	No
write (W)	No	No

Figure 2.5 Compatibility matrix

At this point we make the following important observations:

1. If actions other than R and W are introduced, we need to specify a compatibility matrix for the p different actions in the action set. This matrix tells us which of these actions can be applied to the same data object concurrently by two or more transactions. It plays an important role in the analysis and evaluation of the schedules, since two schedules in which the order of the conflicting actions is different may yield different results affecting the consistency of the database.
2. In the syntactic model we simply ignore the meaning of any transaction, and the compatibility is essentially checked among the primitive actions and not with regard to the actual nature of the two transactions involved. Thus one cannot necessarily guarantee the semantic correctness of a schedule. We will comment briefly on this matter in the following section.

2.7 TRANSACTIONS: SEMANTICS AND MULTILEVEL ATOMICITY

So far we have treated a schedule of interleaved transactions at the syntactic level. That is, we have not been concerned with the nature of transactions and their real-world meaning, and have dealt with them from an operational viewpoint based on the two primitive actions (read and write) purely at the syntactic level. This is because we do not usually have any knowledge of the database systems which would enable us to understand which are correct and which are incorrect interleavings. But we must remember that even the very basic actions which we used, namely, the read/write actions, are powerful enough to generate a complex set of computations, since the read action is an assignment operation and the write action is a function computation at the programming level. Thus a typical schedule can generate an enormous variety of objects of varying types, and different meanings may be assigned to such a complex schedule.

With regard to the correctness of schedules and controlling them for error-free performance, it has been found sufficient to confine oneself to the syntactic level. However, it is desirable to add semantic information about the transactions in a DBMS if we want to improve the concurrency. Furthermore, semantic information is useful in several situations where syntax alone cannot adequately model the system. For example, the actions relating to audit transactions of bank accounts or other monitoring transactions cannot go ahead concurrently or interleave with the actions of the customer account transactions.

As another example, consider the automatic once-a-quarter payment of an insurance premium from a bank account whenever a sufficient amount is available during each quarter. The required amount of funds being available is a non-deterministic condition; we may assume, however, this condition occurs within each calendar quarter. The required logical flag to make such a payment has to be set by the bank once at the beginning of every quarter, and after the deduction is made the flag has to be reset in order to prevent two or more deductions in a quarter. This resetting of the flag is a part of the account holder's transaction, while the setting of the flag is a part of the bank's transaction for several customers. These transactions are subject to a semantic precedence constraint and cannot be interleaved arbitrarily. Such a constraint cannot be easily expressed within the framework of the compatibility matrix of actions, since the types of actions and their atomicity are different. However, such a context dependent or semantic information may have to be necessarily incorporated in any DBMS if the latter is to be useful in real-world problems.

The above discussion suggests that we need to describe compatibility among the different classes of transactions and their types, in addition to compatibility among the basic actions. Obviously, such a description is at a higher semantic level than the compatibility matrix for the action set. The description of compatibility among different classes of transactions would require an understanding of their types and of how their individual tasks of differing granularity would interleave consistently in a schedule in a given context.

Recent research in that direction (see Garcia-Molina 1983; Lynch 1983; Farrag and Ozsu 1989) has shown that the semantic approach can permit a higher degree of concurrency than the syntactic approach in certain instances (see Chapter 5; see also Cellary et al. 1988). But the introduction of semantics and types does not come free of charge; it can be very expensive from the standpoint of software development and of implementation, since:

1. It requires class, type and interleaving descriptors.
2. It also requires the implementation of algorithms in order to partition sets and test for compatibility and consistency.
3. The nature of atomicity (exclusive indivisibility) now pertains not only to a single action but also to a whole sequence of actions (task) of a particular transaction. That is, the interleaving may now take place not only among the basic actions but also among tasks of different size (or granularity) from different programs; this is called 'multilevel atomicity'. To handle the latter,

we need additional control mechanisms. These must be set as punctuation marks (called 'breakpoints') to mark segments in the schedule where interleaving may take place; and with each breakpoint we need to assign the type of transactions that can interleave.

In spite of the overhead costs, some researchers feel that the introduction of semantic information can be of great value in real-world transaction processing. We will deal with these matters in Chapter 5. For further recent work on the semantics of concurrency, see Bondavalli et al. (1989) and Vianu and Vossen (1989).

2.8 RELIABLE TRANSACTIONS

In Section 2.2 we mentioned that both the commit operation and the abort operation should leave the database consistent. The former achieves this consistency by ensuring that all the effects of a transaction are made permanent in the database, while the latter achieves this consistency by removing all the effects of a transaction from the database. Since the transactions are interleaved and interact during a computation, it is absolutely essential that those transactions which have been read earlier by other transactions are not aborted later. This leads to a rule of thumb that states: 'Every transaction should know that it can commit only after the commitment of all those transactions from which it read, and preferably such a transaction should read only those values written by the committed transactions'. Informally this means that a transaction is reliable until its end only if it has dealt with all those transactions that proved themselves reliable until their end, and ended earlier. We will formalize these concepts in Chapter 3.

2.9 PROGRAMMING FOR TRANSACTION PROCESSING

Another important aspect is programming a computer for transaction processing of the database. For that purpose, it is essential to use a high-level concurrent programming language of some kind in which database operations can also be embedded. This is because we need to have two fundamentally different features of computation, namely the concurrency feature and the query processing feature in the database. We need the concurrency feature in order to ensure mutual exclusion among actions, synchronization and protocol execution; and we need the database query processing feature in order to access the database and carry out the required actions. Attempts are currently being made in many directions to achieve these features — for example, attempts to create a binding between a powerful concurrent language such as Ada and the standard database language SQL (Brykczynski 1988); to provide an interface between Ada and relational DBMS; and to use CSP and PROLOG (Woodcock 1987).

In addition to the above features, we need a very powerful new model for parallel programming, such as Sabot's Paralation Model (Sabot 1989), if we want to implement a semantic transaction processing system with class descriptors and set-partitioning algorithms.

2.10 LOCALIZED (CENTRALIZED) AND DISTRIBUTED SCHEDULES

In our elementary introduction, we confined ourselves to localized (or centralized) schedules that operate in a local database in which objects are in a local storage. This is very restrictive, since some databases have necessarily to be dispersed in different geographic locations. In some cases, owing to lack of computational resources, we may need to store the overflowing data in another location. Furthermore, to protect against possible loss of information of critical data as well as to improve reliability and security, we may have not only to disperse the database but also to replicate some data objects at different locations (called sites). In such cases, one has to achieve the required global consistency of the total database by actions taken locally at different sites. Because of possible communication delays and possible failures at different sites, the synchronization problem also becomes extremely complex.

The replication of data is useful for speeding read actions, since it allows data objects to be read from the nearest site, but it slows down the transaction since the write actions have to be carried out now at all sites. In addition, write actions may be affected by communication failures, thus causing the entire transaction to abort.

Moreover, since the transactions now occur at different sites and interact, we cannot establish a total order among the different actions, as we do not know the temporal order of events at different sites on account of possible delays and communication failures. Apart from the concurrency features already introduced in the control, we need to introduce features that can handle distributed communication and the execution of the corresponding protocols.The design of such a distributed concurrency control system is a difficult task, which we will deal with in Chapter 5. In the next chapter we will deal with localized schedules and methods for ensuring their correctness.

EXERCISES

1. Consider a bank database consisting of only the savings accounts of customers. What are its different states? What are the consistency conditions?
2. What is the granularity of a data object? Examine this concept with respect to some known databases.
3. Why are read and write actions adequate to describe any database computation?
4. Why do we *restrict* a transaction to read or write only once? What will happen if this restriction is not obeyed?

5. Enumerate the different failures of a computer system that can force transactions to abort.
6. Why is the commit operation the most important one ?
7. Distinguish a 'failed' state from an 'about to commit' state.
8. What is a total order? What is a partial order? Explain why the actions of a concurrent program are a partial order of events in time.
9. Explain single-thread and multithread access control topology with respect to a transaction.Why does it produce side effects?
10. Write a program for encoding triplets such as ixW, ixR and doublets such as iC, iA into a numeral code and for decoding the numeral code back into the triplets or doublets.
11. Write down the compatibility matrix for read and write actions. How can we implement this matrix in practice?
12. Devise suitable data structures to represent the access matrix of a schedule as well as a log of past actions.
13. Why do we insist that every transaction should read only the values written by committed transactions?
14. Why is it difficult to achieve database consistency when a database is distributed and transactions have to access different sites?
15. Give an example to illustrate that the syntax model of transaction is not adequate for many problems (see Garcia-Molina 1983; Lynch 1983; Farrag and Ozsu 1989).
16. Read about the Paralation model of Sabot (1989).

REFERENCES

Bondavalli, A., De Francesco, N., Latella, D. and Vaglini, G. 1989. 'Shared abstract types: an algebraic methodology for their specification'. In *Lecture Notes in Computer Science* 364, 52–67. Springer-Verlag, USA.

Brykczynski, B. 1988. 'Methods of binding SQL to Ada'. *ACM Ada Letters* 8, 38–51.

Cellary, W., Gelenbe, E. and Morzy, T. 1988. *Concurrency Control in Distributed Systems.* North-Holland, Amsterdam.

Farrag, A.A. and Ozsu, M.T. 1989. 'Using semantic knowledge of transactions to increase concurrency'. *ACM Transactions on Database Systems*, 14, 503–25.

Garcia-Molina, H. 1983. 'Using semantic knowledge for transaction processing in a distributed database'. *ACM Transactions on Database Systems* 8, 186–203.

Lynch, N. 1983. 'Multilevel atomicity: a new criterion for database concurrency control'. *ACM Transactions on Database Systems* 8, 484–502.

Sabot, G. 1989. *The Paralation Model.* MIT Press, USA.

Vianu, V. and Vossen, G. 1989. 'Goal-oriented concurrency control'. In *Lecture Notes in Computer Science* 364, 398–414. Springer-Verlag, USA.

Woodcock, J.C.P. 1987. 'Transaction processing primitives and CSP'. *IBM Journal of Research and Development* 31, 535–45.

3 Localized schedules

3.1 INTRODUCTION

In Chapter 2 we defined a schedule as an interleaving of the actions in different transactions. It is therefore very important to ensure that the interleavings will produce correct results. By a 'correct result', we mean the following: for all possible initial states of the given database and all compatible actions, the database reaches a consistent set of final states. For that purpose, we need to use a logical argument based purely on the different actions used and their compatibility, without making any assumptions about the types or values of the objects. In other words, we must use only the uninterpreted model of the transaction or work at the syntactic level and prove that the schedules are correct.

Before we discuss correctness, however, we will illustrate by examples the different categories of incorrect schedules, and how incorrectness arises.

In all our discussions below we will consider localized, single-site or centralized schedules.That is, we assume that the transactions act on a single database at a site using a centralized computer system with a central processor, or a multiprocessor where each processor can have direct access to the shared memory. We will discuss the distributed (or multisite) schedules in Chapter 5. In these distributed schedules, transactions send simultaneous requests to several independent databases (dispersed at the same site or at different sites), using a distributed multiprocessor system in which memory and auxiliary storage are not shared, and communication between different local databases and processors (at the same site or a different site) takes place through message-passing in a communication network.

3.2 INCONSISTENCIES IN SCHEDULES

When a user interacts with a database, it should be transformed from one consistent state to another; otherwise, all the actions carried out should be undone in order to restore the database. There are a variety of ways in which inconsistencies may arise when one is interleaving actions from different transactions to achieve maximal concurrency. These inconsistencies are well known to programmers and are called side effects; they arise when assignment statements from two or more sequential programs sharing variable names are interleaved. These side effects can obviously arise from R and W actions, since R is an assignment statement and W is a function computation (Section 1.2), and two transactions may carry out these actions on the same data object thus producing undesirable effects.

3.2.1 Example

Consider the schedule in which there are two transactions 1 and 2 which do the following:

T1: 1xR, 1xW; T2: 2xR, 2xW

where

1xW = x + 1; 2xW = x + 2

We can interleave the actions of T1 and T2 in various ways; one such interleaving is:

1. 2xR, 2xW, 1xR, 1xW: if x = 1 initially, this schedule gives finally x = 4.

Another interleaving is:

2. 2xR, 1xR, 2xW, 1xW: if x = 1 initially, we see that although T2 wrote x = 3, it was overwritten by 1 again to x = 2, since T1 has its prevalue x = 1.

Yet another interleaving is:

3. 1xR, 1xW, 2xR, 2xW; if x = 1 initially, we finally get x = 4.

Obviously, the first and third interleavings are equivalent, while the second is not.

The lesson from this example is this: read (assignment) and write (function computation) actions cannot always be interleaved among transactions because they may produce undesirable outcomes. We see that in the first and third schedule the execution order was T2, T1 and T1, T2 respectively. In both cases the transactions preserve the invariance of data because each transaction ended before the other began, without interleaving actions. Such executions are called 'Serial executions' and are safe. But these serial executions will be too slow, since they are not using the power of concurrency arising from the interleaving of actions. We need to know, therefore, when these interleaved transactions can produce the same results as the serial executions and when these interleavings are serializable. That is the main subject of this chapter. Studying it will enable us to ascertain the conditions under which interleaving can be done.

3.2.2 Example

Consider a schedule in which:

T1:1xR, 1xW, 1yR, 1yW; and T2: 2xR, 2xW, 2yR, 2yW

where 1xW = x − 1; 1yW = y + 1; 2xW = 2x; 2yW = 2y.

Let us initially set x = − 2,y = 2 so that x + y = 0 is the consistency condition.

The consistency will be preserved by the serial schedule T1, T2 (yielding x = – 6, y = 6) and the serial schedule T2, T1 (yielding x = – 5, y = 5), but not by the interleaving:

1xR, 1xW, 2xR, 2xW, 2yR, 2yW, 1yR, 1yW

which will yield x = – 6; y = 5.
Note that we have 1xW earlier than 2xW, while 2yW is earlier than 1yW; that is, the W–W conflicts among transactions 1 and 2 are reversed with respect to two different data objects x and y. As we will see later, this is the source of inconsistency.

3.2.3 Types of inconsistencies

Usually, inconsistencies are classified into three categories: lost update, uncommitted dependency and inconsistent analysis, as illustrated below.

Lost update
Consider the schedule:

1xR, 2xR, 1xW, 2xW

where T2 overwrites T1; this is called *lost update.* Note that there is a forward R–W conflict between T1 and T2, and a reverse R–W conflict between T2 and T1; thus each transaction reads the old values and not the new ones.

Uncommitted dependency
Consider the schedule:

2xR, 2xW, 1xR, 1xW, 2A

If initially x = 100$ and 2xW = x + 400$, then 1xR = 500$; but since T2 has aborted, x is set back to 100$; but T1 is under a false assumption, since it has not read a committed transaction. This inconsistency is called *uncommitted dependency.*

Inconsistent analysis
Consider the schedule:

1xR, 1yR, 2zR, 2zW, 2xR, 2xW, 2C, 1zR, 1tW

Let x = 100$, y = 200$ and z = 300$ initially, and let the task of T1 be to find their current total t = x + y + z; let 2zW = z – 100$, and 2xW = x + 100$; we will find that finally t = 500$, which is absurd.

This has arisen because T1 has not read the new overwritten value of x after T2 has committed and has used the earlier x, while t is always supposed to add up the current x, y, z values.This is called *inconsistent analysis.*

Note that there is an R–W conflict on x among T1 and T2 and a reverse W–R conflict on z among T2 and T1. Thus one data object has been read before another updates it, and another data object has been read after update; as a result, inconsistency arises.

On the basis of the observations in the above examples, we will now proceed to study the serializability aspects.

3.3 SERIAL SCHEDULES

A basic method of ensuring the correctness of a schedule is to use the notion of a serial schedule that we mentioned in Section 3.2.1. If each transaction is correct (that is, if it maps a consistent set of initial states of a database to a consistent set of final states), then in a schedule consisting of many transactions, if each such correct transaction is executed independently and in succession, that schedule must be correct. Such a schedule is called a *serial schedule.*

A serial schedule is easily visualized from the topology of the access control flow (see Figure 3.1). Each of the transactions T4, T3, T2 and T1 starts, executes independently and commits before the next one starts. Thus there is no interleaving of actions. It must be remembered, however, that each transaction has left a permanent and consistent change in the database, since none were aborted.

Note that any other permutation of {T1, T2, T3, T4} is also a valid serial schedule; in fact, if there are t transactions there are factorial t (or t!) possible serial schedules.

Thus in terms of the access matrix representation, a schedule is serial if the single thread or multithread of control flows through the action entries of any row, in any order, and then commits or aborts without revisiting the same row again. In other words, each transaction behaves like an independent sequential program with no interaction.

3.4 EQUIVALENCE AMONG SCHEDULES AND SERIALIZATION

We will now consider the problem of equivalence among schedules. The notion of equivalence among any set of objects is always established with respect to a set of relevant criteria. A set of the simplest criteria for equivalence among schedules is given below:

1. The number and nature of operations and the number of transactions are identical in the two schedules.

2. The two schedules have carried out the conflicting actions in the *nonaborted* transactions in the same temporal order.

Such an equivalence is called *conflict equivalence* because it uses the second criterion as its basis. Note that we can establish this equivalence only among the subset of transactions that are committed in the schedule; such a subset is called the *committed subset* of a schedule.

Later, we will choose another set of criteria and establish another kind of equivalence on the basis of these new criteria.

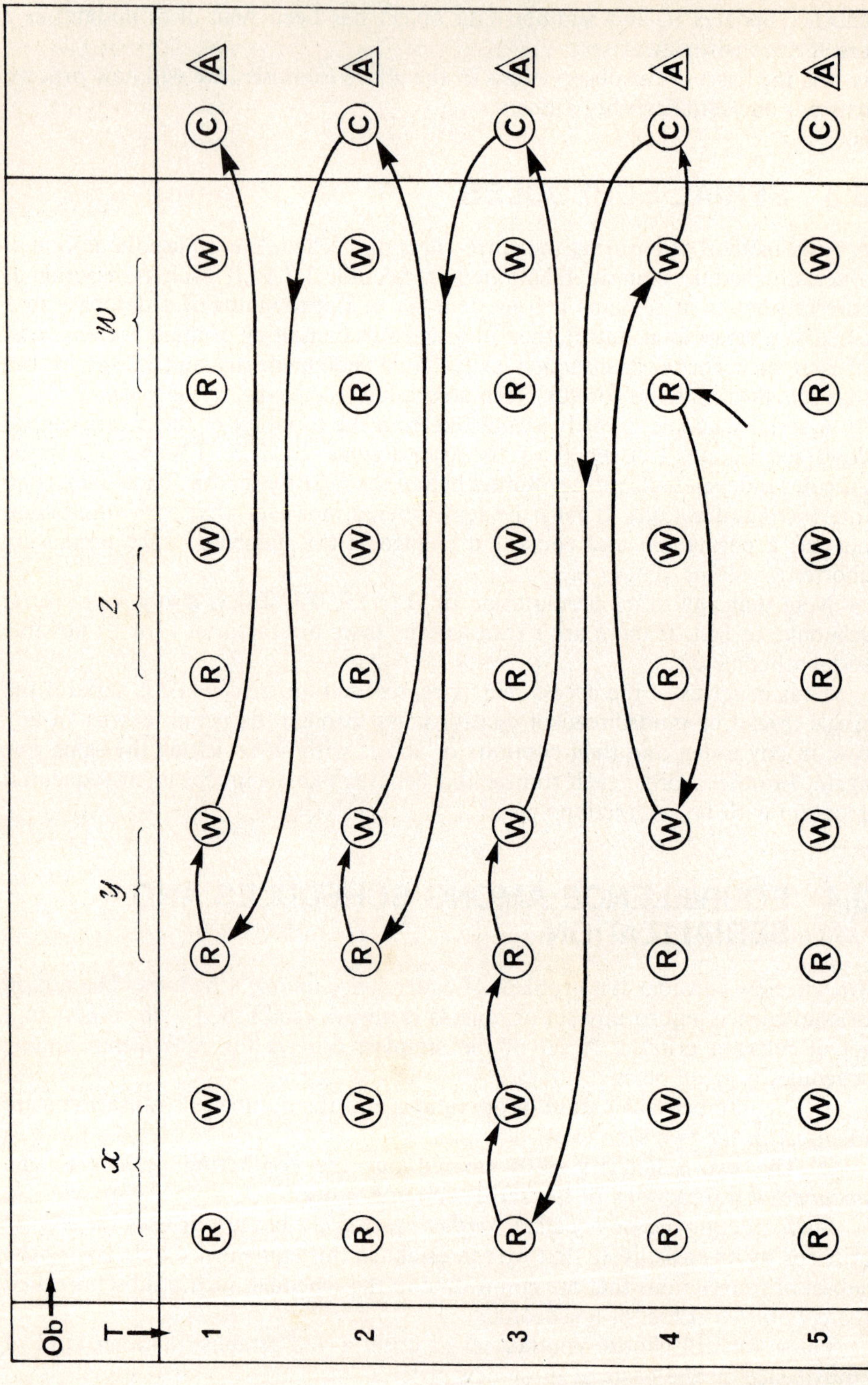

Figure 3.1 Serial schedule

Obviously, two different serial schedules satisfy the above criteria and hence are conflict-equivalent. Thus in order to prove the correctness of a schedule that is not serial, we must devise a standardization procedure which will decide whether the schedule is conflict-equivalent to a serial schedule. Such a procedure is called *conflict serialization*. The questions one has to ask then are:

1. Is there a computational algorithm to make this decision?
2. Is such an algorithm efficient in terms of computational time and space requirements?
3. Is the algorithm applied in a static mode (that is, all the information about the actions of different transactions is predeclared and preanalyzed)?
4. Is the algorithm applied in dynamic mode (that is, on line, where only partial information of the schedule is available up to that time the algorithm is applied and actions are to be interpreted on the fly!)?

The answers to the first two questions are 'yes'. There is a computational algorithm based on the access matrix to decide whether a schedule is conflict-serializable; and it has a complexity of order $O(p^2t^2d^2)$ for p actions, t transactions and d data objects in a schedule. The third and fourth questions have different answers, depending on the application areas, type of technology used and resources available.

We will first explain the principles of the algorithms before describing them and their modes of operation.

3.5 PRINCIPLE OF THE ALGORITHM FOR CONFLICT EQUIVALENCE

This algorithm is based on the construction of a conceptual or relational graph that describes the order in which conflicting actions, such as read-write (R–W), write-write (W–W), and write-read (W–R), happen in different transactions. In other words, such a graph (called a *conflict graph*) describes the intertransaction conflicts in a schedule. Obviously, to verify conflict equivalence with a serial schedule, we must ensure that the order is preserved among the conflicting actions. That is, we must show that there are no cycles present in this graph that prevent us from deciding the true order of precedence among the conflicting actions.

We first illustrate this aspect by an example, in which we assume that there are only two actions R and W in the schedule:

> (p = 2), number of data objects is four (d = 4), and number of transactions is five (t = 5); all these are predeclared.

In other words, we are assuming a static mode where all information is available.

3.5.1 Example

Consider the interleaved schedule given by the access matrix in Figure 3.2. We

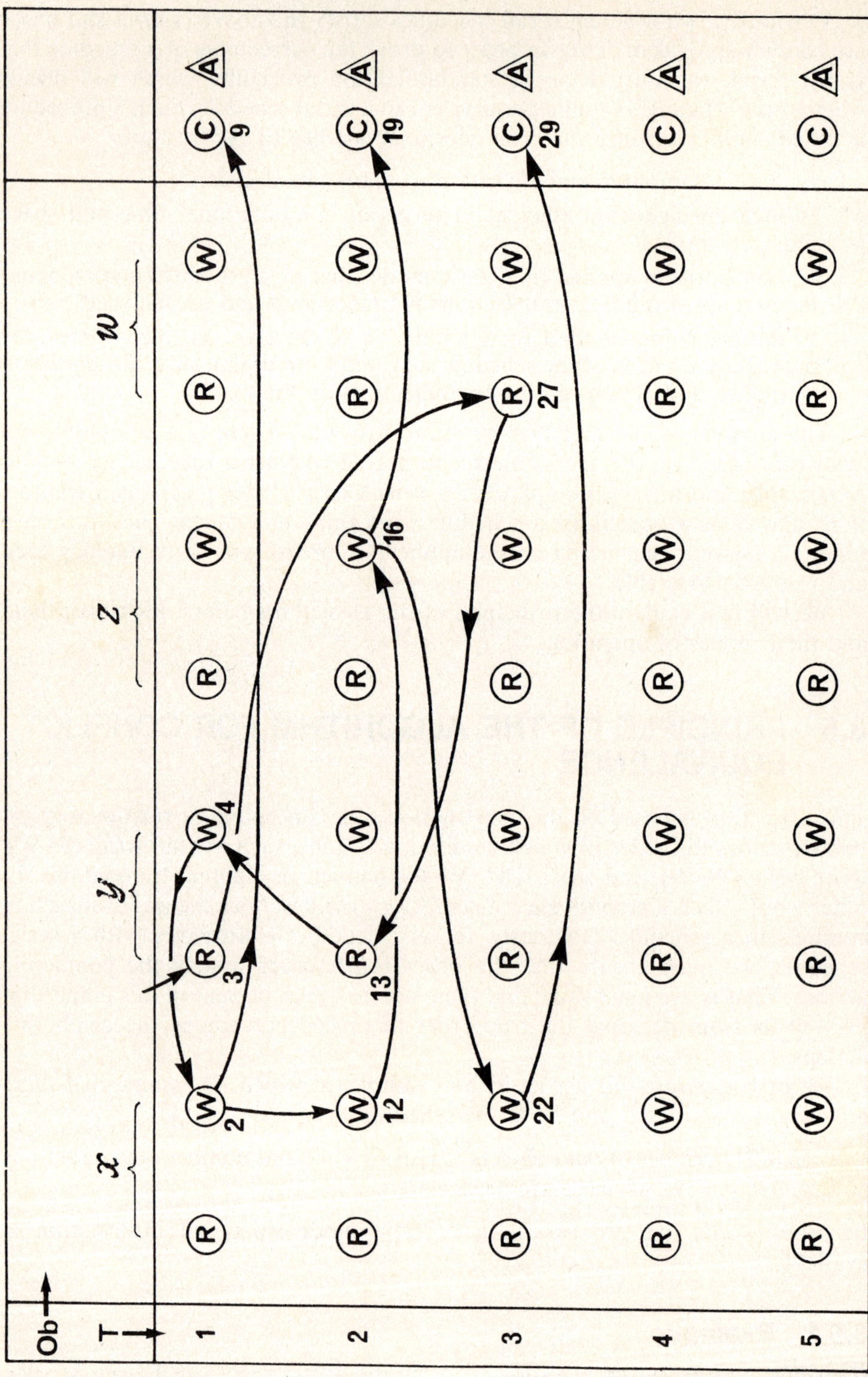

Figure 3.2 Interleaved schedule

will show that this schedule is not conflict-serializable. This schedule has the row-order adjacency list:

{(2,9), (2,12), (3,27), (4,2)}

{(12,16), (13,4), (16,19), (16,22)}

{(22,29), (27,13)}

These edges indicate an ordering of events a and b. We indicate this by the notation a < b (less than) to signify that action a was earlier than action b in the positive time axis. From this edge list we enumerate the various paths that give the required precedences, and we then decode the following correspondences using the algorithm in Section 2.5.6. Thus for the above example, we obtain by enumeration and elimination the paths and their correspondence:

(2,12): 1xW < 2xW; (13,4): 2yR < 1yW

(12,16) and (16,22): 2xW < 3xW

(2,12) and (12,16) and (16,22): 1xW < 3xW

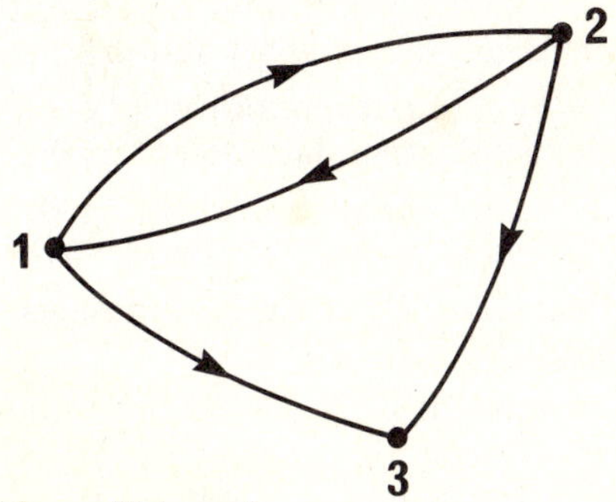

Figure 3.3 A cyclic conflict graph

Using these, we can draw a conflict graph with three nodes 1, 2, 3 having directed edges (1,2), (2,1), (2,3) and (1,3).This contains a conflict cycle (1,2) and (2,1) that prevents us from ordering the transactions 1 and 2 serially (Figure 3.3). Hence this schedule is not conflict-serializable.

3.5.2 Algorithm

The above example is simply an illustration; in practice, we need an efficient algorithm to carry out these operations. Such an algorithm works in two stages:

Stage 1

We extract the required information about the R–W, W–R and W–W conflicts on the same data object from the access matrix either statically or dynamically.

Stage 2

We draw the conflict graph (statically or dynamically) and decide whether it has a cycle; if it does, no serialization is possible, and one of the offending transactions is chosen to be aborted. (If there is no cycle, the nodes of the acyclic graph can be reordered so that if there is a directed edge from node i to node j, then i appears before j in the left-to-right order. That is, if edges were to be redrawn again from each of these nodes, they would all go one way from left to right. Such an order is called a *topological order* and gives the equivalent serial schedule. Fortunately, we need not execute the topological ordering step, since acyclicity guarantees the existence of an equivalent serial schedule.)

In stage 1, we take as input the adjacency list of the access matrix; then for each left element x in the ordered pair of the adjacency list, we trace all possible directed paths to a right element y, thus:

(x,a), (a,b), . . . , (., k)(k,y)

This is nothing but the set of nodes that can be reached from a given node by traversing the edges in the direction indicated. In other words, we need to find the *transitive closure* of the given graph (see Sedgewick 1988). From all such possible pairs (x,y) we eliminate or filter out those nonconflicting or unwanted pairs for which:

1. y = (2d + 1) mod (2d + 2) and y = 0 mod (2d + 2); this eliminates from consideration the commit and abort actions;
2. x is odd and y = (x + 1) or x is even and y = (x − 1); this eliminates the R–W or W–R actions on the same data object in the same transaction;
3. (x − y) mod (2d + 2) is other than +1 or − 1 or 0; this eliminates R–W, W–W and W–R actions on different but nonadjacent objects;
4. x is odd and (x − y) mod (2d + 2) = 0 ; this eliminates the same data objects subject to R–R actions;
5. x is odd and (x − y) mod (2d + 2) = 1; this eliminates R–W actions on different adjacent data objects;
6. x is even and (x − y) mod (2d + 2) = − 1; this eliminates W–R actions on different adjacent data objects.

The above selection rules are applicable only for p = 2; for p not equal to 2, we need to modify them suitably. Although they permit the decoding of only the relevant pairs for the construction of the conflict graph, one may also use the standard decoding algorithm after obtaining each pair and eliminate the nonconflicting or unwanted pairs. The above rules carry out that task in one pass. Also, recall what we stated in Section 2.5.8 concerning the choice of a composite data structure to pick up the relevant conflicting pairs by pattern matching when we encounter many actions, many copies or versions of data objects (see Section 3.10).

In Section 3.5.1 the number of pairs turns out to be 48; of these, 44 pairs are unwanted and we eliminate them using the above rules.

Rule 1. This eliminates the twenty pairs:

(2,9), (2,19), (2,29), (3,9), (3,19), (3,29), (4,9), (4,19),
(4,29), (12,19), (12,29), (13,9), (13,19), (13,29), (16,19),
(16,29), (22,29), (27,9), (27,19), (27,29)

Rule 2. This eliminates the pair (3,4).
Rule 3. This eliminates the fifteen pairs:

(2,16), (3,16), (3,27), (4,2), (4,12), (4,16), (4,22), (12,16), (13,16), (16,2), (16,22), (27,2), (27,4), (27,12), (27,13)

Rule 4. This eliminates the pair (3,13).
Rule 5. This eliminates the seven pairs:

(3,2), (3,12), (3,22), (13,2), (13,12), (13,22), (27,16)

Rule 6. No applicable pair.

Finally, we are left with the four pairs (2,12), (13,4), (12,22) and (2,22), which decode into the triplets with the following precedences:

1xW < 2xW; 2yR < 1yW; 2xW < 3xW; 1xW < 3xW

We now proceed to stage 2 of the algorithm and obtain the cyclic conflict graph in Figure 3.3, which contains the 1–2, 2–1 cycle. Transaction 2 has to be aborted and its node is to be removed from the conflict graph.

3.5.3 Complexity of the algorithm

The dynamic algorithm for stage 1 essentially requires a depth-first search of the access graph, starting from each left member of the pair in the adjacency list. (For a static algorithm, adjacency matrix representation can be used to compute the transitive closure using Warshall's algorithm; see Sedgewick 1988.) For each such element, we need to check all the edges to obtain the required paths and conflicts. Hence for all the different pairs, the complexity is proportional to the square of the number of edges in the access matrix or square of the number of action steps in the schedule. Thus the complexity for the first stage is at most $(ptd)^2$.

The algorithm for stage 2 requires the detection of cycles in the conflict graph constructed either statically or dynamically. Since the conflict graph has t nodes, it can have at most t(t-1) edges. To detect cycles and for topological ordering of the nodes, we need to use again the depth-first search procedure, and the complexity of this procedure is proportional to the number of edges t^2. Thus the overall complexity is at most $p^2.t^2.d^2$. This is considered acceptable, since the complexity function is a quadratic polynomial.

3.5.4 Example

Consider another schedule given by the access matrix in Figure 3.4. This schedule is conflict-serializable. Here also we assume p = 2, d = 4, t = 5. The adjacency list is given by:

{(1,2), (2,4), (2,21), (4,9)}
{(11,2), (11,14), (14,4), (14,19)}
{(21,22), (22,29)}

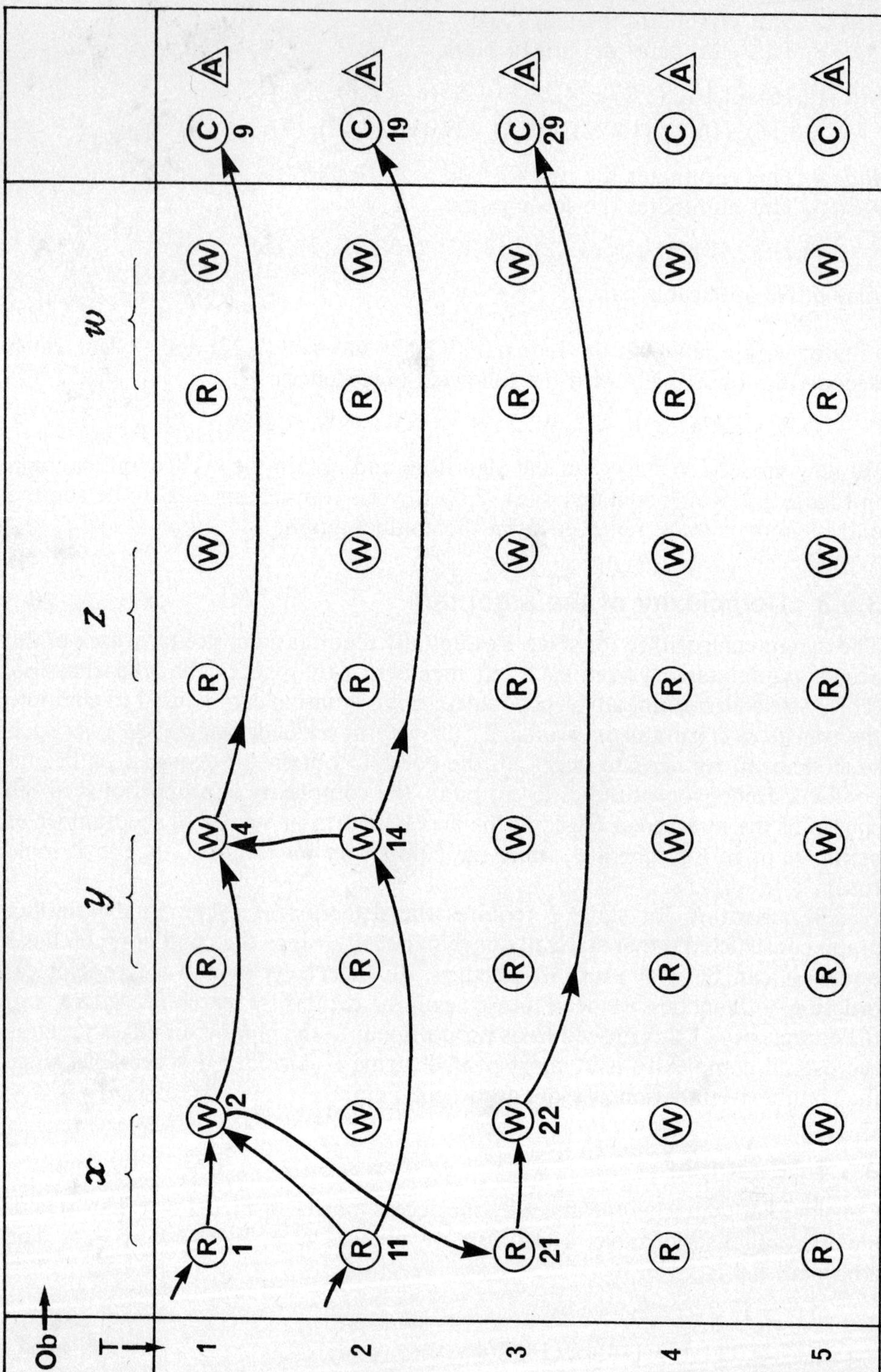

Figure 3.4 A conflict-serializable schedule

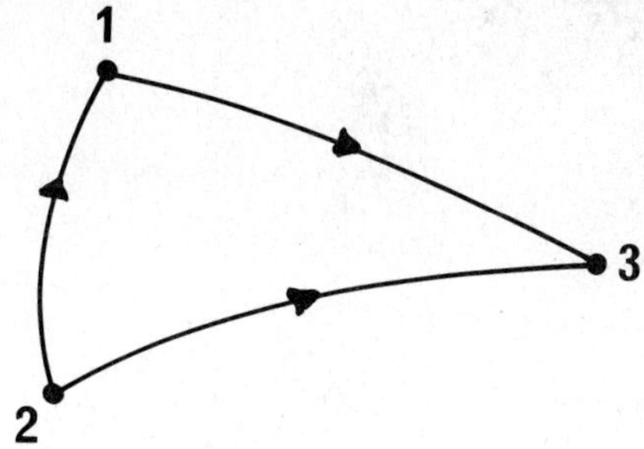

Figure 3.5 An acyclic conflict graph

Using the rules given in Section 3.5.2 we obtain the following conflicting pairs:

(1,22), (2,21), (2,22), (11,2), (11,22), (14,4)

which respectively correspond to:

1xW < 3xR; 2xW < 3xR, 2xW < 3xW; 2xR < 1xW; 2xR < 3xW; and 2yW < 1yW

This gives us the conflict graph in Figure 3.5, which is an acyclic directed graph (this means that there is no conflict among the transactions). Hence this schedule can be serialized in the order 2, 1, 3. That this serial order is conflict-equivalent to the given schedule may easily be verified by looking at the order of preservation of the conflicting actions.

In this example, we found just one topological order, 2-1-3, among the nodes of the conflict graph, so that if there is a directed edge from node i to node j, then i appears before j in this ordering. As mentioned earlier, such a topological sort is possible if and only if the graph is *not* cyclic. In our example we had only one such topological sort. In general, there may be many different topological sorts. To obtain all these, we need to use another algorithm on the conflict graph; but in practice we do not need to do the topological sort, since acyclicity implies serializability for single-site schedules (but not for multisite schedules). We will describe these algorithms in detail in the next section.

3.6 ALGORITHM FOR CONFLICT SERIALIZABILITY

As mentioned in Section 3.5.3, the basic procedure we need to use is the depth-first search (DFS). It can be used for finding paths, finding cycles and also finding the topological order by very simple changes in the algorithm. It is also possible to use matrix operations on the adjacency matrix. All these algorithms can be speeded up using many processors.

In order to use these algorithms we need to represent the access matrix as an adjacency list L[x]. This lists the adjacent nodes for each node x in the graph. For Example 3.5.1 (Figure 3.2), the adjacency list looks like this:

NODE : NEIGHBORS
2 : 9,12
3 : 27
4 : 2
12 : 16
13 : 4
16 : 19,22
22 : 29
27 : 13

3.6.1 Depth-first search

To carry out the depth-first search, we need to visit each node in turn. To remember which node was visited, we mark each one visited; initially, however, all the nodes are left unmarked.

```
procedure DFS (x: nodeType);
var
    y: nodeType;
        begin
    visit and mark x;
    while there is an unmarked node y adjacent to x do
        DFS(y)
    end {while}
end {DFS}
```

We will now explain how to find transitive closure, cycles and topological sort.

1. *Listing all the nodes that can be reached (transitive closure)*

In the above procedure, if we print out all the nodes that are visited we can obtain the required pairs (x,y). But we must remember that not all nodes in the graph will be visited starting from the same node; therefore, we need to perform DFS from each node. Thus the complexity of the transitive closure is $(ptd)^2$. The pairs obtained are then filtered using the rules.

2. *Finding cycles*

In the DFS procedure, we will encounter an already marked node during the search if there are cycles. Thus cycles can be detected.

3. *Topological sorting*

Topological sorting can also be done by DFS if we use the following principle and a trick in printing the result. Performing a topological sort on a graph in which the direction of each edge is reversed leads to a reverse topological sort. In such a sort the sequence of nodes will be ordered as in a mirror reflection;

that is, from each node all the directional edges will now go from right to left. To obtain this neat result, we simply print out the name of the starting node last and print out earlier all the other nodes searched and visited in the reverse order. Thus the modified DFS algorithm, known as revtopsort, is as follows:

```
procedure revtopsort (x: nodeType)
var
   y: nodeType;
begin
   visit and mark x;
   while there is an unmarked node y adjacent to x do
      revtopsort(y)
   writeln(x)
   end {while}
end {revtopsort}
```

The complexity of this algorithm is proportional to the number of edges in the graph.

3.6.2 Example

Consider the graph represented by the following adjacency list:

1: 2,3
2: 6
3: 6,8
4: 2,5,7
6: 7
8: 7

Application of DFS, starting at node 1, would give us the following paths:

```
1–2-6–7; 4–5
|
3–8
```

The use of procedure revtopsort would give us the reverse topological order of the nodes:

7, 6, 2, 8, 3, ***1***, 5, ***4***

where the initial nodes are underlined and bolded. Note that we now have the directions of edges going from right to left for all the nodes in the sequence.

3.7 RECOVERABILITY AND RELATED ASPECTS

We mentioned earlier that the reliability of a database management system depends on retaining all the effects of committed transactions and undoing all the effects of aborted transactions. The latter process may result in a situation in which several other transactions have to be aborted. As an example, consider the following schedule:

2xW, 1xR, 1yW

If for some reason T2 is aborted, since its writing affects x in T1 we have to abort T1. Also in this process, we must restore or recover the value of y which might have been modified by the value of x.

Cascade aborts is the term used to describe a sequence of aborts that may take place; and the restoration of the original consistent values in such a situation is called *recoverability*. In order to state the conditions for recoverability and avoidance of cascade aborts we define a relationship called *reading from* between any two transactions.

3.7.1 Reading-from relationship

We use the notation a > b for a *after* b (or a *later than* b) and a < b for a *before* b (or a *earlier than* b) to denote temporal order. Let i and j be the index of two transactions; then j reads from i, if (for any named data object, say, x):

1. jxR happens after ixW; that is, jxR > ixW;
2. iA (abort of i) does not happen before jxR; that is, iA > jxR;
3. any other transaction k such that kxW occurring in between ixW and jxR aborts before jxR; that is, ixW < kxW < kA < jxR.

Putting the above together, we obtain:

ixW < kxW < kA < jxR < iA

Algorithm for read-from relationship

We can use DFS for analyzing the read-from relationship. After obtaining each pair of nodes, we must now test whether the above rules hold — namely, if there is a W–W conflict between two transactions i and k and following this a W–R conflict occurs among k and j, then the W–W conflict among i and k should have been resolved earlier by aborting the intruding transaction k.

The implementation of the above algorithm (as well as other algorithms to be described below) demands a wait-and-watch priority queue data structure with facilities for delaying an event until the occurrence of another desired event or reassigning a new lower priority number. We describe one such useful data structure below.

Priority queues: simple and conditional

A simple priority queue is defined as a set in which each element has been assigned a priority number; when such a set is processed:

1. A higher priority element (indicated by a smaller number) is processed before any lower priority element.

2. Elements with the same priority (or those in partial order) are processed in the order of their position in the queue.

A conditional priority queue can contain an additional constraint — namely, the priority of certain elements are to be reassigned dynamically to a lower priority number or they are to be suspended and queued in a buffer for execution until some other element x occurring later in the original queue is processed.

Although there are many ways of realizing the priority queue, the two-dimensional array representation given below is time-efficient when priorities are to be altered dynamically just before the execution of a particular process in the queue. Furthermore, this representation permits concurrent processing of elements with the same priority, provided that they are mutually exclusive processes.

For each level i of priority, a separate queue is formed as successive elements in the row i of a two-dimensional array. Also, we store the column numbers j and k respectively of the beginning element (denoted by iB) and ending element (denoted by iE) in each row i. Hence to alter the priority number of an element, it is necessary only to remove that element from its place and put it into the required new row following the current end element. The algorithms for 'priority execute' and 'alter priority' are as follows:

Algorithm for 'Priority Execute'

Step 1. Find the row with least i whose iB and iE are nonzero (smaller i indicates higher priority).

Step 2. Execute the process in iB if its priority is unaltered. (If its priority number is to be lowered to a new value, go to the algorithm for 'alter priority'; if its priority is to be reassigned so as to follow a desired element x, go to the algorithm for 'buffer'.) If iB is the desired element that activates the processes (if any) in BUFF[x], execute them and go to step 3.

Step 3. If iB = iE, set iB = iE = 0 and go to step 1; otherwise, set iB: = iB + 1 and go to step 2.

Algorithm for 'alter priority of iB to p'

Step 1. Insert element in iB as the last element in row p; set pE: = pE + 1. Go to step 3 of the algorithm for 'priority execute'.

Algorithm for 'buffer'

Comment: BUFF[x] is another simple priority queue.

Step 1. Place iB in the BUFF[x]. Go to step 3 of the algorithm for 'priority execute'.

Example

Consider the following set with priority assignment as shown:

A	L	C	D	E	F	G	H
1	2	4	4	5	2	3	4

Here the second row specifies the predeclared priority number. Let us assume that after this predeclared assignment of priority we require to suspend G when it arrives until the element E is processed and also change the priority of F to a later value 4. The algorithm works as follows:

The two-dimensional array is:

	1	2	3	4	5
1	A				
2	L	F			
3	G				
4	C	D	H		
5	E				

Also, we have initially:

i	iB	iE
1	1	1
2	1	2
3	1	1
4	1	3
5	1	1

Thus we execute in the order:

A, L, Send F to row 4 as element 4; set 4E = 4;
send G to BUFF(E), C, D, H, F, E, BUFF(E) = G.

3.7.2 Definition of recoverability

We can now define recoverability in terms of the read-from relationship. The execution of a schedule is said to be recoverable if for every transaction i that commits, the commit action happens after the commit action of every other transaction from which i has 'read from'. As an example, the following schedule is not recoverable:

3xW, 1xR, 1yW, 1C

because 1 has read x from 3, but 3 is not committed and is still active when 1 commits. This situation is quite bad, since if 3 aborts, 1 will not be consistent; and if we abort 1, we will violate its commit operation.

We can formalize recoverability by the following statement: if j reads from i, then jC > iC; that is, if j reads x from i, then j commits after i.

Example

The schedule:

2xW, 2yW, 3xW, 3yR, 3yW, 3C, 2zW, 2C

has 3yR > 2yW and 3C < 2C; hence it is not recoverable.

Algorithm for recoverability

To test for recoverability, we need to put in the additional condition given in Section 3.7.2; that is, when there is a W–R conflict among i and j, we must check whether i is committed earlier than j is committed.

3.7.3 Avoidance of cascade aborts by delayed reading

A schedule is free from cascade aborts if each transaction reads from only the committed transactions. This can be achieved by delaying the reading of a value of a data object x until all those transactions that have written x are either committed or aborted. As a result, the speed of concurrency that can be achieved is limited.

We can formalize the cascade-abort-free schedule by the following statement: if j reads from i, then iC < jxR; that is, transaction j can only read later the value earlier written by a committed transaction i.

Example

The schedule:

2xW, 2yW, 3xW, 3yR, 3yW, 2zW, 2C, 3C

has 3yR earlier than 2C; hence it is not free from cascade abort.

Algorithm for cascade-abort freedom

As before, we need to incorporate the condition in Section 3.7.3; that is, when there is a W–R conflict between i and j, then iC should lie in between.

Example

The schedule in the previous example can be rearranged thus:

2xW, 2yW, 2zW, 2C, 3xW, 3yR, 3yW, 3C

by delaying transaction 3 to avoid cascade abort.

3.7.4 Restoring values after abort

One of the essential tasks we need to perform is the restoration of the correct values to data objects under abort. This becomes difficult when a sequence of W actions by different transactions takes place on the same data object. These transactions essentially rewrite the values over and over. In such cases, if a few of these or all of these transactions abort, original values have to be restored correctly. Thus it is preferable to delay W of later transactions until the earlier ones have committed or aborted. If a schedule is restricted so that it delays all reads and writes for any data object x until all those earlier transactions that have written x are committed or aborted, it is called a *strict schedule*.

We can formalize a strict schedule thus:

if ixW < jxR or ixW < jxW
then either iC < jxR or iC < jxW
or iA < jxR or iA < jxW

That is, no data object may be read or rewritten later by a transaction j until the transaction i which earlier wrote that object commits or aborts.

Example

Consider the schedule:

2xW, 2yW, 3xW, 2zW, 2C, 3yR, 3yW, 3C

Here 3 rewrites x after 2, but before 2 commits; hence it is not strict.

To make it strict, this schedule can be rearranged by delaying 3xW thus:

2xW, 2yW, 2zW, 2C, 3xW, 3yR, 3yW, 3C

Such a rearrangement requires facilities for jumping over queues.

Algorithm for enforcing the strictness condition

We use the condition given in Section 3.7.4 to enforce strictness. That is, if there is a W–R conflict or a W–W conflict among i and j, then i commits before j reads (or writes) or i aborts before j reads (or writes). Syntactically, this can be expressed by:

ixW < {iC | iA} < {jxR | jxW} where | is exclusive-or.

3.7.5 Relationship among properties

It has been proved by Bernstein et al. (1987) that the set of strict schedules is contained within the set of cascade-abort-free schedules which is contained within the set of recoverable schedules. Also, the set of serial schedules is contained within the set of strict schedules. However, the set of conflict-serializable schedules intersects with all these sets, but is incomparable. In this sense there are conflict-serializable schedules that are not strict, cascade-abort-free or recoverable (see Figure. 3.6).

3.8 CONFLICT SERIALIZABILITY FOR MORE THAN TWO ACTIONS

When actions other than R and W are involved—for example, increment (I) and decrement (D)—the access matrix should include them. By design, the I and D actions do not return a value to the transaction issuing it; they atomically increment or decrement values that are numbers. Furthermore, they commute

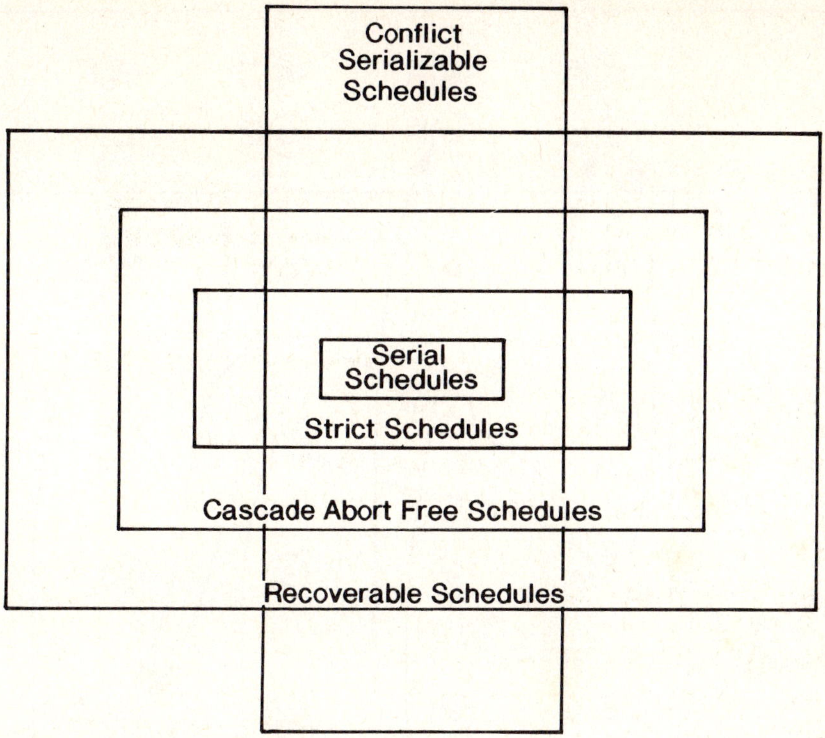

Figure 3.6 Containment of schedules

and do not conflict; that is, 1xI, 1xD has the same effect as 1xD, 1xI for specific increments and decrements. This aspect is reflected in the compatibility matrix (see next section).

3.8.1 Example

Figure 3.7 describes a schedule with additional actions I and D. In this access matrix we have five (t = 5) transactions, four (d = 4) data objects and four (p = 4) actions R, W, I, D; thus there are ninety (ptd + 2t) entries. The adjacency list is given by:

NODES	NEIGHBORS
2(1xW)	17(1C), 37(3xR)
6(1yW)	17(1C), 25(2yI), 43(3yI)
22(2xD)	35(2C), 56(4xW)
25(2yI)	22(2xD), 59(4yR)
37(3xR)	22(2xD), 43(3yI)
43(3yI)	53(3C), 59(4yR)
56(4xW)	62(4yD)
59(4yR)	56(4xW)
62(4yD)	71(4C)

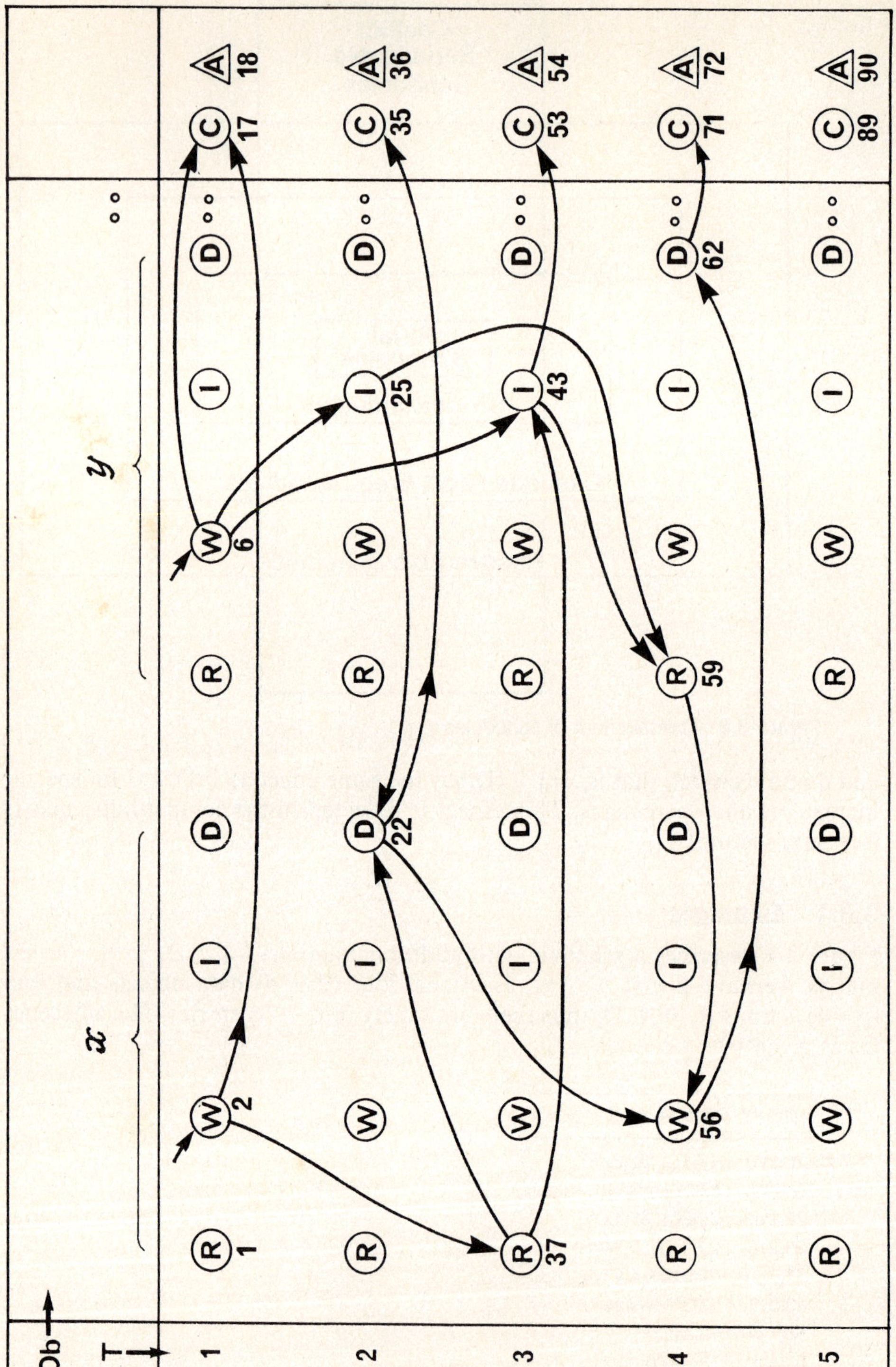

Figure 3.7 Schedule with four actions

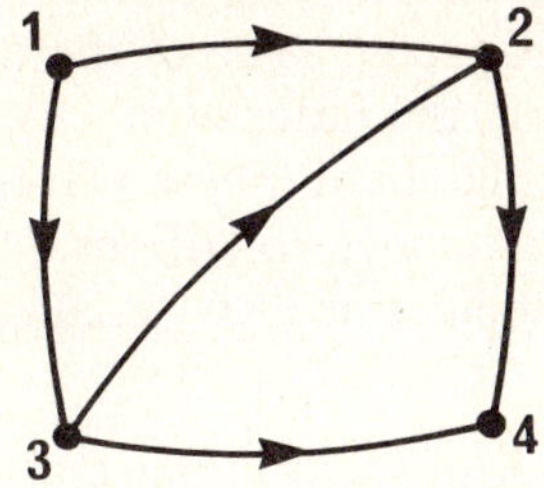

Figure 3.8 Conflict graph

To obtain the conflict serializability, we need to specify the compatibility matrix for these four operations R, W, I, D. This matrix is an extended form of Figure 2.5 and is given below:

	Tj			
Ti	R	W	I	D
R	Yes	No	No	No
W	No	No	No	No
I	No	No	Yes	Yes
D	No	No	Yes	Yes

This table lists eleven incompatible pairs: RW, WR, WW, RI, IR, RD, DR, WD, DW, WI, IW. We now use the algorithms in Sections 3.5 and 3.6 to obtain:

$1yW < 2yI < 4yR$; $1xW < 3xR < 2xD < 4xW$; $1yW < 3yI < 4yR < 4yD$; $1yW < 4yR$

which results in the conflict graph (Figure 3.8). This graph is acyclic and topological sorting yields a serialization: 1-3-2-4.

In this example the simplified rules in Section 3.4, used for two actions R, W, are not applicable. We therefore use the standard decoding algorithm for each of the pairs and eliminate the nonconflicting or unwanted pairs.

3.9 VIEW EQUIVALENCE OF SCHEDULES

Another way of looking at the equivalence of schedules is to use *view equivalence*. This ensures that each read action by the same transactions reads the same values in both schedules; that is, they both see an identical view of the states of the database. Since they read the same values, their write actions should obviously write the same values. Thus we must make sure that the following conditions hold for a committed subset of transactions:

1. Every corresponding transaction in each schedule reads from corresponding write actions.
2. The final read of the values agrees for corresponding data objects in each schedule.

To achieve that we assume the existence of two hypothetical transactions, called initial and final. The former *reads none* of the data objects but *only writes* the initial state of the database; the latter *writes none* of the data objects but *only reads* the final state of the database. These two transactions provide the boundary conditions satisfying the above conditions.

We now define two schedules as view-serializable if the following conditions are met:

1. They have the same set of transactions and identical action sets.
2. If i and j are two transactions such that

   ixW < jxR

   in one schedule, then it should be so in another schedule.
3. If i is not the initial and j is not the final, and k (not initial) is another transaction so that k writes x either earlier than the write step of i or later than the read step of j in one schedule, that is:

   either kxW < ixW *or* jxR < kxW

   then it should be so in another schedule.

   The following should be noted:

1. If i is not initial, we can assume that it reads from the initial transaction.
2. If i is initial and j is not final, then we have for k (not initial):

   jxR < kxW
3. If j is final, then obviously:

   kxW < ixW

3.9.1 Equivalent definition

We can also provide an equivalent definition based on the read-from relationship (Section 3.7.1). Two schedules S1 and S2 are view-equivalent if they satisfy the following conditions:

1. They consist of the same set of transactions and have the same action sets.
2. For any transactions i and j such that iA, jA belong to S1 (and not S2) and for any data object x, if i reads from j in S1, then i reads from j in S2.
3. For each data object x, if ixW is the final write in S1, then it is so in S2.

3.9.2 Conflict serializability and view serializability

As mentioned earlier, the algorithms to prove conflict serializability are executable in polynomial time. However, detection of view serializability cannot be done by polynomial time algorithms. This is because the third condition for view serializability in Section 3.9 requires testing for the acyclicity of the serialization graph for the two possible choices, namely, whether kxW < ixW or jxR < kxW for each data object. That is, we must test for acyclicity by choosing one of the two possible alternative edges (k,i) or (j,k); if there are r such pairs of them, 2^r trials would be required. Hence testing view serializability, which is exponential in nature, should not be attempted. Fortunately, this is not a dead end, since it has been proved by Papadimitriou (1986) that conflict-serializable schedules are view-serializable, but not conversely. In other words, the set of view-serializable schedules is a larger set (providing a greater degree of concurrency) that contains as a subset the conflict-serializable schedules. Hence the latter is a smaller set and is more restrictive from the point of view of the degree of concurrency achievable. On the other hand, since the testing of conflict serializability can be done in polynomial time, it is the only method currently advocated for practical reasons.

3.9.3 Example

The schedule S:

1xW, 2xW, 2yW, 2C, 1yW, 3xW, 3yW, 3C, 1zW, 1C

can be view-serialized but is not conflict-serializable, since there are cyclic W–W conflicts: 1xW < 2xW and 2yW < 1yW.

3.10 MULTIVERSION SCHEDULES

So far we have been concerned with schedules in which each write action by a transaction on a specific data object overwrites a new value on the same memory location(s). This can cause difficulties in recoverability when certain transactions are to be aborted.

For example, consider the schedule:

2xR, 2xW, 3xR, 3yW, 2yR, 2zW, 3C, 2C

There is a W–R conflict between 2 and 3 involving x, and a W–R conflict between 3 and 2 involving y; hence this schedule is not conflict-serializable. Therefore, 3 has to be aborted and as a consequence 2 has to be aborted with no way of recovering the lost value of y, since 2 has read from 3, which has overwritten y. One way of avoiding this mishap is to retain older values that can be read when needed.

In Section 3.7.3 we suggested that delayed reading could be useful in avoiding cascade aborts. This scheme delays reading until all those transactions that write a data object are committed or aborted. In such cases, the previous version produced by an unaborted transaction can be supplied to the waiting reader without aborting it. This improves the speed of transaction processing.

On the basis of the above observations, it seems desirable to have a scheme in which older values or versions of data objects are retained. Although such a scheme would certainly cost more from the point of view of storage and concurrency control, the extra expenditure would be worthwhile because:

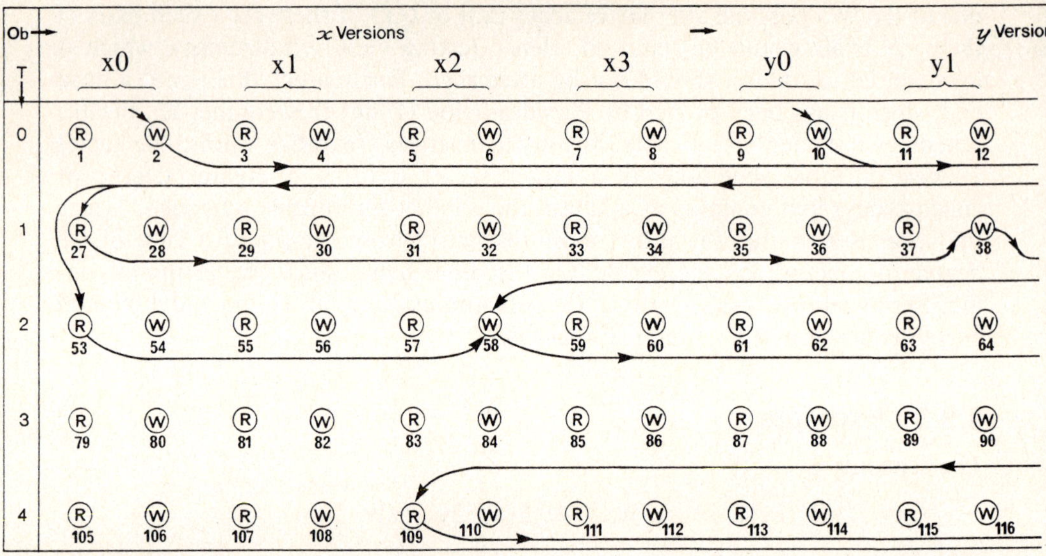

Figure 3.9a Multiversion schedule

1. Recovery is a very important issue in the database management system.
2. The ready and explicit availability of older values on demand can result in a significant improvement in the speed of transaction processing.

In order to implement a scheme of this sort we need to ensure that each write action of a transaction produces a newer version of each data object in a newer memory location, thereby retaining all the older versions. Thus any succeeding read action may read any one of these available versions. Such a schedule is called a *multiversion schedule* (MVS). Since the MVS is more costly, there should be a periodic review of the versions to be retained and those to be purged. This is a cost added to the cost of concurrency control.

Before studying the MVS in greater detail, we will list some of the important points relating to it:

1. We need to introduce a hypothetical initial transaction T0 which reads none of the data objects but only writes the initial version of the database, and a final transaction Tf which writes none of the data objects but only reads the final version.
2. Since each W action of a transaction Ti produces a new version of a data object, each version is assigned a unique new name ixiW specifying which transaction wrote it. If subsequently another transaction Tj reads this version, we denote this by jxiR.
3. Since each transaction reads or writes a data object only once in its lifetime, the number of new versions produced must equal the number of transactions that handled a given data object.
4. W–W conflicts between different transactions are not possible, since each W action of a transaction i produces a unique version, indicated by ixiW.

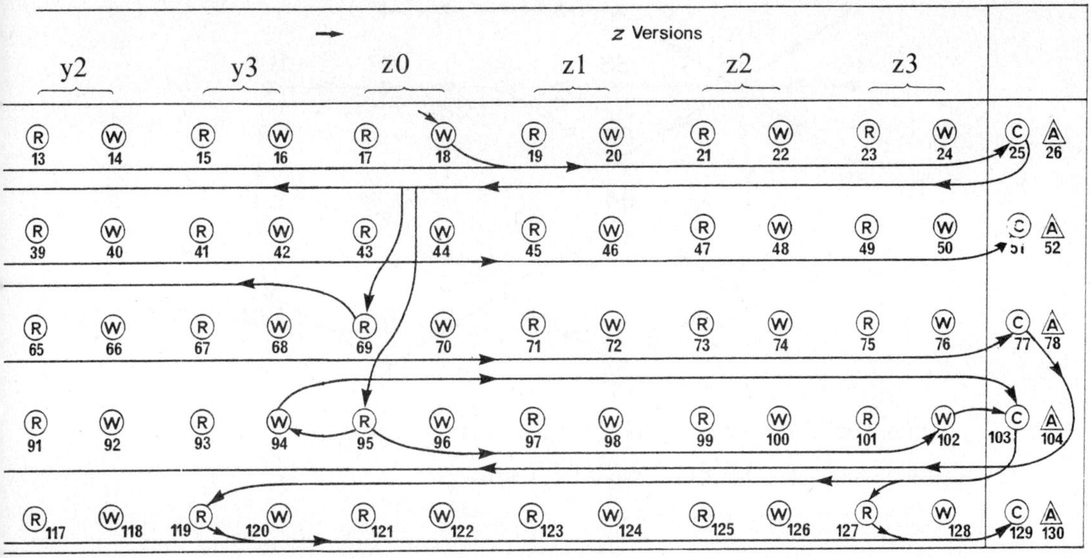

5. R–W conflicts of the form jxiR < ixiW are not possible, since xi is not produced yet and so j cannot read it.
6. W–R conflicts of the form ixiW < jxiR are the only possible conflicts between different transactions, the same data object and the same version.
7. W–R and R–W conflict may arise between different transactions and the same data object with different versions.

3.10.1 Multiversion schedule numeral encoding

A multiversion schedule is shown in Figure 3.9a, and its abstract graph form in Figure 3.9b.The multiversion schedule consists of five transactions, three data objects each with four versions denoted by x0, x1, x2, x3 and y0, y1, y2, y3 and z0, z1, z2, z3.The access matrix has a total of 130 entries.

We can extend the numeral coding scheme in Section 2.5.4 (for the monoversion schedule) to the case of a multiversion schedule. But we must now remember that there are t transactions, d data objects, v versions and p actions where:

$$0 \leq T \leq t;\ 1 \leq D \leq d;\ 0 \leq V \leq v - 1;\ 1 \leq P \leq p$$

These are represented by the quadruplets:

Transaction label (T): Data object (D): Version (V): Action (P)

The doublets **TA** and **TC** are respectively the commit and abort. They are encoded using:

$$TC = (T + 1)(pdv + 2) - 1 = N;\ TA = (T + 1)(pdv + 2) = N$$

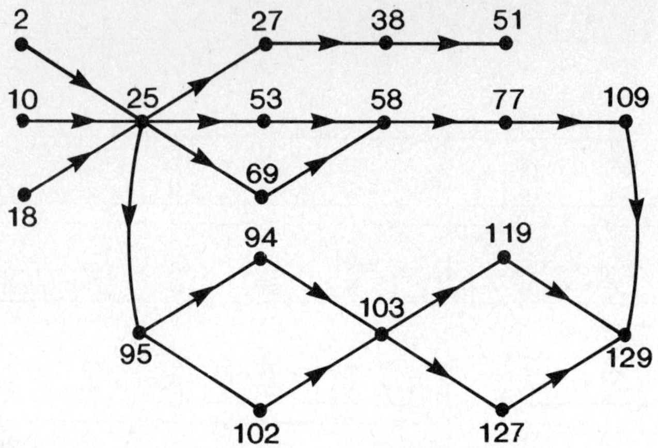

Figure 3.9b Abstract graph form of the multiversion schedule

Quadruplets such as TDVP are encoded using:

$$N = T(pdv + 2) + [(D - 1)p.v + V.p] + P$$

The minor changes in the formula from that in Section 2.5.4 have arisen because the initial transaction has received a label zero and there are v versions (zero to (v − 1)). Remember, however, that the actions as well as the data objects are labelled from 1 to p and 1 to d respectively. For example, in Figure 3.9a, where t = 5, d = 3, v = 4, p = 2:

0C = 1.26 − 1 = 25; 3A = 4.26 = 104

3z0R = 3(24 + 2) + [2.2.4 + 0] + 1 = 95

4z3W = 4(24 + 2) + [2.2.4 + 3.2] + 2 = 128

3.10.2 A multiversion schedule–decoding a numeral code

The following algorithm, which is an extended form of the algorithm in Section 2.5.6, enables decoding of the numeral code assigned to each element of a multiversion schedule.

Step 1. Find N mod (pdv + 2) = r;
if r = 0, then find [N/(pdv + 2)] − 1 = T; it is an abort;
if r = (pdv + 1), then find [(N + 1)/(pdv + 2)] − 1 = T;
it is a commit.

Step 2. If r equals neither zero nor (pdv + 1), then find r mod p = P; if P = 0, it is a W action; otherwise if P=1, it is an R action.

Step 3. Find (r − P) mod pv = s; then V = s/p.

Step 4. Find 1 + [(r − P− Vp)/pv] = D.

Step 5. Find T = (N − r)/(pdv + 2)

3.10.3 Example

Consider the case of the access matrix in Figure 3.9a, where

p = 2, v = 4, d = 3, t = 5

1. If N = 77, we have 77 mod 26 = 25 = r; then [(77 + 1)/26] – 1 = 2; hence the result is 2C.
2. If N = 104, we have 104 mod 26 = 0; find [104/26] – 1 = 3; hence the result is 3A.
3. If N = 95, then 95 mod 26 = 17 = r; then 17 mod 2 = 1 = P; hence action is R.
   Also (17–1) mod 8 = 0 = s; so V = 0;
   D = 1 + [(r – P – Vp)/pv] = 3 = z; T = (95–17)/26 = 3.

Thus the decoded quadruplet is 3z0R.

4. If N = 58, then 58 mod 26 = 6 = r;
   then 6 mod 2 = 0 or P = 2; hence action is W.
   Also (6–2) mod 8 = 4 = s ; so V = 4/2 = 2;
   D = 1 + [(r – P – Vp)/pv] = 1 = x; T = (58–6)/26 = 2

Thus the decoded quadruplet is 2x2W.

3.11 CONFLICT SERIALIZABILITY OF THE MVS

The main purpose of introducing multiple versions is to improve the speed of transaction processing by providing readers with values from nonaborted transactions. Such a scheme should be examined from the point of view of serializability and performance. Studies along those lines have provided much valuable information (Papadimitriou 1986; Bernstein et al. 1987; Cellary et al. 1988). We will summarize in this section some of the key results that are of great practical utility.

1. The computational complexity of transaction models other than action and restricted models (see Section 3.2.1) for both mono version and multiversion serializability problems is exponential (NP-complete).
2. The degree of concurrency of the MVS improves by increasing k, the number of versions; that is, the concurrency degree of k-version (k = 1, 2, 3. . .) MVS improves as k becomes larger.
3. For unrestricted transaction models the hierarchy of sets of conflict-serializable and view-serializable schedules for any specified k-version does not overlap.
4. For restricted and action transaction models, however, the hierarchy of sets of conflict-serializable and view-serializable schedules overlaps for a specified k-version.
5. For restricted and nonrestricted transaction models both single-version and k-version conflict serializability can be tested by polynomial time algorithms.

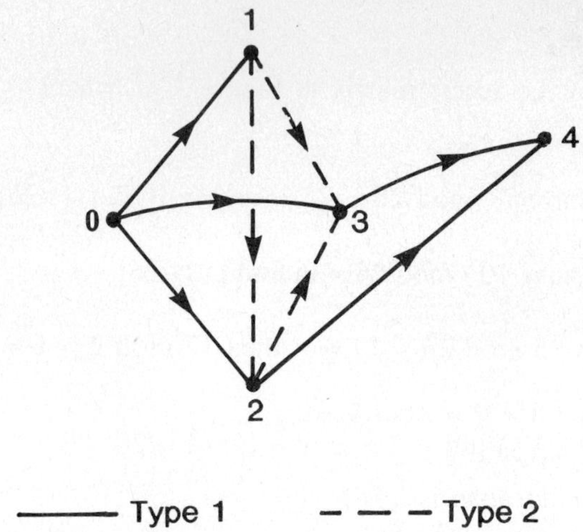

Figure 3.10 MVS conflict graph

In the following section we will define multiversion conflict serializability and an algorithm to recognize it. This algorithm checks whether there exists a total order among the different transactions and their different versions for conflicting actions. Later, in Section 4.4.6, we will describe how timestamps can ensure this total order.

3.11.1 Algorithm for conflict serialization of the MVS

We recall the following from Section 3.10:

1. Among different transactions, W–R conflicts of the form ixiW < jxiR are the only possible conflicts for the same data objects and the same versions.
2. W–R and R–W conflicts may arise between different transactions and the same data object with different versions.

A conflict serialization graph is constructed using the following algorithm.

Step 1. In this algorithm, we consider a pair of nodes labelled by quadruplets of the form, (T,D,V,P) and (T', D', V', P') in the given MVS in order to obtain the two types of edges of the conflict graph.

Type 1 edges: those graph edges which describe the W–R conflict among different transactions on the same data objects with the same version.

Type 2 edges: those graph edges which describe W–R and R–W conflicts between different transactions on the same data objects with different versions.

Type 1 edges are obtained as follows:
if T<>T', D = D', V = V', P = W, P' = R, and P<P' (that is T' reads D' from T) direct an edge from node T to node T' (we use <> for not equal to; = for equal to; and < for earlier).

Type 2 edges are obtained as follows:

if T<>T', D = D', V < V', P = W, P' = R, direct an edge from node V to node V';
If, however,
T <> T', D = D', V < V', P = R, P' = W, direct an edge from node T to node T'.

Step 2. If the conflict graph constructed in Step 1 is acyclic, the MVS is conflict-serializable; otherwise, the MVS is not conflict-serializable.

3.11.2 Example

We consider the same example of MVS given in Figure 3.9a:

Node:	T D V P:	Node:	T' D' V' P' :	*Edge*
	Type 1 edges			
2	: 0 x 0 W :	27	: 1 x 0 R	: 0-1
2	: 0 x 0 W :	53	: 2 x 0 R	: 0-2
18	: 0 z 0 W :	95	: 3 z 0 R	: 0-3
58	: 2 x 2 W :	109	: 4 x 2 R	: 2-4
102	: 3 z 3 W :	127	: 4 z 3 R	: 3-4
	Type 2 edges			
27	: 1 x 0 R :	58	: 2 x 2 W	: 1-2
38	: 1 y 1 W :	94	: 4 y 3 R	: 1-3
69	: 2 z 0 R :	102	: 3 z 3 W	: 2-3

The conflict graph obtained is shown in Figure 3.10. It is acyclic and has a topological sort 0, 1, 2, 3, 4; hence the MVS in Figure 3.9a is conflict-serializable.

EXERCISES

1. Explain the three types of inconsistencies that arise when interleaving the R and W actions of several transactions.
2. What is conflict equivalence among schedules? Illustrate it with a few examples.
3. Program the algorithm described in Section 3.6 to detect conflict serializability of a schedule.
4. What is a 'topological sort'? Write a program for it.
5. Write a program for priority queue. Apply this program to convert a schedule into a strict schedule, a cascade-abort-free schedule or a recoverable schedule.
6. Extend your program for detecting conflict serializability in Exercise 3 to include the two additional actions I (increment) and D (decrement) in the transactions.
7. Illustrate with an example why the detection of view serializability is more time-consuming than the detection of conflict serializability.

8. Encode a multiversion schedule into a numeral code using the algorithm in Section 3.10.
9. Decode a numeral code into a multiversion schedule using the algorithm in Section 3.10.
10. Write a program to detect conflict serializability of a multiversion schedule using the algorithm in Section 3.11.

REFERENCES

Bernstein, P.A., Hadzilacos, V. and Goodman, N. 1987. *Concurrency Control and Recovery in Database Systems.* Addison-Wesley, USA.

Cellary, W., Gelenbe, E. and Morzy, T. 1988. *Concurrency Control in Distributed Database Systems.* North-Holland, Amsterdam.

Papadimitriou, C. 1986. *The Theory of Database Concurrency Control.* Computer Science Press, Rockville, Md.

Sedgewick, R. 1988. *Algorithms.* Addison-Wesley, USA.

4 Locks, timestamps and certifiers

4.1 INTRODUCTION

In the previous chapters we studied the syntactic structure of a transaction as well as the conditions under which a set of transactions, when executed concurrently, can be serialized. In this chapter we will describe the three basic mechanisms used for concurrency control: *locks*, *timestamps* and *certifiers*.

Locks and timestamps permit temporal ordering of each action (such as R, W, I and D) within a transaction by accepting, delaying or rejecting conflicting actions. They ensure that the actions are carried out atomically without interference from actions of another transaction, and that at the same time the database remains consistent.

Certifiers behave in a different manner. Here no action is delayed or rejected, and the transaction runs to a near completion until it is ready to commit; at that moment, a certification or validation test checks for the serializability of the transaction. If the test fails, the transaction is aborted or rolled back and restarted; otherwise, it is committed. The use of this mechanism results in a method called an *optimistic method*, since this method works on the assumption that most probably a serializable execution will result. If any mishap results, it pays the price required to correct the schedule by aborting and restarting a transaction; hence it is also called a *rollback method*.

4.1.1 Locks

A lock is associated with every action on a data object in the database. When a transaction i wants to access a data object, it must acquire an appropriate lock before performing any action on the data object. If the latter is already exclusively locked by another transaction j, which is performing a conflicting action, i must wait until j releases the lock. However, if the actions are not conflicting, i can jointly access the data object sharing that action lock. Thus mutual exclusion is achieved for conflicting actions among transactions while an exclusive lock is in force. By using the lock suitably we can therefore introduce an order restriction (synchronization) in accessing shared data.

The following points relate to the use of a lock:

1. *Granularity*

   One should determine the size of the items to be locked—for example, a block, a page, a file, a record of a file, and so on. This is called the degree of granularity, and it should be chosen optimally in order to ensure maximal concurrency and performance.

2. *Lock compatibility*

   Compatibility among locks intended for different actions among different transactions should be determined; that is, a compatibility matrix should be associated with the granule locks for simultaneous actions (same or different) by different transactions.

3. *Atomicity, fairness and freedom from deadlock*

   Since a lock by itself is a shared device, we must ensure the following:

   (a) Its implementation for each action and a given granularity is atomic.

   (b) Its access is fair to each transaction.

   (c) No transaction holds the lock for ever, thus blocking the lock.

   (d) There is no contention among different transactions holding locks, thereby causing deadlocks; that is, two transactions do not get into a situation in which both mutually wait for ever to gain access to each other's locks.

4.1.2 Timestamps

A timestamp resembles a queuing discipline. Here each transaction i is assigned a unique positive number from a set of totally ordered (monotonically increasing) positive numbers. Such a number can be simply the clock reading at which each transaction starts if we confine ourselves to local events and use a local clock (which generates a totally ordered set of positive numbers). In this case, we need to ensure that the clock is sufficiently fine-grained to distinguish between any two events so as to assign each of them a unique number. This unique number serves as a mechanism called a timestamp. We denote it by TS(i) for a transaction i. The timestamp totally orders all the transactions in a local schedule; that is, either TS(i) < TS(j) or TS(i) > TS(j) if i is not equal to j. In fact, if i is the sequence numbering assigned at the time of the birth of each transaction, then it serves as a timestamp; in this case, we map the ascending set of positive integers to a set of monotonically increasing successive clock readings.

The following points should be noted:

1. Timestamps can specify priority.

If we define the priority of a transaction as the inverse of its timestamp, we can use the timestamp to assign a priority among transactions as follows: the older a transaction, the smaller its timestamp, and the higher its priority.

2. Timestamps can avoid deadlocks.

Suppose that a transaction i waits for j and j waits for i to acquire a lock X, thus resulting in a deadlock. In this situation, if i has a higher priority over j, we can allow i to wait to access the lock; otherwise, i is aborted. Hence cycles are eliminated in the wait-for graph, since each transaction has a unique priority.

A question that arises immediately is: when a transaction is aborted in this way, should it be restarted with the same timestamp or given a new timestamp? We will consider this aspect below.

3. New timestamps can cause livelocks.
Consider the partial schedule:

i(2)xX, i(2)xW, j(1)yX, j(1)yW, i(2)yX?

where transaction i has been assigned a timestamp 2 (that is, it has a lower priority), and j has a timestamp 1. When we reach i(2)yX?, where i is awaiting X lock, it has to be aborted owing to its lower priority.

At this point, if we give a new timestamp 4 for i and restart, it is possible that we have:

k(3)xX, k(3)xW, i(4)xX?

Thus i is aborted again, is restarted and aborted again indefinitely. This situation is called a *livelock*. Unlike in a deadlock, where a transaction is not prevented from executing, here it is prevented from completing, thus resulting in a situation where no useful work is done.

Therefore, in order to avoid a livelock the same original timestamps should be used; otherwise, no transaction will get older and priority cannot be assigned. However, in some instances, when there are conflicting but slow-moving requests from transactions, we need to use new timestamps, as explained below.

4. New timestamps are essential for sluggish transactions.
For example, when a particular transaction i with a lower timestamp is sluggish in its request for actions, a conflicting action of another transaction j with a higher timestamp might have been completed. Consequently, nothing can be done to j if it is committed and gone! Therefore, the timestamp rule is not followed, and we need to abort i and restart. Here we cannot use the old timestamp for i again, since all actions have to start afresh. But how can one determine whether a particular transaction is sluggish? To do so, we need to footprint the timestamp on the data object, as explained below. This is very useful for detecting sluggish transactions and thus improving the speed and reliability of transactions when one is dealing with single or multiple versions of data objects.

5. Footprinting can be used to reject or accept transactions.
Since each data object x is read or written by some transaction, we can test and maintain an ordered pair of the maximum timestamps of transactions which did R and W actions on x. We call this pair a *footprint of transactions* on x or FP(x):

FP(x) = [∀i (ixR)Max TS(i), ∀i (ixW)Max TS(i)] = [r,w], where ∀ denotes 'for all'.

Here r denotes the read footprint, that is, the maximal TS(i) for a transaction i that read x; while w denotes the write footprint, that is, the maximal TS(i) of a transaction i that wrote x.

Initially, for a virgin data object x, FP(x) = (r,w): = (0, 0); then after any first encounter ixW, FP(x) = (0,TS(i)); then followed by a second encounter jxR, FP(x) = (TS(j), TS(i)). Eventually, given such a FP(x) when we receive any kxR, if TS(k) >TS(j), FP(x) = (TS(k), TS(i)); else FP(x) = (TS(j), TS(i)). However, given such a FP(x) when any kxW arrives, if TS(k) >TS(i), FP(x) = (TS(j), TS(k)); else FP(x) = (TS(j), TS(i)).

For any transaction i, the decision to abort, the choice of a timestamp for the transaction and the footprinting on the data object are carried out using the following rules:

Case 1: if ixR arrives

When ixR arrives, if TS(i)< w (irrespective of whether TS(i) < r or TS(i) > r), then ixR is rejected and i is aborted since a conflicting W action of a transaction with a larger timestamp has already been carried out. We then assign the new timestamp greater than all existing timestamps. Otherwise, that is if TS(i) is greater than or equal to w, we permit ixR; if TS(i) < r then we retain the present value of r for x; if TS(i) > r, we set a new value for r, namely r: = TS(i).

Case 2: if ixW arrives

When ixW arrives, we reject this if TS(i) < r or TS(i) < w, since W conflicts with both R and W. We then need to abort i and assign a new timestamp greater than all existing ones. Otherwise, that is if TS(i) is greater than or equal to max(r, w), we permit ixW and set a new value for w, namely w: = TS(i).

In summary, the footprinting takes place thus:

If transaction i gets through and reads: if TS(i) >r then set r: = TS(i); else retain r.

If transaction i gets through and writes: set w: = TS(i).

If transaction i aborts: assign new TS(i).

4.1.3 Certifiers

Certifiers work on the assumption that the probability of a conflict between two transactions is very low and that a transaction would therefore pass the serializability test almost always. Numerous algorithms have been developed for certification (see Bernstein et al. 1987; Cellary et al. 1988). Certifiers fall into four categories:

1. serialization graph certifiers;
2. lock-like certifiers;
3. timestamp certifiers;
4. three-phase (read, validate, write) certifiers.

The serialization graph certifier maintains the summary information about

R–W and W–W conflicts, which is updated whenever any action is performed. When the transaction finally wants to commit, the certifier checks its conflict graph; if it is acyclic, it is permitted to commit, or else it aborts.

The lock-like certifier uses the same principle of conflict detection as in the serialization graph, by checking for conflicts among a set of imaginary locks that could have been assigned to the transactions during their execution before the commit. Since this is done at the end of a transaction, deadlock is avoided.

The timestamp certifier performs the same task as the timestamp procedure, except that it does the checking at the end without rejecting the actions. For the execution produced so far, i checks whether conflicting actions of two transactions have been performed in the permitted timestamp order, as described below:

1. For each ixR that succeeds jxW it checks whether TS(i) is greater than or equal to TS(j).
2. For each ixW that succeeds jxR or kxW it checks whether TS(i) is greater than or equal to j or k.

If both these conditions are satisfied, the transaction i is certified; otherwise i is aborted as required by the timestamp rule (see Section 4.1.2).

The three-phase certifier, as the name implies, consists of three phases:

1. *R phase.* Here only reading is performed and new write values are determined but not written in the database.
2. *V phase.* Here the transaction is tested for the validity of all its actions. If it is consistent, the transaction is allowed to proceed to the W phase; otherwise, it is aborted and restarted.
3. *W phase.* This phase is permitted only after the V phase accepts the transaction; then W action takes place on the database.

The certification method has the following advantages:

1. Read-only transactions are not delayed.
2. It is suitable for distributed database systems, where data is stored at different sites, since the exchange of information takes place only at the end of a transaction but not during its execution.
3. Deadlock and livelock are avoided.
4. It is possible to combine this method with locks and timestamp mechanisms (see Section 4.6).

However, it has the following disadvantages:

1. It is suitable only when the probability of conflicts among transactions is very low.
2. Overhead is needed for collecting and storing summary information about R–W and W–W actions.
3. A transaction may suffer from infinite restarting.

4.2 LOCK TYPES, COMPATIBILITY, 2PL, PROMOTION, AND ESCALATION

As mentioned above, the locks are set on each data object. Thus we need different types of locks, depending on the nature of the action performed. We say that a lock of a specific type is *compatible* or *nonconflicting* with respect to a pair of actions arising from two different transactions if it can be accessed by those transactions simultaneously and each can perform its specific action on the same data object; otherwise, the lock is said to be *incompatible* or *conflicting* for that pair of actions. For example, if we assume that there are only two actions R and W, we can have two types of locks on a data object: read-lock (RL) and write-lock (WL), or no-lock (NL). Their compatibility is then specified for two different transactions i and j and is given by the matrix: (Yes = compatible; No = conflict) (Figure 4.1).

j \ i	RL	WL	NL
RL	Yes	No	Yes
WL	No	No	Yes
NL	Yes	Yes	Yes

Figure 4.1 Lock compatibility matrix

This matrix shows that if there is no-lock (NL) held by any transaction, the request for RL or WL is granted. If a transaction holds RL, this lock can be held simultaneously (or shared) by two or more different transactions to perform R action; but WL cannot be held simultaneously along with RL or WL, since W action is to be excluded from both R and W actions of the other transaction. We therefore call RL a *shared lock* (S) and WL an *exclusive lock* (X) (observe the parallel with the conflict matrix in the read-write model in Figure 2.5).

The S and X locks together constitute what is known as a *two-phase lock* (2PL). This terminology derives from the manner in which these locks are allocated: in the first phase, called the growing phase, the locks are acquired by the transactions; and in the second phase, called the shrinking phase, they are released by the transactions.

Also in the growing phase, a transaction that has acquired a S lock can be promoted to acquire the X lock (if it is free) without releasing its S lock; this is called *lock promotion*. Note that the lock promotion will not cause conflict, since it is set by the same transaction; further, it will not disobey the 2PL protocol, since the S lock is not released in the growing phase.

If the locks used are of various granularities, they are called *multigranularity locks*. In this type of lock, it may sometimes be necessary to vary the level of the lock from a fine to a coarse level; this is called *lock escalation*.

The allocation, promotion and escalation of locks require compliance with specific rules for achieving compatibility. Such rules are called *lock protocols*.

4.2.1 Locking for serializability

We now describe how locks can be used to ensure serializability of a schedule. For this purpose, we introduce the following additional actions in the access matrix described in Chapters 2 and 3:

> ixS: Transaction i share-locks (S lock) data object x.
>
> ixS*: Transaction i unlocks its S lock from data object x.
> (We use * to denote the inverse operation unlock.)
>
> ixX : Transaction i exclusive-locks (X lock) data object x.
>
> ixX*: Transaction i unlocks its X lock from data object x.

In order to achieve maximal concurrency, we must be able to interleave these actions together with R and W actions in different transactions and prove that the resulting schedule is serializable. In the limiting case of least concurrency, these locks simply act as mutual exclusion devices that permit each transaction in succession to ensure serialisation. However, to obtain more concurrency from the schedule, we need to maximize interleaving and at the same time ensure serializability. This is achieved by using the following basic 2PL protocol:

1. When a transaction i wants to access a data object x for an action, it is granted a lock provided that the compatibility matrix permits the lock allocation; otherwise, i waits. Formally, this means ixX < ixW and ixS < ixR. This protocol prevents concurrent access of incompatible locks.
2. Once i is given a lock for its action on data object x, it should not release that action lock until the action is complete. Formally, this means ixW < ixX* and ixR < ixS*. For committed transactions we then have ixX < ixW < ixX* and ixS < ixR < ixS*. This protocol ensures mutual exclusion, thereby avoiding collisions.
3. If i releases its lock on any data object, it will not be eligible to hold any lock subsequently for any other data object. This protocol emphasises that lock acquisition and release should occur in two phases. In the first phase (called the growing phase) the locks are acquired but not released; in the second phase (called the shrinking phase), the locks are released but not acquired. Hence all pairs of conflicting operations in any two transactions are carried out in the same order to ensure serializability.

It can be proved that a schedule that satisfies the above Basic 2PL protocol is *serializable* (see Bernstein et al. 1987).

But how did we avoid the steps of graph algorithms that look for conflict cycles? In fact, we have not avoided these algorithms totally because, in accordance with Rule 1, a transaction needs to wait to acquire a lock, and this may lead to an eternal waiting called a *deadlock*. Since this is not desirable, we need to find a method to detect such deadlocks and correct the situation. Such a method involves the detection of cycles in another kind of graph, called a *wait-for graph* (WFG), in which nodes i and j denote transactions, and if i waits for j we draw a directed edge from i to j. Eternal waiting among a number of transactions is reflected by a directed cycle in this WFG.

4.2.2 Violating 2PL protocol

We now give an example of a nonserializable schedule that violates the 2PL rules. As one would expect, violation of the rules will lead to a cycle in the conflict graph. To construct such a directed graph, we need to use the following rules, which are suitably extended rules used in Section 3.5 that look for R–W, W–W and W–R conflicts incorporating the additional rules of 2PL:

Rule 1. Assign each transaction a node with the same label.
Rule 2. If ixS < jxX, draw a directed edge from i to j.
Rule 3. If ixX < jxX, draw a directed edge from i to j.
Rule 4. If ixX < kxS < jxX, draw a directed edge from i to k.

Example

Consider the following schedule:

1xS, 1xR, 1xS*, 2xX, 2xW, 2yX, 2yW, 2xX*, 2yX*, 2C, 1yX, 1yW, 1yX*, 1C

This has a conflict graph with a cycle 1–2–1 because of 1xS, 2xX and 2yX, 1yX. This has arisen because 1xS* < 1yX, which is a violation of Rule 3 of the 2PL protocol —namely, that once a lock is released no further locks can be allocated.

Example

Consider the modified schedule below, which is obtained by rearranging the schedule in the above example:

1xS, 1xR, 1yX, 1yW, 1C, 1xS*, 1yX*, 2xX, 2xW, 2yX, 2yW, 2C, 2xX*, 2yX*

This is serializable, since it obeys the 2PL protocol.

4.2.3 Deadlock, wait-for graph and conflict graph

As mentioned above, deadlock results when two or more transactions wait for each other in a cycle, so that ultimately each transaction is waiting for itself, thus resulting in a blocking. In order to keep a watch on this phenomenon, we must construct a WFG in which each transaction is represented by a node with the corresponding label. We then draw a directed edge from j to i, if j waits for i to acquire a lock.

The WFG is closely related to the conflict graph; for committed transactions the direction of each of their edges is simply reversed. This is because if i has acquired a X lock on x and j is waiting, then ixX < jxX; thus in the conflict graph we have the direction from i to j. However, in WFG, since j waits for i, we will have the direction of edge from j to i. Note that the conflict graph contains the information pertaining only to committed transactions, while the WFG contains more information since it describes the current state of transactions, including nonaborted ones.

To break a deadlock, we must abort one transaction from the cycle in the WFG; if more than one independent cycle exists, we must abort one transaction from each cycle. Therefore, if one transaction appears as a member in more than one cycle, it should be aborted. We will now illustrate a deadlock by means of an example.

Example

Consider the partial schedule:

1xS, 1xR, 2yX, 2yW, 2xX, 2xW, 1yX, 1yW, . . .

This schedule cannot progress because 2 has to wait for X lock on x, which is under S lock of 1; and similarly 1 has to wait to have X lock on y, which is under X lock of 2. Thus we will have a cycle 1–2–1 in the WFG, indicating a deadlock.

Note that the rules described in 4.2.2 can be used for detecting a deadlock, since they essentially detect conflict serializability by constructing a conflict graph, which as mentioned earlier, is a reversed WFG (recall the comments made in Section 3.6.1).

4.2.4 Lock promotion deadlock

A deadlock may sometimes arise while one seeks to promote a transaction from S to X lock. Consider the partial schedule:

1xS, 1xR, 2xS, 2xR, 1xX, 1xW, 2xX, 2xW, . . .

In this case, 1 has to wait to acquire promotion from S to X since 2 is also sharing S; in addition, 2 cannot be promoted from S to acquire X since 1 is sharing S. But 1 and 2 cannot unlock their S lock and also cannot acquire their X lock; this results in a deadlock.

We will discuss later a number of different strategies that are used for breaking deadlocks.

4.2.5 Variations in basic 2PL

The basic 2PL can be used in two different ways: static (conservative) or dynamic (strict). In the *static* 2PL, all transactions acquire their locks before any operations begin; that is, each transaction has to declare its R and W actions on the named data objects. Then each transaction is assigned a lock only if no conflicts arise, and so deadlocks are eliminated. In this sense the static 2PL limits the degree of concurrency to a minimum. Thus the set of static 2PL schedules is properly contained within the set of conflict-serializable schedules.

In the *dynamic* 2PL, the R and W actions are not predeclared; hence we have information only about the actions already performed. This no doubt increases the concurrency degree but at the same time can cause cascade aborts. Therefore, to ensure recoverability, all the locks acquired by a transaction are released simultaneously when it terminates. The reason for this is explained below.

The set of dynamic 2PL schedules is properly contained within the set of conflict-serializable schedules and properly contains the set of static 2PL schedules.

Use of strict 2PL

We mentioned in Section 3.7.5 that the set of strict schedules is contained within the set of cascade-abort-free schedules which is contained within the set of recoverable schedules. We will now consider whether it is possible to make a 2PL schedule strict so that the schedule is recoverable and free from cascade aborts.

In Section 4.2.1 we stated that:

1. $ixX < ixW < ixX^*$
2. $jxX < jxW < jxX^*$ or $jxS < jxR < jxS^*$

Since iW and jR or jW conflict, we must have (from Section 3.7.4, p. 53) for strictness:

3. $ixW < (iC|iA) < (jxR|jxW)$

Using 1., 2. and 3. together we get:

4. $ixX < ixW < (iC|iA) < (jxX|jxS) < (jxW|jxR)$

(Here | denotes mutually exclusive-or in each pair ordered correspondingly.)

Further, we need from 2PL:

5. $ixX^* < jxS$ or jxX

This means that we can carry out ixX* only when we know iA or iC; that is, the earliest moment we can unlock X on x is when we know that i is aborted or committed. On the other hand, S lock may be released sooner, but in accordance with the 2PL protocol.

4.2.6 Locking additional actions

In Section 3.8 we mentioned that additional actions such as increment (I) and decrement (D) can be incorporated. From the compatibility matrix given there we see that I and D conflict with R and W; hence we cannot share locks in these actions. However, since I and D are compatible we can use a shared lock, provided that we are able to achieve those actions atomically.

4.2.7 Use of 2PL for 2-version schedules

When single-version (or monoversion) schedules use 2 PL, the X lock on a data object prevents us from obtaining a S lock on the same data object; thus concurrent W and R actions are not possible. However, when two versions are used on the same data object we can avoid the lock conflicts as follows: if i writes into x, we can set a lock on the new version ixi so that other transactions may not do R or W action on this new version but can read from the previous version. Consequently R action will not be delayed by a concurrent W operation, thus providing greater concurrency in the schedule.

The 2-version 2PL (2V2PL) scheme works in the following manner. At the end of a transaction execution, the transaction and the items it wrote go through a certification step, which consists of a two-phase locking procedure. This consists in certify-locking all data objects accessed by transaction i for W action. The certification is complete when all certification locks are set and the following conditions are satisfied:

1. At the moment of certification of i, the version of all the data objects read by i is certified.
2. For each data object x that i wrote, all those transactions that read the certified version of x are certified.

Finally, we retain only that new version written by a committed transaction, discarding the older version. By using this scheme we are able to achieve both greater concurrency and recoverability.

To implement such a scheme we use three types of locks:

1. S lock: the shared read-lock;
2. X lock: the exclusive write-lock;
3. OK lock: the certification lock.

For any two transactions i and j, these locks satisfy the compatibility matrix shown in Figure 4.2.

	i		
j	S	X	OK
S	Yes	Yes	No
X	Yes	No	No
OK	No	No	No

Figure 4.2 2V2PL lock compatiblity matrix

The locks are set as follows:

S lock

Before reading any data object x, we attempt to set ixS. Since S conflicts only with OK lock, it can be set as long as no other transaction holds an OK lock. If i already has X lock on x, then i has written x; hence ixS is translated to ixiR (to indicate that i read its own writing). If, however, there is an OK lock on x, i waits until it can set a S lock on x. When OK lock is released from x by a transaction j, the version read by i is due to j, and hence it is labelled ixjR (see Section 3.10). Since this is a committed version, we can avoid cascade abort and ensure recoverability.

X lock

To set X lock for W action on a data object x, the following logic is used: since X lock conflicts with X and OK locks of other transactions, W action is to be delayed until these locks are unlocked; otherwise, X is set and the version written bears the label ixiW.

OK lock

To set OK lock for certification: when the transaction i is about to commit, we attempt to convert all its X locks into OK locks. Since OK locks conflict with S, X and OK locks of other transactions, we can do this conversion only if no other transactions hold such locks.

Deadlock due to lock conversion

As mentioned in Section 4.2.4 (see also Section 4.3.3, p. 81–3), the lock conversions may result in deadlock. For example, consider the schedule:

ixS, jxX, ixX(?), jxOK(?)

where i has S lock on x and j has X lock on x and i seeks X and j seeks OK, this schedule will be deadlocked.

Trade-off factors in 2V2PL

Usually the time taken for certification of a transaction is less than the execution time; hence the time delay in R actions due to 2V2PL certification locks is less than that caused by 2PL X lock on R action. However, since existing S locks may delay OK locks, the resulting improvement in concurrency is achieved through delay in certification and consequently the commitment of a transaction.

4.2.8 Multiversion 2PL

The 2V2PL scheme can be extended to multiversion 2PL, in which many uncertified versions exist. As a result of reading uncertified versions, cascade aborts are possible (see Cellary et al. 1988).

4.3 HOW TO HANDLE GRANULAR LOCKS

As mentioned in Section 4.2, locks can be of various granularities, especially when there is a whole hierarchy of different granules of data. For example, if the data objects are fields of records, the hierarchy of granularity from fine to coarse will be as follows: fields, whole records, blocks of records, files and the whole database. In view of this, it is an advantage to have locks of different granularities in the same database system. If the lock is used at a coarser level, fewer locks will be required, while finer locks will be larger in number. Thus from the lock management point of view, coarse locks incur lower overheads.

But coarse locks permit less concurrency than finer locks since more conflicts are likely. Thus we need to arrive at a balance between size and concurrency. This is not always easy for it requires careful experimentation of the particular database used and depends on the nature of the transactions—whether small or large—and on the mode of access of data—whether random access (that is, the probability of accessing each item is the same and is independent of any previous item accessed) or worst-case access (that is, all transactions require all items). See Ries and Stonebraker in Stonebraker (1986).We will, however, outline some basic principles for handling locks with varying granularities.

4.3.1 Use of hierarchical locks

It is convenient to partition data objects into nonoverlapping sets, each set containing many disjoint subsets that permit a tree representation of the given database. Here, the leaves of the tree correspond to the finest level (fields, for example), while the root corresponds to the coarsest level (the whole database). The different granular sizes appear at different levels of the tree, becoming finer top-down (root to leaves).

In using locks at various levels, we must ensure that conflicting locks are not held on the same data object; that is, we must make sure that two transactions do not hold locks on granules having common elements. This means that before allocation of a lock to a file we must scan through the finer levels (blocks, records, fields) to ensure that no other transaction is holding a finer lock. Such work can be quite tedious. In order to do it more easily, we need to communicate the information that a fine level is locked to its parents and ancestors in the tree. For that purpose we introduce another additional lock, called an *intention lock*. When such a lock is used, we must provide yet another protocol to allocate the locks.

Intention lock

So far we have been using two action locks: S lock and X lock. These locks apply to individual data objects. When a granular hierarchy of locks is desired, we divide the locking in two stages: *intention* and *action*. Intention locks are set at a higher level and action locks at a lower level. When a transaction is holding an action lock, intention lock by another transaction is not permitted except where one holds S lock and the other an intention read-lock. However, two different transactions may share the intention lock at a given granular level. Thus intention locks behave like a macro S lock, which explicitly locks the granule to which it is applied and implicitly locks all its descendants in the tree hierarchy. For example, an intention lock on a record explicitly locks the record and implicitly locks the fields contained within.

We will use the following notation for these locks in different modes:

H: intention share-lock. When this lock is set by a transaction i on a granule, it intends to share access to this granule and read some of its descendants; thus i can set explicit S or H locks on any one of the descendants.

E: intention exclusive-lock. When this lock is set by a transaction i on a granule, it intends to have exclusive access to this granule and to perform W and/or R action on some of its descendants; thus i can explicitly set E, H, S, M or X locks on the descendants.

M: mixed intention read-write lock. When this lock is set by a transaction i on a granule, it intends to have shared or exclusive access to this granule and to perform R-action on it and W and/or R action on some of its descendants. Thus i can set any other locks on descendants, particularly the useful ones X, M and E (note that H and S are not useful in this context).

S: shared read-lock. When this lock is set by a transaction i on a granule, it provides shared access to that granule and all its descendants.

X: exclusive write-lock. When this lock is set by a transaction i on a granule, it provides exclusive access to that granule and all its descendants.

N: no-lock. No-lock is set on any object by any transaction.

In summary, the lock relation between ancestor and descendant is given by the trees:

H	E	M
|	|	|
H or S	Any	Any

This means that a requesting transaction should hold H, E or M on an ancestor to obtain S or X. Further, before requesting X, E or M the transaction must have E or M on an ancestor.

We also denote by S*, X*, H*, E* and M* the unlocking of S, X, H, E, and M respectively. At a given granularity level we can express the compatibility of locks for different transactions i and j by the following matrix (Figure 4.3):

j \ i	H	E	M	S	X	N
H	Yes	Yes	Yes	Yes	No	Yes
E	Yes	Yes	No	No	No	Yes
M	Yes	No	No	No	No	Yes
S	Yes	No	No	Yes	No	Yes
X	No	No	No	No	No	Yes
N	Yes	Yes	Yes	Yes	Yes	Yes

Figure 4.3 Lock compatibility matrix

Access matrix description

In order to describe schedules that use the above locks we can use the access matrix (Figure 2.2). Here each element in the array, such as x, y, z, is now a hierarchical data object represented by a tree (as shown in Figure 4.4) and the twelve actions (R, W, S, X, H, E, M, S*, X*, H*, E*, M*) can be carried out on these data objects. While carrying out these actions and interleaving them for

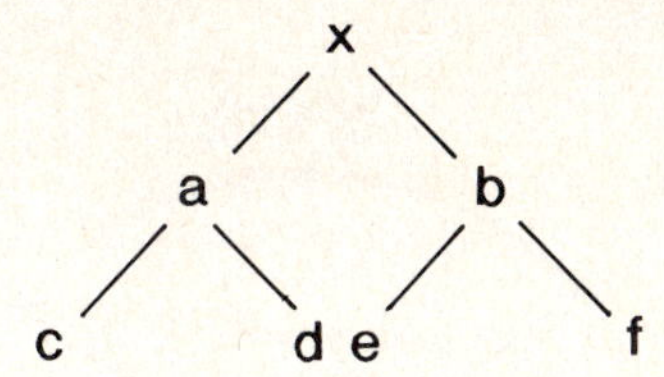

Figure 4.4 Hierarchical data object

maximal concurrency we must ensure that the lock compatibility matrix is satisfied, and that the schedule is conflict-serializable and has no deadlock when this additional fine structure is embedded on each data object.

Example

A typical schedule using the data object in Figure 4.4 is given by:

1xE, 2xE, 1aX, 1bS, 1bS*, 2bE, 2eX, 1aX*, 2aH
2cS, 1xE*, 2cS*, 2aH*, 2eX*, 2bE*, 2xE*

This schedule has no conflicts and is serializable. Note that each lock is compatible. The conflict graph is acyclic (Figure 4.5) and has the following directed edges resulting from conflicts:

1–2: a (X, H); 1–2: b (S, E)

Note also that the lock compatibility is satisfied, as shown in Figure 4.6, at different nodes for different transactions and locks.

4.3.2 Granular lock protocol for tree data object

We now give a basic protocol for the use of granular locks for a tree data object:

1. The first vertex that is requested by transaction i to lock is the root node of the granule.
2. i can set S or H lock on a nonroot node only if i holds a H or E lock on the predecessor node.
3. i can set E, M or X locks on a nonroot node only if it holds a E or M lock on its predecessor.
4. Locks set by the transaction must be released either when it commits or during execution. If the locks are to be released during execution, their release must be in the leaf-root order. For example, no transaction may release an intention lock on a data object x if it is currently holding a lock on any child of x.

4.3.3 Lock escalation

We mentioned earlier that it may be necessary to promote a S lock to a X lock

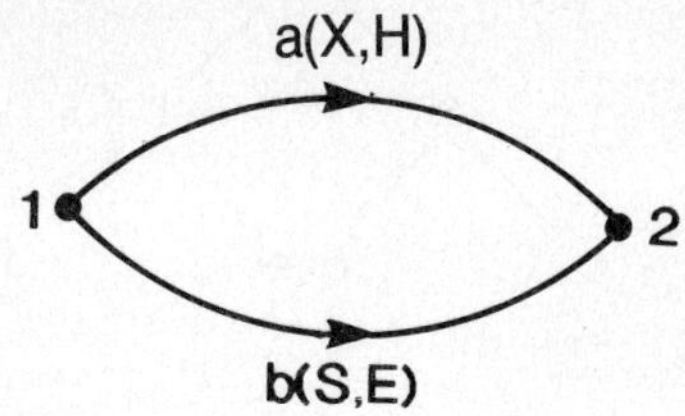

Figure 4.5 Conflict graph

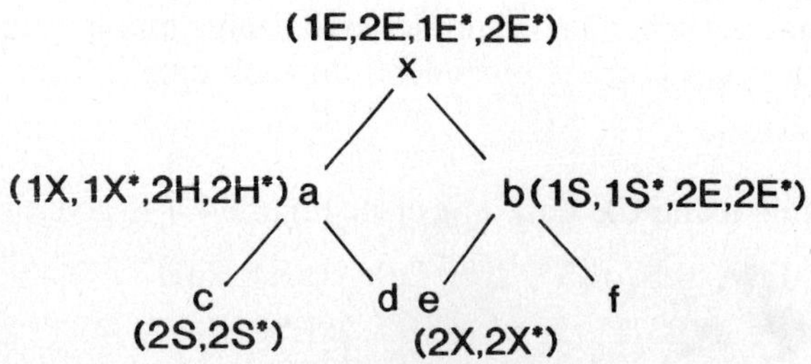

Figure 4.6 Ancestral intention locks

so that a transaction can gain exclusive access while using 2PL without releasing its S lock. An analogous case of strengthening of the lock, called *lock escalation*, is required in granular locking. The rule for escalation of the H, E, M, S and X locks is described compactly by a lattice diagram (Figure 4.7). Figure 4.8 gives a complete lock escalation table, due to Gray (1978) based on the lattice diagram rule.

The rule is as follows: if a transaction holds a lock H it can be promoted to S or E; S or E can be promoted to M; and M can be promoted to X. Each time the lock acquired is strengthened but not weakened when a transaction requests exclusive access. However, each such promotion has to be compatible with the locks held by other transactions; otherwise, the requesting transaction waits; this may result in a deadlock as shown below.

Example (Lock escalation deadlock)

It is quite possible that, owing to lock escalation, deadlock arises in a schedule in a manner similar to that of lock promotion from S to X in 2PL. Consider the partial schedule:

1xE, 2xE, 1aS, 2bE, 2eX, 1bM, 2aX, . . .

where 1 holds S on a and wants M on b, while 2 holds E on b and wants X on a. Using the lock compatibility matrix in Figure 4.3 we note a S-X conflict between 1 and 2 on object a and a E-M conflict between 2 and 1 on object b; thus 2 waits for X (while 1 holds S), and 1 waits for M (while 2 holds E).

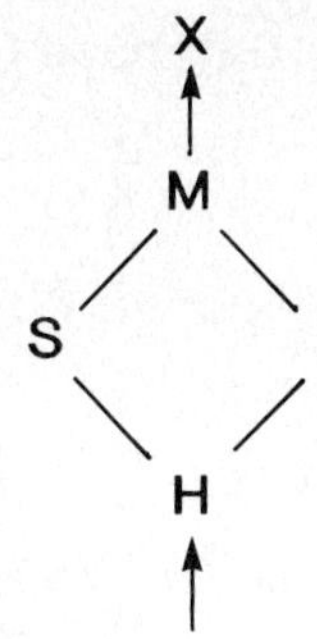

Figure 4.7 Lock escalation lattice diagram

	Old lock held				
New lock wanted	H	E	M	S	X
H	H	E	M	S	X
E	E	E	M	M	X
M	M	M	M	M	X
S	S	M	M	S	X
X	X	X	X	X	X

Figure 4.8 Gray's lock escalation table

In Section 4.3.6 we will see how to avoid deadlocks by using another extra lock, called edge lock.

4.3.4 Relationship between granular lock and 2PL

From the above arguments it is clear that 2PL is contained as a subcase of the granular tree-lock protocol. Korth (1982) has proved that for any two transactions, if the explicit predecessor locks are selected using the compatibility matrix (Figure 4.3), then the implicit locks required on children (S or X) will also be compatible with the 2PL protocol.

4.3.5 Directed acyclic graph locking

A tree-structured hierarchy is very restrictive from a practical point of view when files are indexed, and records may have to be accessed either through files or index as shown in Figure 4.9. This structure is known as a directed acyclic graph (DAG).

In this case, each child can have more than one father, and as a result we have more than one path to reach a desired node. Therefore it is possible that two different transactions may enter into conflicting actions with records—one through the file and the other through the index. Hence we need to modify the tree protocol described in Section 4.3.2 in order to enable us to lock the records suitably so that conflicts are avoided.

Consider the schedule below with reference to Figure 4.9:

1dH, 1iH, 1rS, 2dE, 2fX

Here transactions 1 and 2 hold H and E locks (which are compatible) on d, but

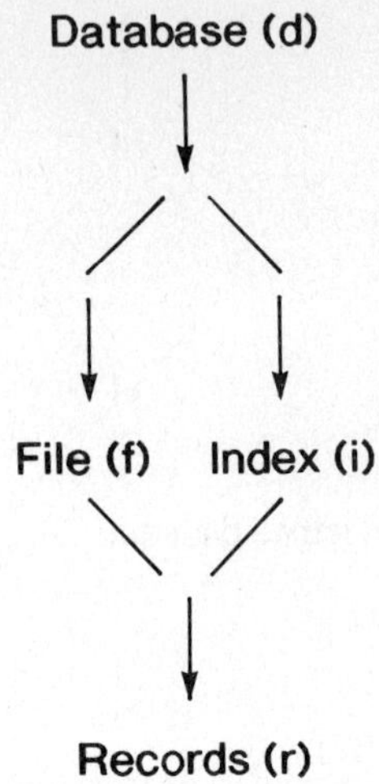

Figure 4.9 DAG data object

1 has a S lock on r and 2 has a X lock on f (which contains r). Such a conflict is undesirable.

To resolve this difficulty we use the modified granular lock protocol for a DAG given below:

1. The first vertex requested by transaction i to lock is a source node of the DAG granule.
2. Transaction i can set S or H lock on a nonsource node only if i holds a H (or M or X) lock to at least one parent and to all ancestors on one of its paths to a source node.
3. Transaction i can set E, M or X locks on a nonsource node only if it holds E or M or X lock on all its parents. This implies that E or stronger locks are held on ancestors and all other transactions hold compatible locks on these ancestors.
4. All locks set by the transaction must be released when it commits or in the leaf-source node order during execution. That is, no transaction may release an intention lock on any data object x if it is currently holding any lock on any child of x. As an example, if (in Figure 4.9) read-write access to records is required through the index, we need to E-lock the database, M-lock the index and X-lock the records.

4.3.6 Korth's edge lock

We have seen that lock escalation can lead to a deadlock. One way of preventing such a deadlock is to use additional locks, called *edge locks*, on the edges that link the nodes in the tree or DAG data object. Edge locks are intention locks and do not behave the same as node locks. This scheme was suggested by Korth (1982). We denote by He and Ee respectively the intention-share edge lock and intention-exclusive edge lock. These locks have the following compatibility matrix for two different transactions i and j:

i j	He	Ee
He	Yes	No
Ee	No	No

Figure 4.10 Edge-lock compatibility matrix

Korth's scheme uses the following lock access and release rules and protocol.

A. Access rules

1. Majority parent rule

A transaction can request a lock of type t on a nonroot node only if it already holds a lock of that type or one stronger on a majority of parents of that node.

2. Majority leading edge rule

A transaction can request a lock of type S (or X) on a nonroot node only if it already holds a lock of type He (or Ee) on a majority of edges leading to that node.

B. Release rule

A transaction i should not release a lock on any ancestor node while holding a lock on a child node.

C. Protocol

A transaction must obey rules A and B, and it has to obtain a lock of type H (or E) on x before getting He (or Ee) lock on edge (x, y). The locks on x and locks on all outgoing edges from x must be requested simultaneously.

Furthermore, lock compatibility must be satisfied and waiting transactions must be served in a FIFO (first in, first out queue order); also, edge lock on (x, y) must be released as soon as the desired node lock on y is obtained.

Example

Consider the same example as on p. 82:

1xE, 2xE, 1aS, 2bE, 2eX, 1bM, 2aX . . .

We can introduce edge locks, thus avoiding deadlock:

1xE, 1(x,a)Ee, 1(x,b)He, 2xE, 2(x,a)He, 2(x,b)Ee . . .

Here 2 will wait in the queue for 1 to unlock (x,a), and (x,b).

Hypergraph protocols

Recently, some studies have been carried out concerning the design of locks for the specific data structure of the database and the structure of transactions. (Cellary, et al. 1988). Their practical performances are yet to be evaluated. For further recent studies on locks, see Lausen and Soininen (1989).

4.4 TIMESTAMPING PROCEDURES

In the introductory Section 4.1.2 we gave a detailed account of the basic principles of the timestamping procedure. As in the case of locking, the timestamping procedure can be classified as basic, strict, single and multiversion, depending on the manner in which it is applied.

4.4.1 Basic timestamping procedure

The basic timestamping procedure uses the procedure outlined in Section 4.1, namely: (Recall(r, w) = FP(x) is the footprint on x where r is the max TS(i) of i that read x and w is the maximum TS(i) of i that wrote x):

Case 1: if ixR arrives

When ixR arrives, if TS(i)< w (irrespective of whether TS(i) < r or TS(i) > r), then ixR is rejected and i is aborted since a conflicting W action of a transaction with a larger timestamp has been already carried out. We then assign the new timestamp greater than all the existing timestamps.

Otherwise, that is if TS(i) is greater than or equal to w, we permit ixR; if TS(i) < r then we retain the present value of r for x ; if TS(i) > r, we set a new value for r, namely r: = TS(i).

Case 2: if ixW arrives

When ixW arrives, we reject this if TS(i) < r or TS(i) < w, since W conflicts with both R and W. We then need to abort i and assign a new timestamp greater than all the exising timestamps. Otherwise, that is if TS(i) is greater than or equal to max (r,w) we permit ixW and set a new value for w, namely w: = TS(i).

The above procedure ensures serializability but not recoverability. In Section 4.4.2 we will show how to ensure recoverability by making the schedule strict.

Example

Consider the partial schedule using a 2PL (Section 4.2.3, p. 75):

1xS, 1xR, 2yX, 2yW, 2xX, 2xW, 1yX, 1yW . . .

This results in a deadlock due to 2 waiting for X lock on x, which is under S lock of 1, while 1 is waiting for X lock on y, which is under X lock of 2.

To avoid this deadlock we can use timestamping:

Let us assume that TS(1) = 1, TS(2) = 2; FP(x) = (0,0); FP(y) = (0,0); consider

1xR, 2yW, 2xW, 1yW;

when 1xR arrives: accept 1xR, r(x): = 1; thus FP(x): = (1,0);

when 2yW arrives: accept 2yW, w(y): = 2; thus FP(y): = (0,2);

when 2xW arrives: accept 2xW, w(x): = 2; thus FP(x): = (1,2);

when 1yW arrives: abort, start with new TS(1) = 3.

The timestamp procedure can lead to infinite restarting or livelock, as will be demonstrated by the next example.

Example (infinite restarting)
From now on, to denote timestamps on a schedule we use the notation:

i(TS(i))xR and j(TS(j))yW

whenever the timestamps used—TS(i), TS(j)—are different from the assigned transaction labels i, j.

Consider the schedule:

1(10)yR, 2(11)xW, 1(10)xR, 1(12)yW, 2(11)yR, 2(13)xW, 1(12)xR

The assignment of footprints on y and x, abort, and assignment of new timestamps and restart take place thus:

FP(y) = (10,0), FP(x) = (0,11), abort 1 and restart 1 with new timestamp 12; FP(y) = (10,12), abort 2 and restart 2 with new timestamp 13; FP(x) = (0,13), abort 1 and restart 1 with new timestamp 14, . . . and so on.

Here each time after an abort we restart the transaction with a new timestamp immediately; this results in infinite restarting.

4.4.2 Strict timestamping procedure

Consider the schedule:

2(5)xW, 3(7)xR, 3(7)yW, 3(7)C

where timestamps are in brackets.

This is a valid timestamp order; but 2 has not committed; hence this schedule is not recoverable. To make the schedule strict, we need:

ixW < (iC|iA) < (jxR|jxW);

that is, we need to delay all jxR and jxW for which TS(j) > TS(i) until iC or iA (that is, i is committed or aborted). Note that this waiting will not cause deadlock since j is younger than i. Thus in the above example 3(7) waits until 2(5) commits or aborts.

4.4.3 Thomas write-ignore rule

In Section 4.4.1 we used the following rule: if ixW arrives after jxW and the timestamps TS(i) < TS(j), reject transaction i, abort and restart. This rule may be relaxed; that is, one can ignore the request without becoming inconsistent and one need not abort i, *but simply ignore its W action* and proceed. This rule is called the Thomas write-ignore rule, and it is obviously an improvement over the basic timestamping procedure in terms of speed. However, this relaxation is not permissible for W–R and R–W actions because the net result of a sequence of W actions of transactions is the same as the result of doing only the W action of a transaction with the largest timestamp. That is, if we have a schedule:

1(3)xW, 2(6)xR, 3(9)xW, 4(5)xW

where each TS(i) is in brackets following i, we should abort 4; but the Thomas rule would ignore the W action and permit 4 to go through.

Example (Thomas rule)
Consider the schedule:

1(8)yR, 2(6)xR, 3(7)zR, 1(8)yW, 1(8)xW, 2(6)zW(Abort 2), 3(7)xW.

The footprint assignment sequence and abort take place thus:

FP(y) = (8,0); FP(x) = (6,0); FP(z) = (7,0); FP(y) = (8,8); FP(x) = (6,8).

In step 6, we reject 2(6)zW since TS(2) = 6 < 7 in r of FP(z) = (7,0) and abort 2. In step 7, using the Thomas rule, we ignore the W action of transaction 3 since transaction 1 with a larger timestamp has already written x as indicated by FP(x) = (6,8)

4.4.4 Two-phase commitment with timestamping

Since commit is a very important operation, it is preferable that it be done only after very careful scrutiny. With this in mind, all W actions can be made to go through two phases—intention write or prewrite (P) and action write (W). The prewrite phase is carried out on a buffer rather than the database and in the write phase the action is on the database. The P action must be requested before W. Once P is accepted in the buffer, the corresponding W will not be rejected; hence this is called a two-phase commitment (2PC) procedure. This procedure is very useful in avoiding cascade aborts and in improving the reliability of distributed transaction processing systems, which we will study in Chapter 6.

In this section we will describe how the basic timestamping procedure (Section 4.4.1) can be modified when a queue is associated with each data object; in this queue the accepted read, accepted prewrite and accepted write requests are buffered. That is, these valid actions are neither executed nor rejected but held in a buffer for subsequent possible execution. The algorithm for accepting R or P and performing final write W is a minor modification of the procedure described in Section 4.4.1. Here the rejection takes place only for R and P actions; those accepted are buffered for execution in a timestamp order. Also, we maintain three other registers—LR(x), LP(x) and LW(x) respectively—to indicate the smallest timestamps of transactions whose R, P and W requests are currently in a buffer denoted by BQ(x) for execution.

We use the notation TS(i) for the timestamp of i; FP(x) = (r,w) for the footprint of x. Initially, we assign FP(x): = (0,0) and assume that LP, LR and LW are initialized to zero.

```
PROCEDURE ixR {When ixR arrives}:
{Comment: ixR action is rejected when TS(i) < w; when TS(i) > w
ixR can execute only when there is no prewrite jxP such that TS(j) < TS(i); that is, R
action is done only when there is no pending P action on x with a lower timestamp.
LP(x) is used to find any jxP with least TS(j) waiting for P action}
  begin
    if TS(i) < w then
    {ABORT i; START WITH A NEW TIMESTAMP}
    else if TS(i) > LP(x) {pending P actions} then
    {PLACE i'S R REQUEST IN BQ(x)}
    else {TS(i) is less than or equal to LP(x)}
      begin
        {ixR}
        r: = max[TS(i),r]
      end
  end
PROCEDURE ixP {When ixP arrives} :
{Comment: P actions are aborted or buffered.}
  begin
    if TS(i) < r or TS(i) < w then
    {ABORT i; START WITH A NEW TIMESTAMP}
    else {PLACE i'S P REQUEST IN BQ(x)}
  end
PROCEDURE ixW {When ixW arrives}:
{Comment: W action is never rejected; it is buffered if there
are jxP with TS(j) < TS(i) or kxR with TS(k) < TS(i); LR(x)
indicates kxR with least TS(k) waiting for R action.That is,
W is performed only when there are no pending P or R on x with timestamps smaller
than TS(i).}
  begin
    if TS(i) > LR(x) or TS(i) > LP(x) then
    {PLACE i'S W REQUEST IN BQ(x)}
    else begin
    {EXECUTE ixW IN DATABASE}
    w: = TS(i)
        end
  end
```

Note that accepted P action at the buffer is to be removed and executed. EXECUTE ixW does this removal from BQ(x) and updates x to a new value. Since the value of LP(x) may increase after this removal, successive retesting of

BQ(x) is needed to perform R or W action of a newly enabled transaction j for which TS(j) < LP(x) now holds. Thus using 2PC reduces concurrency and slows down the schedule.

Example

Consider the partial schedule:

1xR, 1xP, 2xR, 1xW, 3xR, 2xP, 3xP, 4xR

We assume that for each transaction i, TS(i) = i when

1xR arrives: TS(1) = 1; no pending P; do 1xR; FP(x): = (1,0);
1xP arrives: Put in BQ(x); LP(x) = 1;
2xR arrives: 1xP pending; put in BQ(x); LR(x): = 2;
1xW arrives: Do 1xW; no pending P; do 2xR; FP(x): = (2,1);
3xR arrives: No R or P pending; do 3xR; FP(x): = (3,1);
2xP arrives: TS(2) = 2 < r(= 3); abort;
3xP arrives: TS(3) = 3; put in BQ(x); LP(x): = 3;
4xR arrives: 3xP pending; put in BQ(x).

4.4.5 Deadlock-livelock avoidance in locking

We mentioned briefly in Section 4.1 and in the example in Section 4.4.1 that timestamping can be used to avoid deadlocks arising in locking. We will now describe two strategies that are based on timestamps for avoiding deadlock and livelock in locking. These are:
(i) Wait and die (or non-preemptive) method; and
(ii) Wound and wait (or preemptive) method.

With the wait-and-die method, when a transaction i requests an X-lock already held by j, i is permitted to wait until j finishes if i is older than j; otherwise, i is aborted. That is, if TS(i) < TS(j) then i waits; otherwise i aborts. This means that the younger transaction is aborted and restarted with its original timestamp. Note that the older transaction waits to allow the youngsters already in action to continue. This scheme is therefore friendly to 'youngsters'.

With the wound-and-wait method, when a transaction i requests an X-lock already held by transaction j, transaction i is permitted to wait only if it is younger than j; otherwise, j is forcibly aborted (if it has not already escaped by committing or aborting) granting the lock to i. That is, if TS(i) < TS(j), then (try to) abort j, otherwise, i waits.

Here also the younger transaction is aborted; but it may so happen that j escapes unhurt by committing or aborting on its own. This is therefore called wounding rather than killing! After abort, transaction j starts again with its original timestamp; if it conflicts with an older i, it waits, because TS(j) > TS(i). Consequently, this scheme is friendly to 'oldies' which push through the system forcing youngsters to wait. However, this brute force approach can abort a younger transaction about to complete and commit, and this may not be desirable. Furthermore, in the wait-and-die method a younger transaction i may have to be aborted and restarted several times if the older j holds its lock too long. In the wound-and-wait method, however, if a younger transaction is aborted, it has to be restarted only once to acquire the lock. Retaining the original timestamp ensures that the oldest transaction in either strategy cannot die or get wounded. Thus both strategies prevent deadlock as well as livelock.

4.4.6 Multiversion timestamping

In Section 3.10 we described the basic multiversion schedules (MVS). We will now consider how timestamping can be used for MVS. The basic algorithm is given in Bernstein and Goodman (1983). This algorithm uses timestamps to ensure total order among transactions and their different versions for conflicting actions. A younger transaction is only permitted to read a data object written by an older transaction; an older transaction is aborted if it attempts to overwrite a data object already read by a younger transaction. Also, an older transaction cannot read a version written by a younger transaction.

Here, as before, for each data object version x0, x1, x2, . . . , xk we associate the read and write footprint of a transaction with the maximal timestamps that read or wrote them. Thus footprint FP(xk) = (rk, wk) for k = 0, 1, 2 . . . , where rk = Max[TS(j)] of any transaction j that read xk and wk = TS(k).

The footprinting of timestamps on data objects, acceptance or aborts of transactions then take place according to the following rules:

1. When ixR arrives:

   {R actions are never rejected here.}

We first recall that in a single-version schedule ixR is permitted only if w is less than or equal to TS(i). In the multiversion case we read a version xj (that is, we do ixjR) that has the largest write footprint wj that is less than or equal to TS(i); then, if the corresponding read footprint rj < TS(i), we set rj: = TS(i).

2. When ixW arrives:

   {W actions are rejected or accepted; if accepted, they are relabeled}

Recall that in the single-version case we permit ixW only if TS(i) is greater than or equal to max (r, w) and set a new value for w, namely: w: = TS(i). In the multiversion case choose that version xj with the maximum write footprint wj that is less than TS(i). If the corresponding read footprint rj > TS(i), reject ixW and abort i; otherwise, accept and relabel ixW as ixiW and set:

FP(xi): = [TS(i), TS(i)]

Example
Consider the schedule:

1(1)x0R, 2(2)x0R, 2(2)y1W, 1(1)y0R, 1(1)x1W

The advantage of this multiversion schedule is that at step 4 transaction 1 is allowed to read an older version. Note, however, that transaction 1 cannot read the new version y1 since its timestamp is smaller than the write footprint of y1 (which is 2). This can be seen from the footprint assignment sequence:

[we start with FP(x0) = (0,0); FP(y0) = (0,0)]

FP(x0) = (1,0); FP(x0) = (2,0); FP(y1) = (2,2); FP(y0) = (1,0);

now when 1(1)x1W arrives, we abort 1 since r0 [= 2] is greater than TS(1)[= 1].

Example

Consider the schedule with timestamps:

TS(1) = 6,TS(2) = 4,TS(3) = 18,TS(4) = 23; we start with FP(x0) = (0,0); if now 1(6)xR arrives, we accept this and set FP(x0) = (6,0); now, if 2(4)xW arrives, we abort 2 since corresponding r0 = 6 > 4; if now 3(18)xR arrives, we accept and set FP(x0) = (18,0); if we now get 3(18)xW, we accept and relabel 3(18)xW as 3(18)x3W and set FP(x3): = [18,18]. If now we have 4(23)xR, we accept this since w = 18 < 23 and we set FP(x3): = [23,18].

4.5 HIERARCHICAL TIMESTAMPING PROCEDURES

4.5.1 Single-version data object

We now consider the use of timestamping for single-version hierarchical data objects (Section 4.3). As before, the timestamp of a transaction i is denoted by TS(i), but we now use two different kinds of footprint (FP) for a granule:

1. individually assigned read-write FP of granule x, denoted by FP(x): = (r(x), w(x));
2. derived family footprint FF of a granule x denoted by FF(x) = (fr(x), fw(x)): = (max r(x), max w(x)), where max operation is applied to the granule x and all its descendants; hence if x is a leaf (no descendant): r(x) = fr(x)and w(x) = fw(x).

The algorithm for footprinting timestamps on and from data objects, and for acceptance or abort of a transaction i, is as given below:

```
PROCEDURE ixR {When ixR arrives}:
begin
   flag: = T;
for each y ∈ ancestors(x) do
   if TS(i) < w(y) then flag: = F;
if TS(i) < fw(x) then flag: = F;
if flag: = T then
   begin
      ixR;
      r(x): = max[TS(i), r(x)]
      fr(x): = max[fr(x), r(x)]
   for each y ∈ ancestors(x) do
```

```
            fr(y): = max[TS(i), fr(y)]
        end
        else {ABORT i; RESTART WITH A NEW TIMESTAMP}
    end
    PROCEDURE ixW {When ixW arrives}:
    begin
        flag: = T;
    for each y ∈ descendants(x) do
    if TS(i) < r(y) or TS(i) < w(y) then
        flag: = F;
    if TS(i) <fr(x) or TS(i) < fw(x) then
        flag: = F;
    if flag: = T then
        begin
        ixW;
        w(x): = TS(i);
        fw(x): = TS(i);
        for each y ∈ ancestors(x) do
        fw(y): = max[TS(i), fw(y)];
        end
        else {ABORT i; RESTART WITH A NEW TIMESTAMP};
    end
```

Example

Consider the tree data object in Figure 4.11; here FP(x) is within () and FF(x) is within [ ]. If 3(6)cR arrives, it will be accepted and we then set r(c): = 6; fr(c): = 6; fr(a): = 6; fr(x): = 11. If, however, 4(6)xW arrives, 4 will be aborted.

4.5.2 Multiversion data object

The multiversion timestamping procedure can be extended to hierarchical data objects. We will not, however, deal with this aspect here (see Carey 1983).

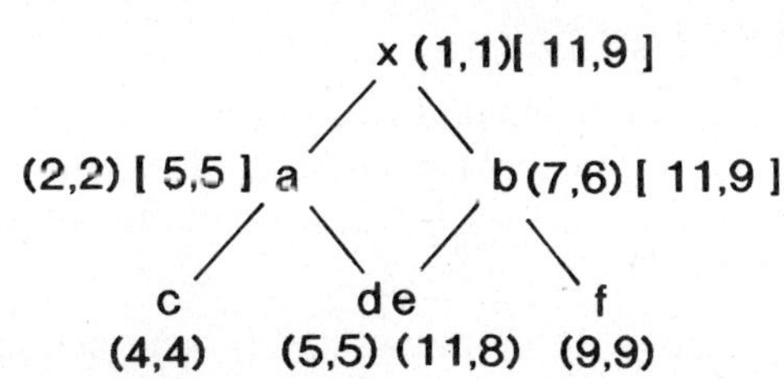

Figure 4.11 Hierarchical timestamping

4.6 CERTIFICATION PROCEDURES

In Section 4.1.3 we outlined the basic principles of the certification or validation procedures (also called rollback or optimistic methods), and mentioned the four different categories of certifier:

1. Serialization graph certifier;
2. Timestamp certifier;
3. Lock-like certifier;
4. Three-phase certifier.

We now describe these in detail.

4.6.1 Serialization graph certifier

Here we maintain a dynamic list of R–W and W–W conflicts that have taken place during the execution of a transaction i. When the action iC is received, the certifier checks whether i lies in a cycle of the conflict graph, as explained in Chapter 3. If so, i is aborted; otherwise, i is certified and committed.

To ensure recoverability we must also abort all those active transactions j that read from the aborted transaction i either directly or indirectly via another transaction k. This is done by checking:

1. whether j has directly read from i; this is indicated by the presence of an edge i-j corresponding to ixW < jxR;
2. whether there is a jxR and ixW such that for every k where kxW is not an action, edge i-k and edge k-j are in the conflict graph; that is, we have ixW < kxR < jxR.

4.6.2 Timestamp certifier

The timestamp certifier performs the same task as a timestamp procedure, except that it performs its actions just before commit action. For each transaction i that comes later than j it checks the following:

1. If ixR > jxW, then whether TS(i) is greater than or equal to TS(j);
2. If ixW > jxR or kxW, then whether TS(i) > TS(j) and TS(i) > TS(k).

If 1. and 2. are true, it certifies the transaction i to commit; otherwise, it rejects and aborts.

4.6.3 Lock-like certifier

The lock-like certifier assumes that imaginary X or S locks have been allocated when conflicting actions take place, and records all the R and W actions of each transaction. When a transaction i wants to commit, it checks whether either of the following is true:

1. for any ixR there is a conflicting jxW (j is an active transaction);
2. for any ixW there is a conflicting jxW or jxR.

If the answer to 1. or 2. is 'yes', then it rejects i and aborts it; otherwise, it certifies i for commit.

4.6.4 Three-phase certifier

The basic principles of the three-phase certifier (3PC) were outlined in Section 4.1.3. These certifiers essentially check for serializability of those transactions that are already in their W phase and those currently being certified. There are two variants of 3PC: serial 3PC and parallel 3PC.

1. Serial 3PC

Here the R phase of a later transaction i overlaps with the W phase of earlier transactions. Hence there should be no common data objects between those read by i and those being written by the overlapping transactions. However, the W phase of an earlier transaction ends before the V phase of another transaction begins; that is, W phase and V phase of different transactions are mutually exclusive.

We assign a sequence number C(i) from a COUNTER C when the transaction i completes its V phase and enters its W phase. At the very beginning this counter C is initialized to zero and whenever any transaction successfully exits its V phase, C is incremented by one and this number is assigned to the transaction. Thus at any time the COUNTER reading tells us how many transactions have been successfully validated and have entered their W-phase.

2. Parallel 3PC

Here also we overlap the R phase of a later transaction i with the W phase of other earlier transactions, as in serial 3PC. In addition, we permit the overlap of the V Phase and W phase of earlier transactions with the corresponding phases of a later transaction i. Hence there should be no common data objects between those read as well as written by i, and those being written by the overlapping transactions. Also, we need to keep a record of active transactions which finished their R phase but not their W phase.

Furthermore, we assign the sequence number C(i) to a transaction only when it completes its W phase; hence the COUNTER is incremented just after the W phase and before C(i) is assigned. Thus at any time the COUNTER reading tells us how many transactions have completed their W phase.

To describe these certifiers we need the following additional notation:

R(i) is the set of data objects read by i; it is called the read-set of i.

W(i) is the set of data objects written by i; it is called the write-set of i.

iB denotes the action begin of i;

iV denotes the action enter validation of i.

C(iB) denotes the counter reading when i begins;

C(iV) denotes the counter reading when i enters for validation after R phase.

Thus the set of transactions with the sequence numbers C(iB) + 1 to C(iV) do W phase concurrently with the R phase of i. We call this set WLAP (i). We must therefore make sure that there is no R–W conflict between i and any member j belonging to the set WLAP(i).

In parallel 3PC we denote by ACTIVE(i) the set which includes i and all other active transactions which completed their R phase and overlap their V phase and W phase with R phase and V phase of i, but have not finished their W phase. Again we must make sure that there is no R–W or W–W conflict among i and any member j belonging to the set ACTIVE(i)-{i}.

We now describe the 3PC serial and parallel certifiers for a transaction i.

Serial 3PC certifier

```
PROCEDURE Serial 3PC(i):
begin
   C(iV): = COUNTER;
   FLAG: = T;
   for each j ∈ WLAP(i) do
      if R(i) ∩ W(j) is not empty then FLAG: = F;
   if FLAG = T then begin
         COUNTER: = COUNTER + 1;
         C(i): = COUNTER;
         {PERFORM W-phase};
            end
   else {ABORT i}
end
```

This procedure should be carried out atomically.

Parallel 3PC certifier

```
PROCEDURE Parallel 3PC(i):
begin
   C(iV): = COUNTER;
   FLAG: = T;
for each j ∈ WLAP(i) do
   if R(i) ∩ W(j) is not empty then FLAG: = F;
for each j ∈ ACTIVE(i)–{i} do
   if [R(i) ∪ W(i)] ∩ W(j) is not empty then FLAG: = F;
   if FLAG = T then begin
         {W-phase};
         COUNTER: = COUNTER + 1;
         C(i): = COUNTER;
         ACTIVE(i): = ACTIVE(i)–{i};
            end
```

```
else begin
ACTIVE(i): = ACTIVE(i)–{i};
{ABORT (i)};
    end
end
```

Example

Consider the parallel 3PC schedule shown in Figure 4.12 with:

R(1) = W(1) = {a,b} = x; R(2) = {c,d} = y; W(2) = {b,e} = z
R(3) = {b,e} = z; W(3) = {a,f} = w; R(4) = {d,f} = u; W(4) = {f} = v.

Here our usual notation appears in a more general form where a data object is replaced by a set of data objects and the new action V is included along with R and W. The V and W phase of 1 overlaps with R phase of 2; 1 gets through before validation of 2; 2 is permitted because there is no R–W conflict between R(2) and W(1). Now 3 overlaps its R phase with R, V and W phase of 2 and V and W phase of 1, but 3 is aborted owing to R–W conflicts with both 1 and 2, since [R(3) ∩ W(1)] and [R(3) ∩ W(2)] are not empty. For 4, there is no conflict with 1 and 2, but 4 has R–W and W–W conflict with the active set with 3.

The 3PC is due to Kung and Robinson (1981). We see that its approach is similar to finding the conflicting R–W actions among read and write sets after the transactions pass through the read phase.

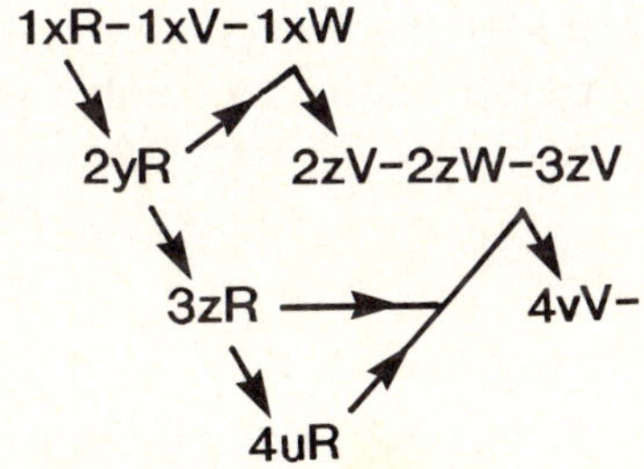

Figure 4.12 Parallel 3PC schedule

4.7 DEGREE OF CONCURRENCY AMONG CLASSES OF SCHEDULES

At this point we will recall the important properties concerning the degree of concurrency achieved in the different classes of schedules.

1. Containment

The set of serial schedules is contained within the set of strict schedules, which is contained within the set of cascade-abort-free schedules, which is contained

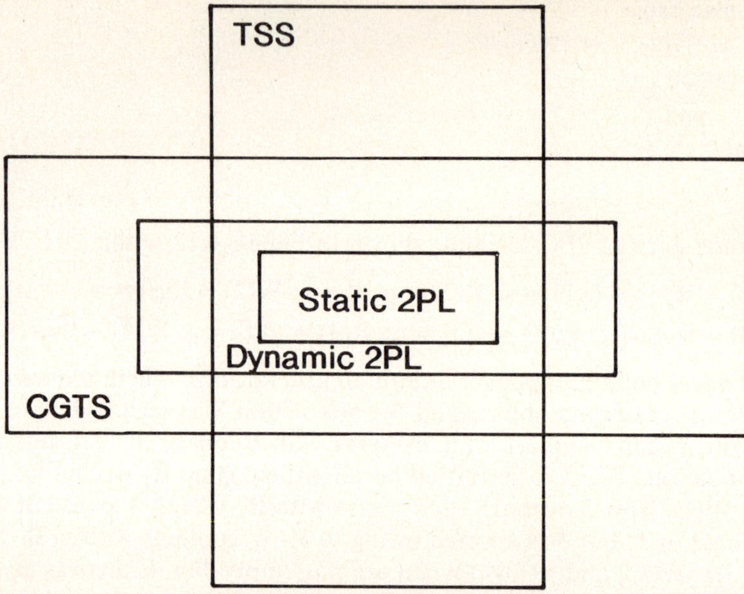

Figure 4.13 Degrees of concurrency under different mechanisms

within the set of recoverable schedules. The set of conflict-serializable schedules intersects with all these sets but is incomparable (see Section 3.7.5).

2. Complexity

The set of conflict-serializable schedules is contained within the set of view-serializable schedules. Although the former is more restrictive with regard to the degree of concurrency available, testing for conflict serializability can be done in polynomial time, whereas testing for view serializability cannot (see Section 3.9.2).

3. Use of multiversion

The computational complexity of transaction models other than action and restricted models for both monoversion and multiversion serializability problems is exponential. The degree of concurrency can be improved by increasing the number of versions. Conflict serializability of single-version and multiversion can be tested in polynomial time (see Section 3.11).

4. 2PL, conflict-graph-tested and timestamped schedules

The degrees of concurrency of the schedules that use 2PL locks, the conflict-graph test and timestamps satisfy the following property (see Figure 4.13). The set of timestamped schedules (TSS) and the set of conflict-graph-tested schedules (CGTS) intersect, while the set of 2PL schedules is properly contained within the CGTS. The static 2PL schedule is properly contained within the intersection of the TSS and the CGTS. In addition, the dynamic 2PL properly contains the static 2PL and is properly contained within the CGTS. However, the set of dynamic 2PL schedules is not contained within the TSS, although they intersect.

The above properties are useful for choosing the appropriate mechanisms that will produce maximal concurrency in designing the schedulers.

EXERCISES

1. Describe, with examples, the basic philosophy of the three different concurrency control schemes.
2. How does timestamp prevent deadlocks? When does it create a livelock?
3. Classify the different types of certifiers.
4. Give an example of a 2PL protocol that makes a schedule serializable.
5. How does one check whether a 2PL protocol leads to a deadlock?
6. What happens if a 2PL protocol is violated?
7. Explain why lock promotion causes deadlock.
8. What is the difference between dynamic and static 2PL?
9. How does one make a 2PL schedule recoverable and free from cascade aborts?
10. What are granular locks? Write a program to find the conflict graph of a schedule using a hierarchical object and granular locks (Section 4.3.1).
11. What are edge locks? How do they prevent deadlocks?
12. Read about hypergraphs and how they are used for devising a lock protocol (Cellary et al. 1988).
13. Read about the geometry of locking and devising safety conditions (see Lausen and Soininen 1989).
14. What is the Thomas write-ignore rule? Why does it work?
15. What is the difference between basic and strict timestamping procedures?
16. Program the algorithm for two-phase commitment with timestamping, using a suitable datastructure.
17. Program the hierarchical timestamping procedure.
18. Program the serial 3PC certifier.
19. Program the parallel 3PC certifier.
20. Write an essay on the degree of concurrency among the different classes of schedules (see Cellary et al. 1988).
21. How can one statistically examine the performance of the different mechanisms such as locks, timestamps and certifiers?

REFERENCES

Bernstein, P.A. and Goodman, N. 1983. 'Multiversion concurrency control: theory and algorithms'. *ACM Transactions on Database Systems* 9, 596–615.

Bernstein, P.A., Hadzilacos, V. and Goodman, N. 1987. *Concurrency Control and Recovery in Database Systems*. Addison-Wesley, USA.

Carey, M.J. 1983. 'Granularity hierarchies in concurrency control'. *Proceedings of the 2nd SIGACT SIGMOD Conference on Principles of Database Systems*, Atlanta, pp. 156–65.

Cellary, W., Gelenbe, E. and Morzy, T. 1988. *Concurrency Control in Distributed Database Systems*. North-Holland, Amsterdam.

Gray, J.N. 1978. 'Notes on database operating systems'. In *Lecture Notes in Computer Science* 60, 393–481. Springer-Verlag, USA.

Korth, H.F. 1982. 'Deadlock freedom using edge locks'. *ACM Transactions on Database Systems* 7, 632–52.

Kung, H.T. and Robinson, J.T. 1981. 'On optimistic methods for concurrency control'. *ACM Transactions on Database Systems* 6, 213–26.

Lausen, G. and Soininen, E.S. 1989. 'Locking policies and predeclared transactions'. In *Lecture Notes in Computer Science* 364, 317–36. Springer-Verlag. USA.

Stonebraker, M., ed. 1986. *The INGRES Papers*. Addison-Wesley, USA.

5 Multisite (or distributed) schedules

5.1 INTRODUCTION

In Chapter 3 we considered the serializability of schedules at a single site (called 'localized schedules' or 'centralized schedules') and in Chapter 4 we described the basic mechanisms — locks, timestamps and certifiers — that are used for concurrency control to achieve serialization of schedules at a site. We will now consider 'multisite schedules' or 'distributed schedules'; that is, schedules operating simultaneously at many sites connected by a computer network.

The centralized schedule and distributed schedule and the mechanisms called 'schedulers' that control these schedules can be defined as follows:

1. Centralized schedule and centralized scheduler

This schedule consists of interleaving transactions on one single database located at one site, and has a centralized computer system with a central processor (or a multiprocessor) where each processor can have direct access to the shared memory. The mechanism that controls a centralized schedule is called a centralized scheduler.

2. Distributed schedule and distributed scheduler

This schedule consists of interleaving transactions that can send simultaneous requests to several independent local databases (dispersed at the same site or at different sites) using a distributed multiprocessor system in which memory and auxiliary storage are not shared. Communication between different local databases and different processors (at the same site or at different sites) takes place through message passing in a communication network. Accordingly it is possible to have varying degrees of distribution of databases, hardware/software modules, and control. Such a degree of distribution determines whether it is a central uniprocessor system at one end of the spectrum or a totally distributed processor, distributed database and distributed control network at the other end of the spectrum. The mechanism that controls a distributed schedule is called a distributed scheduler.

The practical design considerations for the centralized and distributed schedulers turn out to be quite different because of the following reasons:

1. The degree of distribution of database, hardware/software and control determines the complexity of a distributed system. The degree of cooperation among the different processors determines the intercomputer message rate and the complexity of control.
2. The centralized scheduler needs to take care of the internal consistency of a single database at one site. The distributed scheduler, however, has to ensure the consistency of different local databases (at the same or different sites) in which replication and multiversion data objects may be used; at the same time it needs to ensure the global consistency of the whole collection of databases. Thus the distributed scheduler is essentially a scheduler of schedulers.
3. In the design of a centralized scheduler we need to consider only issues related to improving concurrency in computation and reducing the complexity of detecting serializability. In the distributed system no one site may hold all the global information to ensure a global consistency check. Hence one has to obtain information about actions at different sites and then combine all the information to obtain the global information on consistency. We should therefore either have a central coordinator or assign the coordination job to one site. Thus we need to consider communication costs between sites and deal with issues related to communication delays and failures.
4. The conflict graphs, locks, timestamps and certifier techniques introduced in Chapter 4 depend on the fundamental notion of total ordering of events in time, and were based on such *temporal logical connectives* as *earlier than* and *later than* at a given single site. We must somehow extend these techniques in order to design a distributed scheduler, although we cannot readily synchronize clocks at different sites to realize a total order among different events.

In this chapter we will first devise a notation to describe multisite schedules based on our earlier notation for the localized schedules. We will then deal with the different concurrency control mechanisms used for the serialization of the distributed schedules to design efficient schedulers.

As already mentioned, in a distributed schedule each transaction performs actions at several sites 1, 2, . . . s. The sequence of actions performed by a single transaction at any one site is called a subtransaction. The sequence of actions performed by different transactions on a database at any one site is called a *local schedule*. Thus when many transactions are performing their subtransactions at many sites, we have a schedule of many local schedules. Hence to ensure the serializability of a distributed schedule it is necessary that each local schedule be serializable; this is not sufficient, however, to ensure global consistency and serializability, since local information is incomplete.

In order to achieve a multisite or global serialization we need to combine the local information obtained from different sites at a coordinating site, and look for multisite or global consistency. Since it is clear that such a compilation of information is communication-intensive, one should look for ways and means of minimizing the communication overhead. All the techniques described earlier for the serialization of local schedules can be extended for that purpose. They have, however, different communication and computational complexities, a brief account of which is given below.

1. *Extending the concept of local conflict graph*

   This extension is communication-intensive among the different sites, and requires potentially unbounded memory space because we need to compile all the information pertaining to local conflict graphs sent by messages across a network. Using these individual local graphs, we must then obtain their union with the messages to obtain the global conflict graph. The latter has to be checked for a global cycle and used for controlling the actions at various local sites. It has been shown by Papadimitriou (1986) that this method requires a rate of information processing far higher than that needed to process each transaction in order to ensure that no transaction involved in a global cycle commits. Although a space-efficient algorithm for that purpose has been designed by Bernstein et al. (1987) using only active transactions in the schedule and their transitive closure, it is not considered to be reliable since communication failures can create problems.

2. *Extending the locking technique*

   This extension has a polynomial time complexity; but the associated deadlock detection can add additional complexity since we need to develop a coordination among the different sites to construct a global wait-for graph. But in this case the complexity of the deadlock detection algorithm is not as expensive as in the checking of a cycle in a global conflict graph. Further, since the transactions cannot proceed here owing to deadlock, they cannot commit. Thus we can be sure of their reliability even if we are slow. We will discuss the locking techniques in Sections 5.5 and 5.6.

3. *Extending the timestamping technique*

   This technique is most readily extended to the distributed environment. The crucial issue here is to achieve a total ordering of events at different sites with different local clocks. How to synchronize these different clocks first and then how to achieve a global total ordering of events are the key questions. Fortunately, the synchronization of local clocks can be done by using the concept of relative time at sites. Each message from a site bears a local timestamp based on its local clock. It is passed on to reach another site; if it arrives at an earlier local clock time, the local time is incremented to a value greater than the timestamp of the received message, since a message cannot be received at another site earlier than it was sent! In this way, all the clocks can be relatively synchronized. The assignment of a unique global timestamp for total ordering is based on each local clock time, the total number of sites and the site label. We will discuss this aspect in Section 5.7.

4. *Extending the certifier technique*

   This technique is the least expensive among all the others from the communication point of view. It can be combined with voting strategies to arrive at a global decision, but it suffers from frequent aborting and infinite restarting. We will describe the certifier techniques in Section 5.8.

All the abovementioned approaches are syntactic and are essentially based on the notion of serializability. Another important approach is based on semantic knowledge (see Section 2.7). Two different methods, one due to Garcia-Molina (1983) and improved by Lynch (1983), and the other due to Farrag and Ozsu (1989), are discussed in Section 5.9. These methods are also called *semantic locking methods*, as they also use locks; they permit consistent nonserializable schedules, thereby improving concurrency. However, since an extra overhead is incurred in utilizing the semantic information, it is necessary to explore the trade-off between additional concurrency and the overhead for storing and using the semantic information.

In practice, a combination of these different techniques are used. We will consider these aspects in detail in the following sections.

5.2 DESCRIPTION THROUGH ACCESS MATRICES

The notation and the access matrix description which we used earlier for a localized schedule can be readily extended to describe the multiversion-multisite schedules by using the quintuple format:

Transaction label(T): Data object(D): Version(V): Action(P): Site label(S)

Here we make the following assumptions:

1. Each transaction receives a unique global label at the site of its birth; at other sites, it executes only subtransactions.
2. Each site has a unique global label.
3. Every data object has a unique name in all sites; that is, there are no name collisions.

In the examples below we also use the convention that when there is a single version, we omit the version label.

As an example, consider Figure 5.1:

```
1xR1–1xW1–2yR1–2yW1–1yR1–1yW1–2xR1–2xW1
 |    |    |    |    |    |    |    |
1xR2–2xW2–2yR2–2yW2–1yR2–1yW2–2xR2–1xW2
```

Figure 5.1 Distributed schedule

This describes a single-version distributed schedule of two transactions 1 and 2 at two sites 1 and 2 on data objects x and y. Here the pairs of actions (1xR1, 1xR2), (1xW1, 2xW2), (2yR1, 2yR2), (2yW1, 2yW2), (1yR1, 1yR2), (1yW1, 1yW2), (2xR1, 2xR2), (2xW1, 1xW2), indicated by links in Figure 5.1, are concurrent at different sites 1 and 2; that is they are partially ordered and we do not know whether they are earlier or later. But the actions at each site are totally ordered.

5.2.1 Numeral encoding and decoding in access matrices

From the above example it is clear that we need to provide the access matrix description of a localized schedule at each site, as in Figure 3.9(a). Thus there will be as many access matrices as the number of sites in the network. While communication within a local schedule takes place through memory sharing, intersite communication among the transactions and the different access matrices takes place through message passing. This enables a transaction born in one site to read from or write into a data object in another site by using communication primitives based on handshaking or remote procedure call.

Thus a distributed schedule consists of a global schedule that controls the many local schedules through message-passing channels. The controller of this global schedule is called a 'coordinator'.

We can extend the numeral-encoding scheme of Section 3.10.1 to a multiversion distributed schedule described below. For pedagogical reasons, we assume that all the sites are accessible to all transactions whether they are active or not at some sites. Also, we assume that the number of versions of data objects available is identical at all sites, so that the access matrices have a regular structure to derive a simple formula. In a practical situation this requires modification.

Let us assume that there are t transactions, each uniquely labeled globally, d globally named data objects, each with v versions, and p actions, and that in total there are s sites. Thus:

$$0 \leq T \leq t,\ 1 \leq D \leq d,\ 0 \leq V \leq v\text{-}1,\ 1 \leq P \leq p,\ 1 \leq S \leq s$$

The triplets for commit and abort are encoded using the formula:

$$TCS = (T + 1)(pdv + 2) - 1 + (S-1)t(pdv + 2);$$

$$TAS = (T + 1)(pdv + 2) + (S-1)t(pdv + 2);$$

where T is the transaction label and S is the site label.
The quintuplets are encoded using:

$$N = T(pdv + 2) + [(D-1)\ pv + V.p] + P + (S-1)\,t\,(pdv + 2)$$

where D is the data object label, P the operation label, V the version label, S the site label and T the transaction label.

5.2.2 Decoding algorithm

In decoding, first we identify the site by taking the lower integral part of the quotient $q = N/[(pdv + 2)t]$; then $S = q + 1$. After this step we proceed with the same algorithm described in Section 3.10.2, using the remainder in the above division, namely: N mod(pdv + 2)t as the input value N.

5.2.3 Examples (encoding)

Consider the case p = 2, t = 5, v = 4, d = 3, s = 2; then

$$3C2 = 4(26) - 1 + 130 = 233;\ 2A2 = 3(26) + 130 = 208$$

$$4y1W2 = 4(26) + (8 + 2) + 2 + 130 = 246$$

5.2.4 Examples (decoding)

let N = 246; t(pdv + 2) = 130; q = 1; therefore S = 2; N mod (pdv + 2) t = 116. Using this as the input to the algorithm in Section 3.10.2 we obtain:

116 = 4y1W;

thus the quintuplet is 4y1W2. Similarly, if N = 208, its decoding gives 2A2.

5.3 GLOBAL SERIALIZABILITY CONDITIONS

We will now describe the global serializability conditions of a distributed schedule:

1. At each site the local schedule is serializable.
2. At each site the serialization order of transactions dictated by every other site is not violated. That is, for each pair of conflicting actions among transactions i and j, an action of i precedes an action of j in any local schedule if and only if i precedes j in the total ordering of *all transactions at all sites.*

   For the example in Section 5.2, we have:

   2yW1 < 1yR1 < 2xW1.

   Hence 1 and 2 cannot be ordered either as 1, 2 or as 2, 1 to bring in a total order.

We will now give additional examples.

5.3.1 Examples

1. Consider the distributed schedule with the local schedules:

1xR1, 1yW1, 2yR1, 3xW1 (site 1)

1yW2, 2zW2 (site 2)

2zW3, 3zR3 (site 3)

There is a R–W conflict on x between 1 and 3 in site 1; that is, 1 < 3; and W–R conflict on y between 1 and 2 with 1 < 2 in site 1. At site 3, there is a W–R conflict on z between 2 and 3. Thus the total order of transactions 1 < 2 < 3 is preserved at all sites, including site 2, with no conflict.

2. Consider a modified form of the above schedule:

1xR1, 2yR1, 3xW1, 1yW1

2zW2, 1yW2

2zW3, 3zR3

There is a R–W conflict on x between 1 and 3; thus 1 < 3 in site 1. Also 2 < 1 due to R–W conflict on y in site 1; and 2 < 3 due to W–R conflict on z in site

3. But the only possible total order 2 < 1 < 3 is violated at site 1 by 3xW1 < 1yW1.

3. Consider another modified form of the above schedule:

1xR1, 1yW1, 2yR1, 3xW1
2zW2, 1yW2
2zW3, 3zR3

Here the total order consistent within each local schedule is 1 < 2 < 3, but this is violated at site 2.

To make the above analysis simple, we can introduce the construction of a conflict graph that describes the situation more effectively.

5.3.2 Conflict multigraphs

The conflict graph of a centralized schedule is a directed graph in which the nodes denote transactions and the directed edges describe the conflicts among these nodes at a single site. Thus no more than two different directional edges occur between any pair of nodes. However, the conflict graph of a distributed schedule represents several sites in which each node corresponds to a transaction that can operate at different sites. The edges now describe R–W, W–R or W–W conflicts among transactions at different sites. Consequently this graph turns out to be a multigraph in which more than two directed edges can occur between any two nodes. This is because each transaction can read and write at different sites and as a result conflicts can arise at different sites. It is convenient to mark each such edge with the nature of the conflict and the site label. For example, the conflict multigraph of the second modified form in Example 5.3.1 is given in Figure 5.2. The graph is acyclic, and a topological sort 1-2-3 that gives the total order is unfortunately violated by site 2.

Thus in order to use the conflict multigraph approach to detect serializability, we need to carry out the following steps:

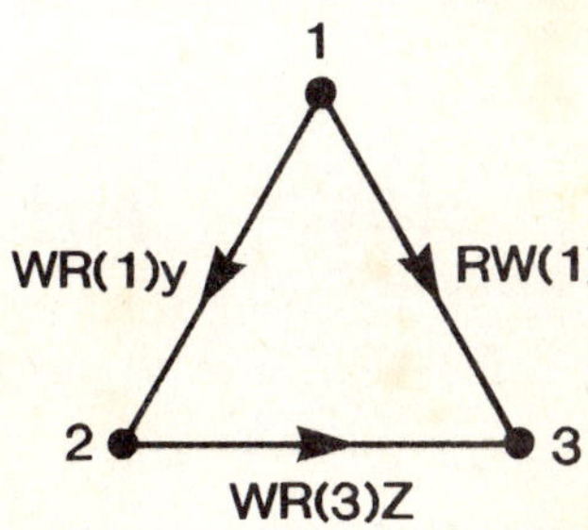

Figure 5.2 An acyclic conflict multigraph

1. Collect all the local information and draw a global graph for all sites.
2. Find whether the graph is cyclic; if it is, then the multisite schedule is not serializable and one of the offending transactions in the cycle is to be aborted and rolled back.

3. If there is no cycle, find a topological sort that is consistent with each site. This step is an extra step over the centralized schedule conflict detection, since there acyclicity is sufficient to proceed, without finding a topological sort (Section 3.5.4). However, in the case of a distributed schedule, besides the acyclicity we need to ensure that there is one serial order of transactions that is consistent with all sites. If no such order exists then it cannot be serialized and the schedule is incorrect. This is the extra price we pay for distribution.

   Consider, for instance, the second modified form in Example 5.3.1. It is not serializable, although there are no cycles in Figure 5.2. The topological order 1-2-3 is not consistent with site 2. Thus acyclicity of the conflict multigraph is necessary, but it does not guarantee the correctness of a distributed schedule unless the right serial order is enforced.

   As another example, consider the three transactions given below; here we use the notation 1xRW2 to denote transaction 1, which does R and W actions on x at site 2.

```
1xRW2–1zRW2   2uRW1–2vRW1   3wRW1, 3yRW2–3xRW2
     |      ;      |      ;
   1vRW1         2yRW2
```

How do we schedule them in order to have serializability? If we interleave them as below:

```
2uRW1–2vRW1–3wRW1–1vRW1 (site 1)
3yRW2–2yRW2
   |
 1xRW2–3xRW2–1zRW2 (site 2)
```

we see that the conflict multigraph has a cycle 2-1-3, indicating nonserializability (Figure 5.3).

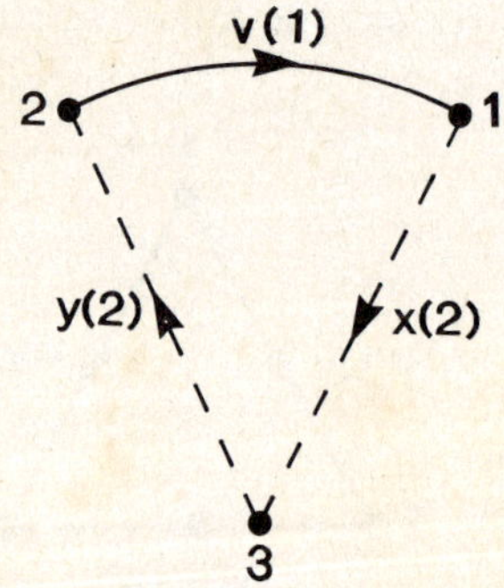

Figure 5.3 A cyclic conflict multigraph

5.3.3 A conflict multigraph scheduler

The conflict multigraph scheduler works in the following manner. A copy of the multigraph is stored at each site. As soon as a step arrives, each site communicates with other sites for information about their conflict graphs. When the reply is received, the site sends its multigraph to all sites and checks for cycles. If a cycle is present, it rejects that step and sends messages to other sites about its decision so as to enable them to abort a transaction. If there are no cycles, it checks for a consistent topological sort at that time that will make the schedule serializable, and enforces this order.

For example, the multigraph in Section 5.3.2 is stored at sites 1 and 2 partially from local knowledge (solid lines) and is completed by global communication (dotted lines as shown in Figure 5.3). When the step 3xRW2 arrives at step 2, the cycle is detected in site 2 rejecting this step.

Hence this scheduler will delay all steps if there is a failure in communication. As already mentioned, it has been shown by Papadimitriou (1986) that excessive communication costs will be involved in using this method; it is therefore not a practicable method.

5.4 DECOMPOSITION OF CONFLICT SERIALIZABILITY

Before we proceed further to discuss other distributed scheduling procedures, we will describe an ingenious and basic approach proposed by Bernstein and Goodman (1981) which decomposes the conflict serializability problem into two simpler and independent parts — *unlike conflict part:* R–W or W–R conflicts; and *like conflict part:* W–W conflict. The interesting aspect of this decomposition is the following:

1. A schedule is serializable only if the conflict graph for the unlike and like conflict parts is independently acyclic.
2. There is a total ordering of transactions consistent with these independent orderings; that is, the union of these like and unlike part-conflict graphs has to be acyclic in order to ensure serializability.

Hence a scheduler has *three* independent parts: *two synchronizers*, one for the unlike conflict part (called the R–W synchronizer or the R–W rejector) and one for the like conflict part (called the W–W synchronizer or W–W rejector), and a *coordinator* to resolve the like and unlike conflicts in a consistent way.

The conflict matrix for these two synchronizers is given below for two transactions i and j, for R and W actions on a specific data object.

	i	
j	R	W
R	Yes	No
W	No	Yes

R–W synchronizer

	i	
j	R	W
R	Yes	Yes
W	Yes	No

W–W synchronizer

That is, in the R–W synchronizer only R and W actions are incompatible, but W–W action is permissible; while in the W–W synchronizer only W–W action is incompatible, but other actions are compatible. Essentially, if we ignore R–R actions, these two conflict matrices are logically opposite or mutually exclusive. It is this property that permits the decomposition of a conflict graph into two logically independent (R–W or W–R) and W–W conflict graphs.

The above concept can be readily extended to conflict graph, 2PL or timestamping methods.

5.4.1 Conflict graph using R–W and W–W synchronizers

This is a very straightforward method. Here the edges for the conflict graph are added independently at each site for the like and unlike conflict parts whenever an operation is received. The coordinator should ensure that the resulting graphs are compatible. This method is therefore subject to the excessive communication costs described in Section 5.3.3.

5.4.2 2PL using R–W and W–W synchronizers

In a 2PL using the R–W synchronizer, two independent R actions or two independent W actions on the same data object are permissible, whereas R (W) action may be delayed by a transaction holding a write-lock (WL) (read-lock (RL)).

Also, in a 2PL with W–W synchronizer, a W action will be delayed only if another transaction holds a write-lock on the same data object. The 2PL lock compatibility matrix (see Section 4.2) is then given by:

R–W 2PL

	i		
j	RL	WL	NL
RL	Yes	No	Yes
WL	No	Yes	Yes
NL	Yes	Yes	Yes

W–W 2PL

	i		
j	RL	WL	NL
RL	Yes	Yes	Yes
WL	Yes	No	Yes
NL	Yes	Yes	Yes

The coordinator in this case has to ensure that both W–W and R–W locks needed satisfy the 2PL basic protocol (Section 4.2.1). In other words, all locks needed for either purpose should be obtained before any lock is released in either case.

Also, one can think of additional locks with the following properties:

R–W write lock. This lock conflicts only with R locks on same data object.

W–W write lock. This lock conflicts with all other locks except R–W lock on same data object.

R–W–W write lock. This lock conflicts with all other locks except R–W lock on same data object.

Such locks, as we will see later, are useful for dealing with multiple copies of data objects kept at different sites. Their compatibility matrix for two transactions i and j is shown below (Figure 5.4). Also, these locks can be escalated as shown in the lattice diagram (Figure 5.5).

j	S (i)	X (i)	R–W (i)	W–W (i)	R–W–W (i)
S	Yes	No	No	No	No
X	No	No	Yes	No	No
R–W	No	Yes	Yes	Yes	Yes
W–W	No	No	Yes	No	No
R–W–W	No	No	Yes	No	No

Figure 5.4 Multiple-site lock compatibility matrix

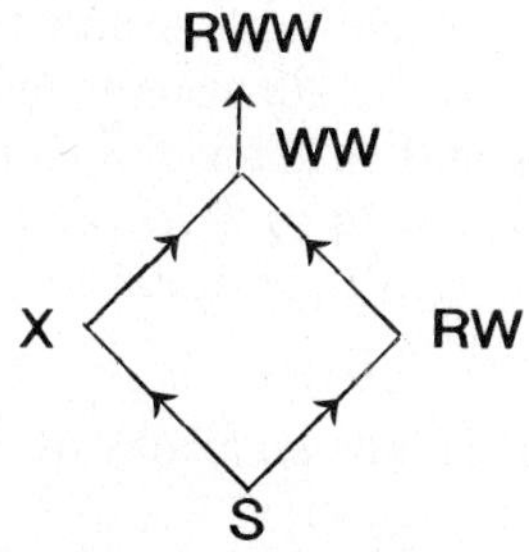

Figure 5.5 Multiple-site lock escalation lattice diagram

5.4.3 Timestamping using R–W and W–W synchronizers

The R–W timestamp system will schedule ixW and jxW in any timestamp order unless there is a kxR such that:

$$TS(i) < TS(k) < TS(j) \text{ or } TS(j) < TS(k) < TS(i)$$

It will permit ixW (or ixR) earlier than jxR (or jxW) only if TS(i) < TS(j).

The W–W timestamp system will permit ixW earlier than jxW only if TS(i) < TS(j); but ixR and jxW or ixW and jxR will be processed in any order. While using the R–W and W–W synchronizers the coordinator should ensure that the same timestamps are used in both cases.

5.4.4 Pure or mixed integrated schedulers

Conventional schedulers which do not use decomposition of conflict types are called pure schedulers, while those schedulers which use the decomposition of conflict types are called integrated schedulers. Further, if R–W and W–W synchronizers belong to the same type — that is, one of conflict graph, lock or timestamp, the resulting scheduler is called a pure integrated scheduler. If, however, two different types of R–W and W–W synchronizers are used, the resulting scheduler is called a mixed-integrated scheduler.

Naturally, there are numerous ways of combining the different techniques, resulting in more than one hundred algorithms (Bernstein et al. 1987). The efficiency of their performance, however, is not known except for a few algorithms. In the following section we will discuss the basic principles of some of the most important algorithms that use locks, timestamps and certifiers.

5.5 LOCKING FOR DISTRIBUTED CONCURRENCY CONTROL

5.5.1 Pure basic 2PL

In this method we assume that a data object has multiple copies stored at different sites and that to each copy is attached an S (RL) and X (WL) lock. Since all the copies have to be consistent, it is necessary that every W action takes place on all copies and that an R action takes place from any one copy. This strategy is popularly known as *write all, read one* strategy. We can employ a distributed form of a basic 2PL protocol to design a pure scheduler using the following rules:

1. *S-lock.* A transaction i holds an S-lock on x if it holds an *S-lock on any copy* of x.
2. *X-lock.* A transaction i holds an X lock on x if it holds an *X-lock on every copy* of x.

Hence no two transactions can hold an S and an X lock simultaneously on the same data object, or X locks on the same data object, thus satisfying lock compatibility. This is so because we can always detect an S–X conflict at a site and an X–X conflict at all sites.

We can compute the communication cost thus:

1. For each R, we need to send a short request message to one site, which if free can S-lock and send the value of x.
2. For each W, we need to send s request messages to ask for X lock. When the reply for lock granting is received from all these sites, the new x-values and X* (unlock) messages are to be sent to them. Thus there are s request and s reply messages which are short and s long messages for passing values.

5.5.2 Primary copy 2PL

In this method we identify a primary site at which R and W actions on a particular data object take place. Such a data object at the primary site is called a primary copy. The use of a primary copy reduces communication costs, especially when most transactions handle a data object at the primary site. Also in this method, S and X locks are requested at the primary site so that lock conflict can be detected. Therefore, we need one short message to read-lock and one long message to read, two short messages to write-lock at the primary site and s long messages to write at all sites.

Bernstein and Goodman (1981) suggest the use of R–W–W lock at the primary site and R–W locks at other sites for W–W synchronization and S lock at any site for R–W synchronization. This would make it possible to wait for propagation of the values to other copies until the R–W–W or W–W lock is granted.

5.5.3 Majority locking 2PL

Here S and X locks are requested on a majority of copies of the data object so that no conflict can arise. We need greater than s/2 short messages to read-lock and one long message to read, and greater than s/2 short messages to write-lock and s long mesages to write. Bernstein and Goodman (1981) suggest setting R–W locks, pending the grant of R–W–W locks, on a majority of copies for W–W synchronization.

5.5.4 Use of centralized 2PL

If a centralized 2PL is used, all lock and unlock requests are made to a central site or node. Thus a S-lock request goes to the central node. If the lock is not granted, the site is informed; otherwise, the central node sends a message to a site where a copy is available. This site then sends a copy to the requesting site. Consequently we need two short messages and one long message for reading.

For a X lock, we need three short messages (two for locking and one for unlocking) and s long messages for writing. In such a case, Bernstein and Goodman (1981) advocate obtaining a S lock or R–W lock on each data object and promoting to R–W–W or W–W locks for writing.

5.5.5 Quorum and generalized majority 2PL

Majority locking earlier described in Section 5.5.3 can be generalized in one of two ways:

1. by using a weighted majority (or quorum);
2. by using k out of n strategy.

In the weighted majority, each site s is assigned a weight called a vote, a positive integer V_s. A transaction must collect a quorum, which is the sum of votes at all sites and is greater than half the total sum of votes V for R or W action. For example, if $V_1 = 2$, $V_2 = 3$, $V_3 = 4$, $V_4 = 1$, then $V = 10$ and so $V_1 + V_3 = 6$ and $V_2 + V_3 = 7$ constitute a quorum, whereas $V_1 + V_2 = 5$ and $V_2 + V_4 = 4$, $V_3 + V_4 = 5$ do not.

In the k out of n strategy, we require that a S lock is placed on at least $n - k + 1$ copies and a X lock on at least k out of n copies, where $k > n/2$.

5.6 DEADLOCK IN MULTISITE SCHEDULES

Whenever any locking technique is used, a natural consequence is the creation of a deadlock where two or more processes or tasks wait for each other eternally in a cycle to acquire a lock! We described in Section 4.2.3 the construction of a wait-for graph (WFG) for detecting deadlock cycles in local schedules. We also mentioned in Sections 4.2.4., and 4.2.7 and in the section on lock escalation deadlock on p. 81–2, Section 4.3.3, how lock conversions, lock promotion or lock escalation can lead to deadlock. In Section 4.3.6 we suggested the use of edge locks for deadlock freedom. Later in Section 4.4.5 we described how to break a deadlock using the timestamps and the two popular strategies: *wait and die*, and *wound and wait*. In this section we will describe certain basic techniques for detecting deadlocks in multisite schedules. This has been a vast area of research in the last decade and great efforts have been made by the best minds to find the best possible solutions for freedom from deadlock. For a detailed study of this subject, see Raynal (1987, 1988).

In a distributed system, where communication takes place through message passing, two types of deadlocks arise:

1. resource allocation deadlock;
2. communication deadlock.

We will describe these below.

1. *Resource allocation deadlock*

   There are n waiting processes P1, P2, P3, . . . , Pn which are passive and want to access a resource (locks, for example). If the resource is free, it is allocated by the controller; otherwise, the processes wait. When processes wait in a simple cycle where they are mutually dependent and blocking each other, deadlock results. For example, if 1 waits for 2, and 2 waits for 3, and 3 waits for 1, there is mutual blocking.The problem is to perceive that such a blocking exists, *not locally* but over several remote sites.

2. *Communication deadlock*

   Here n processes wait for each other in a knot-graph configuration (Figure 5.7) for a message, but no message is in transit. A knot graph is characterized by the fact that it does not lead to sink nodes; that is, each of its nodes has at least one edge directed out. Thus a directed graph is free from knots if and only if each node is a sink or has a directed path to a sink. Hence a directed edge that leads into a knot acts like a suction pump from which nothing can come out.

As an example, the graph in Figure 5.6 is not a knot graph, for it has a cycle that leads to a sink node. Figure 5.7 is a knot graph with a suction arm.

An algorithm to filter out the knot-graph part (if it exists) of a directed graph is given in Section 5.6.3. Since the knot graph contains multiple cycles with shared edges and suction arms, these are to be separately identified.

In this section we will consider only the resource allocation deadlock. For communication deadlock, see Raynal (1987), Chandy et al. (1983) and Natarajan (1986).

5.6.1 Construction of global wait-for graphs

Any algorithm for detecting deadlock should ultimately construct a global wait-

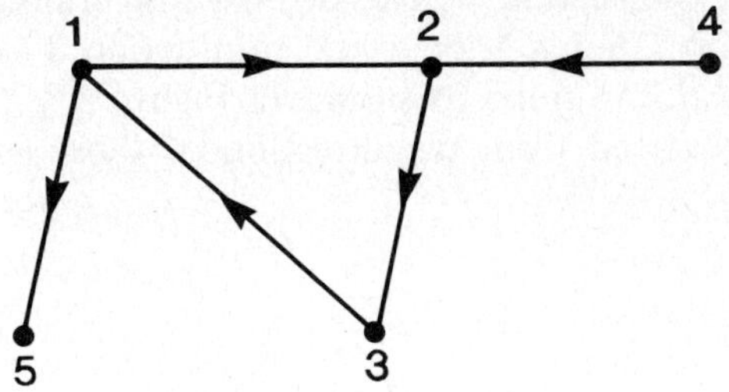

Figure 5.6 Cyclic graph with a sink

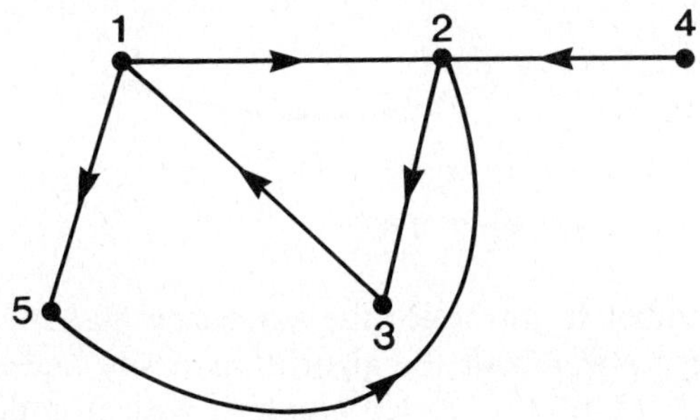

Figure 5.7 Knot graph

for graph based on information from different sites. This can be done by using one of several ways:

1. *Centralized detection.* This involves the use of a central coordinating site where all the information about local wait-for graphs from different local sites is collected and a global wait-for graph is constructed and tested for cycles.
2. *Hierarchical detection.* Here the global wait-for graph is distributed over a tree of controllers and the final decision is made by the root node on the top.
3. *Distributed approach.* Here the potential deadlock warning containing partial cyclic graphs is transmitted along the possible cycle to all other sites.

We will deal only with the centralized and distributed deadlock detection algorithms.

5.6.2 Centralized deadlock detection

Consider the example in Section 5.3.2 (Figure 5.3). Here if locks are used we have the schedule:

2uX, 2vX, 3wX, 1vX (site 1)
3yX–2yX
|
1xX, 3xX, 1zX (site 2)

Thus in site 1, transaction 2 holds X on v and transaction 1 waits for X on v, while in site 2, transaction 3 holds X on y and transaction 2 waits for X on y. Also, transaction 1 holds X on x and transaction 3 waits for X on x. Thus we have a cyclic wait-for graph as shown in Figure 5.8. Note that the direction of edges is just reversed from the direction of those in Figure 5.3 (see Section 4.2.3).

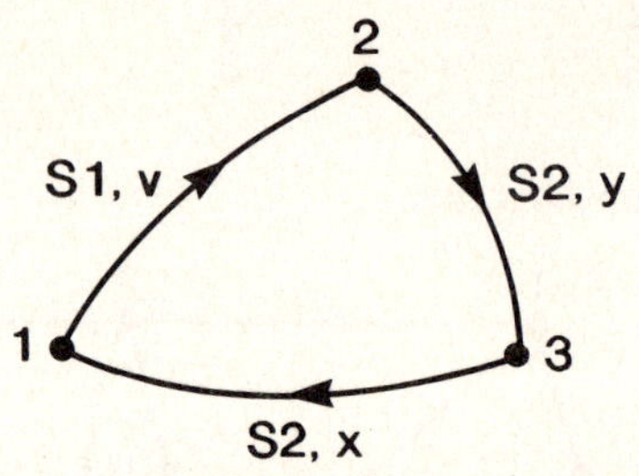

Figure 5.8 Cyclic wait-for graph

It is convenient to introduce the adjacency matrix notation of this directed graph in order to work out the algorithms easily and efficiently. An adjacency matrix $A(G) = ((a_{ij}))$ of a labeled graph G with n nodes is an n x n matrix in which $a_{ij} = 1$ if there is a directed edge from node i to node j; otherwise $a_{ij} = 0$.

Thus the adjacency matrix of the wait-for graph in site 1 is:

	1	2	3
1	0	1	0
2	0	0	0
3	0	0	0

At site 2, we have the adjacency matrix:

	1	2	3
1	0	0	0
2	0	0	1
3	1	0	0

The central deadlock detector should collect both these matrices from site 1 and site 2 and form a Boolean 'or' of the two matrices resulting in:

	1	2	3
1	0	1	0
2	0	0	1
3	1	0	0

The resulting matrix is then subjected to a cycle test and the offending transactions are aborted. In the above case we have a deadlock cycle 1–2-3 and one of the transactions has to be aborted.

The centralized deadlock detection method has the following disadvantages:

1. It can cause pseudo (or false or phantom) deadlock. This arises owing to communication delay which can reverse the order of arrival of messages from different sites at the central site. In the above case, for example, by the time the central site works out the 1–2 edge from the site 1 graph and waits for messages from site 2 to add edges 2–3 and 3–1, 2 might have released the lock in site 1. This message may be delayed. Since this is not known at the central site, it aborts a transaction and rolls it back! This is not desirable. Hence it is preferable to have self-diagnosis at each site by dynamically receiving information from other sites and constructing a wait-for graph.
2. It requires at least two messages per site — one for collecting partial graph information and another for reply.
3. The failure of a central site can cause problems.

Since finding a knot as well as a directed cycle are required for detecting deadlock, we will first describe a simple algorithm for finding a knot based on the array data structure. This filters out the knot part (if any) of the directed graph, thus removing all sink nodes. The depth-first search method of Section 3.6.1 can be applied to the adjacency list to find the directed cycles.

5.6.3 Finding the knot part of a directed graph

To find the knot part, we first reduce the adjacency matrix using the following algorithm:

Step 1

Delete a row with all zero entries; this removes a node which is a sink having no outgoing edges. Then delete the corresponding column from the A matrix. This collapses the order of matrix A to (n-1)x (n-1). Repeat this procedure for each row with zero entries in the collapsing matrix.

Step 2

If the matrix collapses successively to a null matrix, no knot part or directed cycle exists; otherwise, the last noncollapsible form gives the knot part or the cyclic part (if there is no knot part) of the graph.

Step 3

To obtain the actual cycles free of suction arms, delete a column with zero entries and the row with the same index from the collapsed adjacency matrix; this removes incoming or source edges into the cyclic part and collapses the matrix further. Repeat this operation until no zero columns are left. Create an adjacency list, then use the algorithm in Section 3.6.1.

5.6.4 Example

Consider the directed graph in Figure 5.9. Its adjacency matrix is given by:

	1	2	3	4
1	0	0	0	0
2	1	0	1	1
3	1	0	0	0
4	0	0	1	0

For the above example, using the algorithm in Section 5.6.3 results in the removal of row 1 (column 1), row 3 (column 3), row 4 (column 4) and finally element a_{22}. Thus the whole matrix collapses, indicating no knot-part or directed cycles.

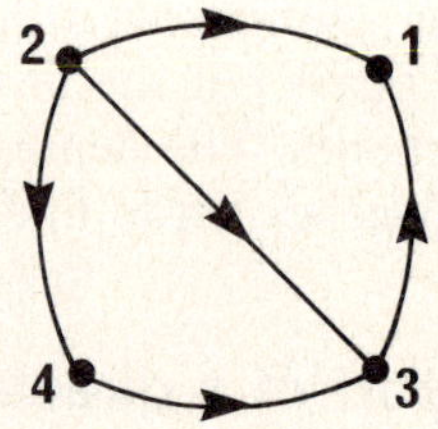

Figure 5.9 Directed graph

5.6.5 Example

Consider the graph in Figure 5.7. Its adjacency matrix is given by:

	1	2	3	4	5
1	0	1	0	0	1
2	0	0	1	0	0
3	1	0	0	0	0
4	0	1	0	0	0
5	0	1	0	0	0

Here no collapsing occurs; in fact, it is a knot with no sinks. The suction arm is 4–2, while the double cycle part is 2-3-1-5-2-3-1-2.

5.6.6 Distributed deadlock cycle detection

This algorithm follows a strategy similar to that used in detecting short-circuit faults in series-parallel (two-terminal) electrical networks by driving a current through the different sites and measuring resistance by a meter.

We assume that at each site one input communication port and one output communication port exist. The input port is a port in which transactions from any external site are waiting to acquire a resource currently used by a transaction at the site. The output port is a port from which a transaction from a site is waiting to use a resource currently used by another transaction at an external site. Thus each site is treated as a two-port input-output system: an input queue of transactions ('the incoming') from other sites waits to perform actions at that site and an output queue of transactions ('the outgoing') from that site waits to perform actions elsewhere. Thus each site knows the first incoming (I) transaction and its first outgoing (O) transaction. Then starting from any site the algorithm drives the information about a connected path, if any, across its I-O. The successive sites which receive this information check whether their I-O path is connected and can contribute to adding additional edges on the partial cycle. Ultimately if the initial sending site receives a message, there is a cycle with specified nodes representing transactions.

For example, if we have a two-site schedule:

1xX1, 5xX1, 1yX1, 3zX1, 2yX1, 2zX1(site 1)

2uX2, 4uX2, 4vX2, 3vX2 (site 2)

we assume that 1, 3, 5 are from site 1; and 2, 4 are from site 2; then at site 1, I is 2 and O is 3; and at site 2, I is 3 and O is 2. If there is no local cycle in the wait-for graph at a site, there is no local deadlock.

In the above example consider site 1: 5 waits for 1 for X lock on x; 2 from site 2 waits for 1 for X lock on y; and 2 waits for 3 for X lock on z. At Site 2, 3 from site 1 waits for 4 for X lock on v, while 4 waits for 2 for X lock on u. Thus no local cycles exist at each site, but globally there is a cycle 2–3–4 causing a deadlock.

The deadlock detection algorithm proceeds as follows:

We assume that each transaction has a homesite where it is born.

Step 1. Each site is assigned a unique label and each transaction is assigned a unique global priority label (which can be the unique global timestamps; see Section 5.7).

Step 2. Each local site ensures that local deadlock, if any, is handled by aborting a suitable transaction.

Step 3. Then each site checks whether there is a path between, the first incoming transaction I, and the first outgoing transaction O. If there is a such an I-O path, it transmits the site label and the actual path list to the site where O is bound. Thus the information travels to all communicating sites; this communication process has to eventually end up if the transactions lie in a cycle.

Step 4. When a message of path list is received from other sites, each site checks whether any local I-O path exists. If no such path exists, the message is discarded and nothing is transmitted. However, if there is an I-O path, each site extends the global graph and transmits the message about the new path to the site of its O. This message will ultimately reach each site in a cycle which detects a global deadlock consisting of one or more independent cycles.

Step 5. When a message is returned through a closed path, each message-sending site checks whether it still has the I-O path. If the path does not exist, it does not transmit any information. But if the path does still exist, it sends through its O the abort action to the transaction with the largest priority number in that cycle. When this message passes through, each site ensures that its I-O path still exists; otherwise, it discards the message. If the I-O path still exists, when the message reaches the site with the highest priority number, the transaction is aborted.

In a dynamic situation the above algorithm requires very careful implementation to save messages and time. We will not describe those technical aspects here.

The above algorithm assumes a one-input, one-output system in which each transaction has a home site and any particular input transaction I from an external site waits at one site at an instant; that is, each I and each O are distinct. This restriction, together with the assumption that local deadlocks are resolved, ensures that only simple closed independent cycles may exist but not multiple cycles sharing edges as in a knot configuration (see Figure 5.7).

The above algorithm has several advantages:

1. It does not report false deadlock, since message reversals do not happen in transmission.
2. It requires less communication than does centralized detection.
3. Site failures can be more easily handled, since there is no single central site.

5.6.7 Example

Let the transactions with priority labels be at sites 1, 2 and 3 with I, O as given below:

Site 1	Site 2	Site 3
1,2,7	3,4,9	5,6,8
I = 6,O = 2	I = 2,O = 4	I = 4,O = 6

Let the local wait-for graph be:

site 1: (1–2), (7–2); site 2: (3–4), (3–9); site 3: (5–6), (8–5)

The I-O paths are:

site 1: (6–1–2); site 2: (2–3–4); site 3: (4–5–6)

Site 1 passes a message to site 2, which extends the global path to 6–1–2–3–4. When this message reaches site 3, it extends the global path to 6–1–2–3–4–5–6; this is passed on to site 1, which, finding that it has already contributed, starts detecting for cycles and reports deadlock. Then it sends an abort message to transaction 6, at site 3.

5.6.8 Example

Consider the following multisite schedule:

Site 1	Site 2	Site 3	Site 4
5,9,2	6,10,3	7,11,4	8,12,1
I = 1,O = 2	I = 4,O = 3	I = 3,O = 4	I = 2,O = 1

The local wait-for graphs are:

site 1: 5–9–2; site 2: 6–10–3; site 3: 7–11–4; site 4: 8–12–1

The site 1 message travels to site 4 and comes back to site 1 with the cycle 1–5–9–2–8–12–1; it aborts 12 at site 4. The site 2 message goes to site 3 and returns to site 2 with the cycle 4–6–10–3–7–11–4; it aborts 11 at site 3. If there is no I-O path in site 3, for example if 7 is not connected to 4, the message of site 2 will be discarded.

5.7 DISTRIBUTED TIMESTAMPING PROCEDURE

In Section 4.4 we described the timestamping procedure for a localized schedule. There we had only a single clock and all the timestamps were issued by that clock alone. However, in a distributed environment we have many sites, each with its local clock. Hence it is a multiclock system. Therefore, in order to timestamp each transaction in a globally unique manner, we need to set up an agreement among the clocks to measure time at different sites and arrive at a convention to differentiate transactions as to whether they are older or younger. Once this is done, we can achieve the total ordering of transactions based on their global timestamps to serialize the multisite schedule. For that purpose, we introduce the notion of logical clock and logical time, which serve as the basis for distributed timestamping.

5.7.1 Logical clock and logical time

Since absolute time measurement at different sites is not physically achievable, the concepts of logical clock and logical time are introduced in the derivation of global timestamps.

A logical clock is a generator of a sequence of monotonically increasing positive integers. A logical time instant is the event of production of each positive integer in the sequence by the logical clock. On the basis of the notion of occurrence of an event and cause and effect in message communication between sites, we can logically synchronize clocks at different sites.

Let the synchronization event be chosen to happen at a site at an arbitrary local logical time T0, a positive integer. This synchronization message is then sent to another site, which on receipt of T0, assigns a value greater than T0 to its logical clock if its value is not greater. In this way local clocks can be aligned to start with, thus taking into account the fact that time duration for communication is a positive quantity.

Assuming that the clocks are not erratic and that they can be synchronized as above, we can generate unique timestamps for events happening at different sites to derive a total order. This requires defining a temporal relation 'happened before' (denoted by <) among any two events.

5.7.2 'Happened before' relation

This relation satisfies the three properties:

1. If an event E1 at site S1 happens before an event E2 at the same site, then E1 < E2.
2. If event E1 from site S1 sends a message to site S2 and the receipt of this message is an event E2 in S2, then obviously (E1 in S1) < (E2 in S2).
3. The relation < is transitive; that is, E1 < E2 and E2 < E3 imply E1 < E3.

Note that the first property is realized easily by a good local clock; this is the principle we used for timestamping in a local schedule. But to realize the second property, we need to use the method in Section 5.7.1 to ensure that any received clock value is checked with the local clock; if the local clock is slow, it is reset to a value greater than the received clock value. We call this the 'clock resetting rule'.

The 'happened before' relation may not always hold good among all events E1 and E2; that is, we may have *neither* E1 < E2 *nor* E2 < E1. In that case, the events E1 and E2 are concurrent and we cannot order them.

We will now describe the assignment of global timestamps.

5.7.3 Unique global timestamps

Let us assume that there are s sites, $1 \leqslant S \leqslant s$; then for an event E occurring at a logical clock time C at a site S the timestamp TS (E) is given by:

$$TS(E) = C.s + S$$

TS(E)mod s gives the site label S and [TS(E)-S]/s = C; hence TS(E) carries the place and time of birth.

We now state the following result: if an event E1 happens in S1 at time C1, before E2 in S2 at time C2 or E1 < E2 (where < is earlier or before), then TS(E1) < TS(E2) (where < stands for less than). This is proved as follows:

Let TS(1) = C1.s + S1 and TS(2) = C2.s + S2.

So TS(2)−TS(1) = (S2−S1) + s (C2−C1).

Thus if E1 has happened before E2, then C1 < C2 or C2−C1 ⩾ 1 by the 'clock resetting rule'. Hence TS(2)−TS(1) ⩾ 1 because −(s−1) ⩽ (S2−S1) ⩽ (s−1). That is, if events are totally ordered, their timestamps are totally ordered and are unique.

Also, if by chance the events are concurrent at S1 and S2; that is, if C1 = C2, then TS(2) will be greater or less than TS(1); but each will receive a unique timestamp. Therefore, while it is true that if E1 < E2 then TS(1) < TS(2), its converse — namely, TS(1) < TS(2) — need not imply E1 < E2.

In order to use the above scheme to assign a timestamp, we must identify a site at which each transaction is initiated. This site is called a 'home site' for that transaction. After the initial setting of the clock at a home site Si, a transaction i is assigned the timestamp TS(i):

TS(i) = C(Si).s + Si

When this transaction i wants to perform actions at another site Sj, we use TS(i) to reset the local clock C(Sj) at site Sj thus:

On the arrival of transaction i compute the clock reading C(Si) at site Si, using the formula:

{TS(i)–TS(i) mod s}/s = C(Si)

If C(Sj)> C(Si), do nothing; otherwise, C(Sj): = C(Si) + 1.

In this way we can ensure that all active cooperating sites have their clocks reset so that their timestamps are not too small (or outdated) for successive rejection and abort.

In all the timestamping procedures described below we assume that when a transaction arrives at a non-home site, the clock resetting rule is executed concurrently with other actions to be carried out.

5.7.4 Basic timestamping procedure

The basic timestamping procedure described in Chapter 4 for the localized schedule can now be easily extended to the distributed schedule.

The rules for acceptance of a transaction for R and W actions at a site S are given below. These rules ensure that conflicting operations are carried out in timestamp order at all sites, thus creating a total order.
[Recall(r, w) = FP(x) is the FOOTPRINT ON x where r is the max TS(i) of i that read x and w is the maximum TS(i) of i that wrote x]:

Case 1: if ixR arrives at a site S

When ixR arrives, if TS(i) < w (irrespective of whether TS(i) < r or TS(i) > r), then ixR is rejected and i is aborted since a conflicting W action of a transaction with a larger timestamp has been already carried out. We then assign the new timestamp greater than all the existing timestamps. Otherwise, that is if TS(i) is greater than or equal to w, we permit ixR. If TS(i) < r, we retain the present value of r for x; if TS(i) > r we set a new value for r, namely r: = TS(i).

Case 2: if ixW arrives at a site S

When ixW arrives, we reject this if TS(i) < r or TS(i) < w, since W conflicts with both R and W. We then need to abort i and assign a new timestamp greater than all the exising timestamps. Otherwise, that is, if TS(i) is greater than or equal to max (r, w), we permit ixW and set a new value for w, namely w: = TS(i).

The above procedure ensures serializability but not recoverability. In Section

4.4.2 we also showed how to ensure recoverability by making the schedule strict.

Example
Consider the following:

```
1xR1, 1xW1, 2xR1, 2xW1
                |      |
             1yR2, 1yW2, 2yR2, 2yW2
```

Let TS(1) = 1 and TS(2) = 2; then at Site 1 after 1xW1, FP(x): = (r, w) = (1, 1); hence at Site 1 the action 2xR1 will be accepted and FP(x): = (2, 1); at Site 2 the action 1yR2 is started and FP(y): = (1, 0); then at Site 1, 2xW1 is accepted since TS(2) = 2 $>$ w = 1 and hence the new FP(x): = (2, 2). Then at Site 2, 1yW2 is accepted and FP(y): = (1, 1); also 2yR2 is accepted and FP(y): = (2, 1); finally 2yW2 is accepted and FP(y): = (2, 2).

Note that the use of locks would cause a deadlock since 1xW1 $<$ 2xW1 $<$ 1yW2 cannot result in a total order.

However, consider the modified schedule:

```
1xR1, 2xR1, 1xW1, 2xW1
         |               |
      1yR2,          1yW2, 2yR2, 2yW2
```

Here the action 1xW1 will be rejected since FP(x) = (2, 1); then we restart 1 with a new timestamp, say TS(1) = 3.

5.7.5 Conservative timestamping

It is possible that basic timestamping causes too many aborts and restarts. Such a situation can be improved by delaying the execution of younger transactions until all the older transactions have finished their actions. This approach is called a *conservative* approach, and the earlier approach which attempts to schedule all actions without delay is called an *aggressive* approach. Thus in the aggressive approach we attempt to maximize concurrency at the expense of aborts and restarts, while in the conservative approach we delay actions to avoid conflicts at the expense of concurrency. The use of delay has been earlier discussed in the context of strict timestamping (Section 4.4.2) and two-phase commitment with timestamping (Section 4.4.4).

Conservative timestamping method has the following features:

1. *Execution at a home site*
   A transaction is executed at one particular site, called a home site; it can request R or W actions at other sites but cannot execute any remote programs.
2. *Timestamp-based protocol*
   Each site s receives a request for R or W from every other site t in the timestamp order. For that to happen, all R-action requests are issued first in

timestamp order followed by all W-action requests in timestamp order. This can be achieved by delaying jxR until all ixR are finished and delaying all jxW until ixW are finished for TS(i) < TS(j).

3. *Nonuse of footprints on data objects or access conflicts*
   This method does not use the footprints or access conflicts among data objects. It essentially executes transactions serially in timestamp order.

4. *Nonrejection of reads and writes*
   We assume that each site s has at least one R and one W action waiting (or buffered) from every other site. Such an assumption ensures that older transactions cannot arrive later from any site, since each site sends its actions in timestamp order.

5. *Rules for actions*
   Case (a): when ixR arrives at site S. If there is a jxW waiting with TS(i) > TS(j), then ixR is delayed by being put in the buffer; otherwise, ixR is carried out.

   Case (b): when ixW arrives at site S. If there is a jxR waiting with TS(i) > TS(j) or a kxW waiting with TS(i) > TS(k), then ixW is delayed by being put in the buffer; otherwise, ixW is carried out.

Disadvantages of conservative timestamping

There are two major disadvantages in using conservative timestamping: there is blocking because of silent sites; it is too restrictive. These disadvantages will be explained below.

Our assumption that each site has at least one R and one W action waiting at one site from every other site demands that there be no silence from any site. If for some reason no actions are sent and there is a silence, no output will result. Therefore, each site must communicate with every other site whether or not they have actions to perform. One way of doing that is to send a *null action* with a timestamp so that no blocking occurs. It is also possible to choose a very large integer as the timestamp of a null action; a site which sends this message assumes a meditative state in which it does not want communication as its null action can wait in a buffer. Alternatively, a blocked site can request such a null action from silent sites. All these techniques, however, are costly from the communication point of view.

The actions are ordered according to timestamps irrespective of whether they are conflicting or not. This reduces concurrency. Bernstein and Goodman (1981) have suggested an approach based on transaction classes and conflict graph analysis to improve this situation. We will describe these in the following section.

5.7.6 Timestamping using transaction classes

If we assume that the R and W set of each transaction is known in advance, we can improve the degree of concurrency in the conservative timestamping procedure by limiting our waiting to only those transactions which can cause conflicts. This is done by defining a transaction class C by a R set and W set. A transaction i belongs to this class if its R set and W set are respectively the subsets of the R set and W set of C. A transaction may belong to several classes, since the classes need not be disjoint. In this case, when ixR arrives at a site S, it needs to wait only for W actions of those classes of transactions j with TS(j) $<$ TS(i) and containing x in their W set.

Similarly, ixW wait only for the R actions of those classes of transactions j with TS(j) $<$ TS(i) and containing x in their R set; and the W actions of those classes of transactions k with TS(k) $<$ TS(i) and containing x in their W set. A convenient method of visualizing this situation is to use conflict graphs that describe the intersection among the R set and W set, and W set and W set of transaction classes. This method is a mixture of timestamping and conflict graph procedures and accordingly will exhibit the advantages and disadvantages of both procedures.

5.8 DISTRIBUTED CERTIFIERS

Here at each site we have a certifier of a particular type: a conflict graph, a lock or a timestamp certifier. A coordinator then needs to collect the information at all sites before giving a global certification. In the case of conflict graph certifier, each local graph is transmitted to all other sites. If the global graph constructed using this local information does not have a cycle, the transaction is certified; otherwise, it is aborted. As we mentioned earlier, this is expensive from the communication point of view. Similarly, 2PL or timestamp certifiers can be designed, but they are not useful in practice.

A certifier which is useful in practice is the distributed version of the three-phase certifier described in Section 4.6.4. We will describe this certifier below.

5.8.1 Distributed three-phase certifier

The algorithm described in Section 4.6.4 is modified thus:

1. *Sequence numbering*
   Each transaction is provided with a sequence number on initiation. This number is assigned to all subtransactions of i at each site S.
2. *Validation*
   Each transaction is validated at two levels in local and global validation phases, thus:
   (a) Local V phase
       Each subtransaction is validated at each site S using the algorithm in Section 4.6.4.
   (b) Global V phase
       To validate globally, all subtransactions must be locally certified. For this purpose, each site S maintains a *past history set* of transaction i at

site S denoted by PH(iS); this set contains the sequence numbers of those global transactions which precede i in the serialization order at site S. Then the global validation is performed using the following rule: a subtransaction is valid only if all the global transactions in the PH set have either committed or aborted; if for some reason this information is incomplete, the certification of that subtransaction is suspended. Since such a suspension may cause a deadlock, a time-out is used to abort this transaction (and hence all its subtransactions). This can result in infinite restarting.

3. *W phase*
   When a subtransaction has finished its global V phase, the corresponding message is sent to the transaction's home site. If all validations are positive, it is committed or else aborted.

5.8.2 Disadvantages of the distributed three-phase certifier

The first disadvantage is the deadlock that may result; for example at site 1, i might be preceded by j and at site 2 j might be preceded by i. Then PH(i1) ={j} and PH(j2) = {i}; thus i and j may indefinitely wait for each other's commitment or abortion. This is resolved by using a time-out mechanism. The second disadvantage is the infinite restarting.

Several modifications of the above algorithm have been made to remove these disadvantages (see Cellary 1986).

5.9 SEMANTIC LOCKING APPROACH

We mentioned in Section 2.7 that the use of semantic knowledge can improve the performance of a scheduler by permitting nonserializable but consistent schedules. In this section we will describe the two different methods based on this principle.

The first method is due to Garcia-Molina (1983). Here the transactions are divided into a collection of disjoint classes so that the transactions that belong to the same class are compatible or their actions can interleave arbitrarily, whereas transactions belonging to different classes are incompatible or cannot interleave at all. The compatibility concept has been further refined by Lynch (1983) to improve concurrency, but we will not describe those aspects here.

The second method is due to Farrag and Ozsu (1989). In some instances this method may offer a greater degree of concurrency than Garcia-Molina's method. It uses a command, called a 'breakpoint', in the schedule that permits transfer to another transaction that cannot violate consistency. Such schedules, which are called relatively consistent (RC schedules), contain serializable schedules. Farrag and Ozsu propose a locking mechanism to produce these RC schedules.

5.9.1 Nonserializable consistent schedule

The serializability condition is only sufficient (but not necessary) to ensure database consistency. In fact, it turns out to be too strong and restricts the degree of concurrency. Moreover, the serializability constraint turns out to be inadequate in certain cases where there are a number of dependent transactions. Indeed, in certain situations it is possible that a semantically consistent schedule may never be realizable by using the concept of serialization.

Usually a consistent but not serializable schedule arises when the individual steps of transactions are interdependent tasks of different sizes. For example, consider the following problem of reservation and cancellation of seats in two ferry companies X and Y, each with two ferries, one large with a capacity greater than N and the other small with a capacity N. Initially the occupancy is set to zero and a flag is set to F; then for each new seat reservation we increase the occupancy by one until it equals the capacity of the smaller ferry. When the occupancy exceeds the capacity N, the flag is set to T to indicate the need for a larger ferry. Each cancellation reduces the occupancy by one; however, no provision is made to reset the flag to F when the occupancy equals or is less than N in order to permit last-minute reservations. Thus the companies do not mind using a larger ferry, although the occupancy has not exceeded the capacity of the smaller ferry. Consequently the only consistency condition is that if the occupancy exceeds N, a larger ferry must be used; thus it is still acceptable to use a larger ferry containing not more than N passengers.

We can represent the above situation by the following schedule: here x and y are the number of seats reserved in X and Y respectively. Transaction 1 does the reservation and transaction 2 does the cancellation.

1xR, 1xW, 1yR, 1yW, 2xR, 2xW, 2yR, 2yW where

1xW:x: = x + 1; if x > N, then set flag(x): = T; else flag(x): = F;

2xW: x: = x − 1;

1yW:y: = y + 1; if y > N, then set flag(y): = T; else flag(y): = F;

2yW:y: = y − 1.

Note that the final result of x, y, flag(x), flag(y) depends on the order of execution of transactions 1 and 2. For example, if x = y = N, the above schedule will yield x = y = N, and flag(x) = flag(y) = T. But the modified schedule — 1xR, 1xW, 2xR, 2xW, 2yR, 2yW, 1yR, 1yW — will yield flag(x) = T; x = N; flag(y) = F, y = N. This modified schedule is clearly nonserializable; however, in this case it is semantically consistent. Hence such an interleaving is permissible.

We say therefore that the tasks of transactions 1 and 2 are interleavable to generate a semantically compatible result, although they are not serializable.

However, suppose that we have another transaction 3 whose function is to reset the value of x, y, and a transaction 4 whose function is to reset flag(x) and flag(y). Although the actions of transactions 3 and 4 cannot be interleaved with the actions of transaction 1, the actions of transaction 4, which resets flag(x) and flag(y), can be interleaved with transaction 2. Hence knowing whether two different types of transactions are compatible can permit the interleaving of their tasks without violating semantic consistency and can improve the degree of concurrency. This is the basic principle used in the Garcia-Molina algorithm.

5.9.2 Garcia-Molina semantic locking algorithm

Here we define that two transactions are compatible if we can interleave their steps without violating database consistency. For this purpose, the user defines types on transactions and a compatibility set for each type. The elements of the compatibility set are called 'interleavers'. It is assumed that a given type interleaves with itself if it interleaves with any other type.

Garcia-Molina's algorithm uses two types of transactions: local and nonlocal. A transaction is local if it consists of single atomic steps; otherwise it is nonlocal. Local transactions are executed at a single site; they can have several interleavers. A nonlocal transaction usually consists of many steps, each one of which is restricted to having at most one interleaver.

This algorithm also uses two kinds of locks: local and global. The local locks are local to every site, and they are X locks allowing only exclusive access to data objects. They ensure atomicity of steps at each local site. The global locks are shared locks that permit type-compatible transactions to run concurrently at different sites without violating consistency. For each global lock on any data object x, we store a list IL(x) of types of interleaved transactions which have concurrently accessed x but not yet completed.

Before there is any action on x, a global lock must be obtained on x and then a local lock. A local lock is released after the execution of the action, whereas a global lock is released only after all the transactions that held x concurrently have terminated (this is analogous to hierarchical locking; see Section 4.3).

The global locking protocol is as follows:

1. *Nonlocal transaction accessing a global lock on* x

   A nonlocal transaction can access an unlocked x by setting its global lock and assigning its interleaver to IL(x). If the lock is free, it is given an access; otherwise, the compatibility of its type with IL(x) is tested. If it is compatible, the global lock is allocated; if it is not, the lock is not allocated and it has to wait.

2. *Local transaction accessing a global lock on* x

   Whenever a local transaction accesses a data object x, it must assign one of its interleavers to it. Before this can happen, however, it has to request a global lock on x; if it is unlocked, the appropriate interleaver that is compatible with other transactions that want concurrent access to x is chosen. This choice provides flexibility for selecting the correct interleaver at the run time, depending on other transactions encountered. However, this choice can cause a delay and reduce the speed. A request to set a global lock on a locked data object y such that IL(y) is not equal to IL(x) is rejected.

3. *Release of global locks*

   The global locks can be released only after all the transactions that have currently accessed x have completed.

Performance

The performance of the Garcia-Molina algorithm depends on the specific application area. It is hard to evaluate its complexity as well as the performance measure, because there is no uniform procedure to evaluate them under different semantic constraints even within the same application area. However, there are instances such as banking (see Garcia-Molina 1983), where this algorithm provides a higher degree of concurrency.

5.9.3 Farrag-Ozsu breakpoint locking algorithm

The algorithm proposed by Farrag and Ozsu (1989) differs from that of Garcia-Molina in the following respects:

1. *Use of breakpoint mechanism*

   The Farrag-Ozsu algorithm uses a control mechanism called a 'breakpoint', together with other actions in a schedule, to permit semantically consistent interleavings. Associated with each breakpoint is a set of transaction types; the elements of this set are those transactions that are allowed to interrupt the present transaction at this point. The different breakpoints of a transaction i are denoted by iBn, where i is the transaction number, B its breakpoint and n its occurrence index. For example, if:

   T1: 1xR, 1B1, 1yR, 1B2, 1C

   T2: 2xW, 2B1, 2zR, 2B2, 2C

   denote transactions and if type (T2) is allowed to interrupt T1 at 1B1, we can have a consistent interleaved schedule:

   1xR, 1B1, 2xW, 2B1, 2zR, 2B2, 2C, 1yR, 1B2, 1C

   Farrag and Ozsu extend the concept of the conflict graph (discussed in Chapter 3 and in Section 5.3) to a nonserializable but consistent schedule comprising actions and breakpoints. They call such schedules 'relatively consistent schedules' (RC schedules). It is shown that the resulting conflict graph should be acyclic for the correctness of the RC schedule. However, here in addition we need to obtain a topological sort of the conflict graph that gives the correct schedule, since the acyclicity does not guarantee correctness. (Recall that in Section 3.5 we said that acyclicity guarantees serializability; we therefore need not obtain the topological sort for serializable single-site schedules. Recall also that in Section 5.3.2 we mentioned the need to find a topological sort for checking the consistency of the multisite schedule.) This is the additional price we pay for dealing with the nonserializable schedules.

2. *Use of additional lock mechanisms*

   Instead of the global and local locks used by Garcia-Molina, here the 2PL locks (namely S and X), as well as two other additional locks — called relative S-lock (RS) and relative X-lock (RX) — are used. Each transaction must obtain a S lock for reading and a X lock for writing; however, when these locks are obtained and R and W actions are not performed and the breakpoints are issued, the S and X locks are respectively modified to RS and RX locks. Hence, nonserializable consistent schedules are produced. Of course, deadlocks may arise, but these have not yet been studied from a practical viewpoint.

5.9.4 Practical systems

The notion of types has been used in the system SDD-1, but it is based on syntactic information. Thus it seems that no commercial systems have yet implemented the semantic locking method, although there is a provision in some systems to include the semantic aspects of transaction processing. For example, the distributed transaction processing system Camelot, developed at Carnegie-Mellon University (Spector 1986), does not enforce serializability; hence it permits transactions to interfere at will and allows implementors to make their choice. Such systems can be used for developing hybrid transaction processing schemes.

However, there still remains the question of the effectiveness of semantic concurrency control in systems with a large number of transactions. This is because the correctness of nonserializable schedules is more difficult to prove, and they require additional efforts such as additional control actions and extra locks, and in finding the right topological sort. It is also quite hard to identify the right application area where their performance would certainly be better than the syntactic approaches to warrant the increased overhead.

Furthermore, even in the less complicated area of ordinary deterministic sequential programming, where the program is completely defined to begin with, the semantic approaches have not made a very great impact. Hence the inclusion of semantics in distributed transaction processing seems to be an academic exercise and is highly unlikely to be successful in a commercial environment, where reliability is of greater concern than a marginal increase in speed.

EXERCISES

1. If you have facilities to run an occam or Ada program, simulate a two-site schedule with five transactions (single version), three data objects and two actions by using access control matrices and a coordinator.
2. What is a multigraph? How is it useful in detecting conflict serializability of multisite schedules?
3. Explain Bernstein's decomposition technique for conflict serializability. Apply it to 2PL.
4. Explain the use of R–W, W–W and R–W–W locks for multiple sites.
5. Explain the majority locking 2PL.
6. Explain the distributed timestamping technique.
7. Program for a three-site schedule with the basic timestamping algorithm.
8. Program for a three-site schedule with the conservative timestamping algorithm using queues.

9. Explain the action of a three-phase certifier.
10. Simulate deadlock and infinite restarting situations in the three-phase certifier.
11. Write an essay on semantic locking techniques. Explain where in practice these schemes are required.
12. Can conservative timestamping lead to a deadlock?
13. Program the centralized deadlock detection procedure.
14. Program the procedure to reduce a directed graph to a knot graph.
15. Program the distributed deadlock detection procedure.
16. Program the distributed knot-finding procedure.

REFERENCES

Bernstein, P.A. and Goodman, N. 1981. 'Concurrency control in distributed systems'. *Computing Surveys*, 13, 185–221.

Bernstein, P.A., Hadzilacos, V. and Goodman, N. 1987. *Concurrency Control and Recovery in Database Systems*. Addison-Wesley, USA.

Cellary, W. 1986. *A Classification of Optimistic Approach Methods for Concurrency Control in Database Systems*, Research Report ISEM 047. University of South Paris, France.

Chandy, K.M, Misra, J. and Haas, L. 1983. 'Distributed deadlock detection'. *ACM Transactions on Computer Systems* 1, 144–56.

Farrag, A.A. and Ozsu, M.T. 1989. 'Using semantic knowledge of transactions to increase concurrency'. *ACM Transactions on Database Systems* 14, 503–25.

Garcia-Molina, H. 1983. 'Using semantic knowledge for transaction processing in a distributed database'. *ACM Transactions on Database Systems* 8, 186–203.

Lynch, N. 1983. 'Multilevel atomicity: a new criterion for database concurrency control'. *ACM Transactions on Database Systems* 8, 484–502.

Natarajan, N. 1986. 'A distributed scheme for detecting communication deadlocks'. *IEEE Transactions on Software Engineering* SE 12, 531–7.

Papadimitriou, C. 1986. *The Theory of Database Concurrency Control*. Computer Science Press, USA.

Raynal, M. 1988. *Networks and Distributed Computation*. MIT Press, USA.

Raynal, M. 1987. *Distributed Algorithms and Protocols*. Wiley, UK.

Spector, A.Z. 1986. 'Distributed transaction processing and the Camelot system'. In Distributed Operating Systems, Series F, *Computer and System Sciences* 28, 331–53.

6 Resilient schedules

6.1 INTRODUCTION

A schedule is called resilient or recovering if it can restore the database to a previous consistent state when unexpected failures occur in hardware, software, system or programs. We mentioned this problem briefly in Section 1.5.1. Any restoration operation, as was noted earlier in Section 1.5.1, is communication-intensive and storage-intensive. This is because we need to store all the steps of a schedule (called a 'log') somewhere safe so that we can restore the database when failures occur. Any such process requires communication between a reliable memory system (such as a disk, where all the actions and previous results are stored) and a fallible, but faster memory system (a main memory, or a cache memory which stores and recovers intermediate computations at high speed). In a centralized schedule the recovery issue turns out to be less complex than in a multisite schedule, since a centralized schedule has only a single site and local communication failures are rare. However, in a multisite schedule the site failures and communication failures can cause serious problems. Since the design of a reliable database system depends on how resilient the schedules are when failures strike, it has been a very important area of study (see Shrivastava 1985). In this chapter we will address these issues with respect to both the localized and multisite schedules.

6.2 CATEGORIES OF FAILURES

Three broad classes of failures affect the transaction services:

1. hardware and software failures at a site;
2. information storage failures — that is, irrecoverable device failure and temporary power failure that result in loss of information from the memory (called a 'crash');
3. message communication failures — that is, site failures and link failures.

When one is dealing with a localized schedule, the main issue is to ensure that the stored information is not lost. Hence the design and management of a fault-tolerant memory system for the database system are vital. When one is dealing with multisite schedules, preventing information loss in message communication becomes an additional vital factor. This will also require a fault-tolerant communication system. Accordingly, memory management and communication management are the key issues in the realization of resilient distributed schedules. We will deal with those two issues in this chapter.

6.3 FAULT-TOLERANT INFORMATION STORAGE

Several types of storage media are used in a computer system to improve the overall throughput. These storage media are organized as a hierarchy (called 'the memory hierarchy') in a computer system. They vary in technology, reliability, speed and quantity of access (chunk size), and total capacity. Bandwidth, which is the ratio of chunk size to access time, is used as a measure of speed; for example, if a memory has a 500-nanosec cycle time for a 32-bit chunk, its bandwidth is 64 megabits. The primary goal in the design of a memory hierarchy is to increase the bandwidth by reducing cycle time, increasing word size and improving concurrency, and to match register and processor speeds.

Typically a cache memory lies in between the processor registers and the main memory in the memory hierarchy. It is a bipolar device with 1-word chunk, a 30–100 nanosec access time and a capacity of 2–128 kilobytes. The RAM, which is a central memory, is a MOS memory with a 2–32-bit word chunk, 0.5 to 1 microsec access and 4 kilobyte to 16 megabyte capacity. The disk is a magnetic device with a chunk size of 1 kilobyte to 4 kilobytes, with an access time of 5–15 millisec and a capacity of 8–256 megabytes. The moving head disk is next in the hierarchy, with a capacity varying from 128 to 512 megabytes, a chunk capacity of 4 kilobytes and an access time of 25–75 millisec. Finally, the tape has a capacity of over 50 megabytes, 1–16 kilobyte chunks and an access time of 1–5 sec.

Thus information transfer takes place between a lower level slower device and a higher level faster device to improve the speed of processing of smaller chunks. For example, the virtual memory technique brings the currently needed page from the disk to the main memory; here the main memory is faster than the disk. The cache memory brings still smaller size chunks from the main memory to have a faster access from the cache, which is 5 to 20 times faster than the main memory. The information then reaches processor registers for much faster computation.

Unfortunately, the cache memory and main memory are volatile; that is, they do not retain their contents when power fails. Such a failure is called a 'crash'. But the magnetic disk, though slow, can retain information under power failure, since it uses magnetic recording. Hence it is called a nonvolatile storage. Magnetic disks are subject, however, to failures such as head crash. The magnetic tape is a stable storage and can be used to retain information for a reasonably long period; it is therefore used for archive purposes. As the tape is too slow for storage and retrieval, it is customary to create a stable storage using multiple, independent nonvolatile disk storages which cannot fail simultaneously. We will discuss the creation of a stable storage in the following subsection.

6.3.1 Creating a stable storage

A stable storage is created at two levels. At the first level a 'careful disk' is prepared; this consists of a 'careful write' that is read and verified each time a write operation is carried out. If the verification fails, the block is marked 'bad' and the system crashes. Thus any read will be correct. At the second level, two independent disks are chosen so that their joint failure probability is very small. This technique is called 'mirroring' and is a widely used redundancy technique for improving reliability. A pair of ordered blocks, one from each disk, is chosen. Then a 'careful write' is performed on the first one; if there is a failure, the block is marked 'bad' and the second one is not used. The block marked 'bad' is replaced by a new block and a 'careful write' is performed on the new block and on the second block. Similarly, if the second block fails during the 'careful write', it is marked 'bad', a new block is chosen and a 'careful write' is performed.

The stable storage is also subjected to a periodic checkup, which consists in comparing a pair of blocks. If both are not marked 'bad' and are identical, nothing is done. However, if both are not marked 'bad' but are different, one is copied on the other to make them identical.

The above procedure seems to work reliably with infrequent failures. It is advisable to dump periodically the contents of another nonvolatile storage to a stable storage or tapes.

6.4 STORAGE MANAGEMENT FOR RECOVERY

We will now look at the memory organization for a database management system and how recovery is achieved. In Figure 1.1 we depicted a typical centralized database management system. As already explained, this system has three basic components:

1. a transaction manager which receives the database actions such as R, W, C and A, and passes them on to the scheduler;
2. a scheduler which takes care of the concurrency control and restricts the order in which the data manager performs R, W, C and A so that consistency is achieved;
3. a data manager which consists of the database in stable storage (called 'stable database'), the faster main memory and the cache memory, the cache manager and the recovery manager.

The cache manager fetches an item (usually called a 'page') from the stable storage and places it in an addressable portion of the cache called a 'slot'. If after a computational step, the value of the stored item in the slot differs from the one in the stable storage, a Boolean flag called a 'dirty bit' is assigned the value one.

The storing of items in cache slots is facilitated by using slot addresses and a directory. The 'fetch' operation for acquiring a data item from the stable storage and the 'flush' operation to write back an item in the stable storage take place thus:

Fetch. An empty slot is selected, the value from stable storage is copied, the 'dirty bit' is cleared and the directory is updated.

Flush. If the 'dirty bit' is zero, nothing is done; otherwise, a copy of the value of an item in the slot is sent to the stable storage and the 'dirty bit' is cleared. Since careless flushing can destroy the stable database, the operation is monitored by two control actions: pin, unpin.

Pin. This action prevents the flushing of a slot until unpin is set.

Unpin. This action enables a previously pinned slot to flush.

The recovery manager carries out the following five actions atomically for each transaction i (see Figure 2.1) under the direction of the scheduler in order to produce serializable execution:

> ixR, ixW, iC, iA and restart (that is, bring the database in the stable memory to a consistent committed state).

Two different approaches are used for recovery management. In the first approach, called 'logging', all changes are made to the stable database (that is, the actual database in stable memory) and are later modified when a failure occurs by using a log containing all the required information in the stable memory; hence this approach is also called 'in place update'. In the second approach, called 'shadowing', the changes are made to a copy of the stable database but not to the stable database. When there is a failure, the copy is destroyed; and no modifications are needed. However, when the transactions commit, the new copy replaces the shadow in the stable memory.

6.4.1 Logging (in place update)

We explained in Section 1.5 and Section 2.5.8 that the recovery of a schedule requires storage of the past history of actions that contains the name of the transaction, the actions carried out, and the prevalue and postvalue of the data object in a manner similar to the organization of the access matrix. If the log contains only the prevalue, it is called a 'backward log'; if it contains only the postvalue, it is called a 'forward log'. However, if it contains both the prevalue and the postvalue, it is called a 'bidirectional log'. We will use here only the bidirectional log.

As the actions are carried out the log is recorded in the stable memory (as well as in the volatile memory) in the topological order of execution in the access matrix. For example, if ixW < jxW and iC < jC, they appear in this order.

In order to store the prevalue and postvalue of a data object we use the notation ix (Ix, Fx)W, which means that when the transaction i acts on the data object x, the initial value was Ix before the W action and the final value is Fx after the W action. Thus if we want to 'undo' the W action to recover the prevalue, we need to set x: = Ix; if we need to recover the postvalue, this is called a 'redo' action and we set x: = Fx.

Since a transaction can do R and W action only once in its lifetime, any number of redo x will result in x: = Fx and any number of undo will result in x: = Ix. Hence these undo and redo operations are given the mathematical name 'idempotent operations'; this means that a repetition of any one of these actions for a given transaction is equivalent to doing the action once. As we will see, this is a very useful property when one is handling failures of transactions. The recovery manager carries out these actions as a part of its restart action; when it does 'redo' it sets x: = Fx; when it does 'undo', it sets x: = Ix.

Example

Consider the following schedule:

> 1xR, 1xW, 1yR, 1yW, 1C, 2zR, 2zW, 2C;

Its log in the stable memory appears as below:

> 1x(Ix, Ix)R, 1x(Ix, Fx)W, 1y(Iy, Iy)R, 1y(Iy, Fy)W, 1C, 2z(Iz, Iz)R, 2z(Iz, Fz)W, 2C

This schedule satisfies the log-write-ahead protocol mentioned in Section 1.5.1. Such a protocol ensures that the database in the stable memory (which we shall call 'stable database') will contain the value of the last committed transaction.

Crash effects

Again we recall the recovery model of a transaction which we discussed in Section 2.2.2. This model (Figure 2.1(b)) reflects a practical situation in which failures can happen when a transaction is about to commit. These failures are essentially loss of information from cache or other hardware errors that force the transaction either to redo and commit or abort, undo and restart.

The recovery manager has the following responsibilities:

1. If for some reason a transaction has committed and recorded this information in the log, but owing to a crash could not write the final value of the data object in the stable database, it has to perform redo to reset the database to a consistent state by its restart action.
2. Since writing in log and writing in database are different processes, it is not possible to achieve atomicity and force simultaneity of the two independent nondeterministic events running at different speeds. Thus anomalies can occur: for example, an *uncommitted* transaction *may write* a new value Fx or the *committed* transaction *may not write* the new value Fx in the stable database. In such cases, the actions are to be respectively undone or redone by the restart action of the recovery manager.

   The undo and redo actions of the recovery manager take place as illustrated below.

Rules for undo and redo actions

In order to explain undo and redo actions, we use the notation $ to denote a crash situation. Consider the schedule:

> 1xR, 1xW, 1yR, 1yW, 1C, 2zR, 2zW, 2C

Let 1xW: x: = x – 100; 1yW: y: = y+100; 2zW:z: = z – 200; let Ix = 2000; Iy = 4000; Iz = 1400.

We will consider three different cases:

Case 1

Let the crash happen as described by the following log:

1x(2000, 1900)W, 1y(4000, 4100)W, $(crash)

If the transaction is not committed but the cache has flushed its slot, the database will have:

x = 1900 or 2000; y = 4100 or 4000;

Thus 1 is to be undone to obtain x = 2000; y = 4000.

Case 2

However, if the log is written up to:

1x(2000, 1900), 1y(4000, 4100), 1C, 2z(1400, 1200), $;

then the database will contain:

x = 1900; y = 4100; z = 1400 or 1200

Since 1 has committed but 2 is not committed in the log, we redo 1 and undo 2. The effect is:

x = 1900; y = 4100; z = 1400

Case 3

However, if the log is written up to:

1x(2000, 1900), 1y(4000, 4100), 1C, 2(1400, 1200), 2C, $

We need to redo both 1 and 2 so that the database will contain:

x = 1900; y = 4100; z = 1200

Thus we have the following rules for undo and redo:

Undo rule

If a transaction i has begun but its log does not contain iC, then undo (that is, set x: = Ix in the stable database for all data objects x handled by i).

Redo rule

If a transaction i has begun and iC is in its log, then redo (that is, set x: = Fx in the stable database for all data objects x handled by i).

Since idempotence guarantees correctness, we need not look up the actual values in the stable database; we simply use the above rules.

Saving space and time in logging

There are two disadvantages in using a log:

1. The number of entries in the log can grow enormously (we should therefore purge it occasionally to save space). This can be remedied by using 'garbage collection'.
2. Although undo and redo can be performed many times without causing inconsistency, overdoing them many times results in a severe loss of time and money. There should therefore be another bookkeeping effort in the log to record the last redo and undo actions that need not be repeated. This can be achieved by using 'checkpointing'.

Garbage collection

In the log we can throw away the following entries which are not needed:

1. entries of aborted transactions: ix(Ix, Fx)A;
2. entries of a transaction i which has committed and has been followed by another transaction j which has overwritten x and committed. (However, we must retain entries of i if j has not committed.)

   In notational form, we can delete entries of i if:

   ixW < i A or ixW < iC < jxW < jC

   But we cannot delete entries of i if:

   ixW < iC < jxW but no jC; or if ixW < iC < jA.

Checkpointing

When a crash has occurred and undo and redo have been performed, it is useful to retain the $ symbol in the log in that place. This serves as a checkpoint. When another crash occurs, it is necessary only to go back to the log and check which new transactions started before the first crash. Only those transactions are to be now undone or redone until the new crash.

Logical log

Another way of saving space in the log is to use logical logging. Here the log contains operations that belong to a level higher than the syntactic level of action W. This method may turn out to be more expensive for practical realization.

6.4.2 Shadowing

Here we maintain two pages of information: one page called the 'current page', and the other page called 'a shadow page', which is a copy of the current page in the stable storage. The transactions can alter only the current page. When they commit, the current page becomes the new shadow page. If they abort, however, the current page is deleted and a new current page is created at restart. Thus no undo is required.

In order to use shadowing we need to have a good address-mapping scheme between the main memory and the stable database. This technique has two advantages over the logging method: no log record is maintained and no undo is needed. Hence faster recovery can be achieved from crashes. However, it has two disadvantages: it requires an efficient address scheme and it does not provide an old version of the database.

6.5 COMMUNICATION NETWORKS MANAGEMENT

Since a distributed database system is a collection of centralized database systems in a computer network, we need to concentrate on communication management among the sites in order to realize the resilient multisite schedules. Communication management is concerned with the problem of coping with:

1. site failures: local failures of volatile memory, system failures, hardware and software failures;
2. communication failures: total inaccessibility, loss of messages, corruption, link failures, noise effects.

The question is how to keep the distributed database consistent when these failures occur. Since the reliability of a database is dependent on its commit action, the answer seems to lie in obtaining a reliable message communication scheme for the decision to commit or abort a large number of participant processes at different sites. This is the central issue in communication management.

6.5.1 Modeling distributed commitment

The atomicity requirement that all subtransactions at all sites leave the database consistent can be stated by the following conditions:

1. If a transaction is to be committed, all its subtransactions should agree to commit; that is, committing requires a unanimous decision.
2. If any one subtransaction aborts, the transaction aborts; that is abort is a unilateral decision.
3. If there are failures of sites or links and subsequent repairs, there should be a procedure to arrive at a decision to abort or commit and leave the database consistent.

In order to understand the distributed commitment of a transaction, we need to model each subtransaction as well as the cooperative group behavior of all the subtransactions.

6.5.2 Voting recovery model

The recovery model of a localized transaction, considered in Figure 2.1(b), can be used for modeling each subtransaction; however it needs some modification for the following reason. In the case of localized schedules, when a transaction decides to commit, it is not uncertain about the outcome of commitment, although it is subject to failures. But when a subtransaction decides to commit, this is not a unilateral decision; hence it is in a doubtful state until all the other subtransactions reach the same decision by way of communication. Thus we need to introduce a state D called 'doubtful state' in addition to the 'about to commit state' (which will be denoted by R) and 'failed state' (F), as shown in Figure 6.1.The 'doubtful state' is reached by a subtransaction when it agrees to commit (called 'vote commit') and wait for others' decision. This model will be called the 'voting recovery model', since it is a recovery model with the addition of a voting and waiting state D.

Note that failure can be of two types: site failure and communication failure. Site failure, such as volatile storage failure, is dealt with as described in Section 6.4. However, since both types of failures may occur together in some cases, we put them together as a single state F in Figure 6.1. To move out of state F, recovery or repair is needed.

In order to leave the database consistent we must ensure that no subtransaction at one site enters state C while other subtransactions at other sites are in states that can lead to the A (abort) state. Thus the main issue is to design a cooperative protocol in order to arrive at a unanimous decision in the presence of communication failures, thus leaving the database consistent. This is analogous to the well-known 'Byzantine Generals' Problem' (Raynal 1987). In this problem several generals widely separated in the enemy war front want to arrive at a cooperative decision on the mode of attack by sending to each other messengers who may fail (get killed) or may be unreliable. In the context of the distributed transaction service the subtransactions correspond to the generals and they communicate to arrive at the commitment or abort decision in the presence of site and communication failures. This situation is modeled using a coordinator and participants as explained below.

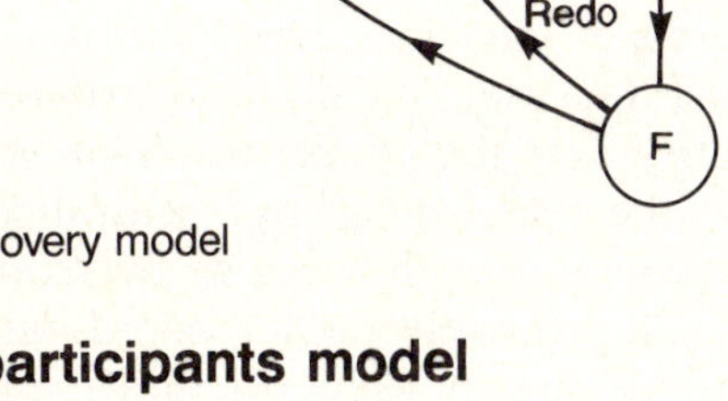

Figure 6.1 Voting recovery model

6.5.3 Coordinator-participants model

Here we assume that each transaction executes at one site, called the home site, and communicates with the controllers at other sites to do R or W actions. The process that executes at the home site is called the 'coordinator' and processes at the other sites are called 'participants'. As in the localized schedule, a transaction does R and W action at the home site and also at other sites. When the coordinator completes its task, it reaches a point called the 'commit point'. It then sends messages to all participants to write in their stable memory. If they all say 'yes', the coordinator sends commit messages to all of them; however, if any participant is unwilling or has failed, the coordinator sends abort messages to all of them.

That is the basic principle to be used. However, it can lead to blocking when a participant fails while in its doubtful state, because it cannot decide to abort or commit without help from the coordinator or other participants. Thus any recovery from such failure is not independent. In fact, there is no method that can guarantee independent recovery of a failed process, since the commit action has to be the result of a cooperative decision.

In order to recover from local volatile storage failures we need to have a logging scheme as explained below.

6.5.4 Logging

The logging of subtransactions should contain the following information:

1. the conversation between the coordinator and participant;
2. the commit/abort record of the participants;
3. the recovery record (redo/undo) and checkpoints.

In order to recover safely:

1. Each site should retain the record of all subtransactions until the local recovery manager processes its A or C action.
2. At least one site should retain the record until all the sites have processed C or A.

Three basic protocols are used for distributed commitment based on the coordinator-participants model in which each participant is modeled by the voting recovery model.

6.6 PROTOCOLS FOR DISTRIBUTED COMMITMENT

The coordinator-participant model reduces the communication overhead. If we did not use this model and use a totally decentralized model where no single participant has authority over the others, we might need $O(n^2)$ messages for n participants. However, the disadvantage of a central coordinator is that when it fails, the whole system fails. But this can be overcome by the remaining participants if they negotiate and re-elect a new coordinator. In this section we will describe the three basic protocols using the message-passing scheme. This is a basic notion in the Communicating Sequential Process (CSP) model developed by Hoare, using Dijkstra's guarded commands. It is used in the programming language occam.

In this model the participants (or processes) and coordinator communicate using two primitives: Send (denoted by!) and Receive (denoted by ?). This mode is called a synchronous mode of communication, where the sender proceeds after the message is acknowledged by the receiver, hence no blocking takes place while a reply is awaited.

The coordinator-participant model can be easily realized as a program in occam, Jones [1987].

The coordinator–participant model is subject to the following failures:

1. participant/coordinator failure;
2. channel disconnection that prevents message sending or receiving.

Thus provision must be made for repairing a participant and also reinserting of a channel. Methods for that purpose are discussed in Raynal (1988); they are based on graph-theoretic algorithms which compute the shortest path among the participants.

We will now discuss three different protocols for commitment of distributed transactions which communicate by message passing among a central coordinator and participants. We will also provide a method of replacing a failed coordinator by a newly elected coordinator among the participants. The three protocols are called simple, two-phase and three-phase commitment protocols (SPAC, 2PAC and 3PAC respectively).

The conversation among each of the n participants Pi (i = 1, 2, . . . n) and the manager or coordinator (M) in the three different protocols proceeds as described below.

6.6.1 Behavior of SPAC

Figure 6.2 illustrates this protocol. We use the symbol M! x to denote send x to M, and M?y to denote receive y from M. Also, we use the following notation:

IP: initial state of Pi; IM: initial state of coordinator M;

vC: vote commit; vA: vote abort; C: commit; A: abort; D: doubtful state;

F: failed state; ∀: for all; ∃: there exists.

Figure 6.2(a) illustrates the behavior of participant Pi and Figure 6.2(b) illustrates the behavior of coordinator M. The plain English description of the behavior is as follows:

Pi: While Pi is in initial state IP, Pi sends vote commit to M and waits in the doubtful state D; or sends vote-abort to M and aborts.

M: While M is in initial state IM, if vote-commit is received from *all* Pi, then M sends commit to *all* Pi. If any one Pi votes for abort, then M sends abort to all Pi (and self-aborts).

Pi: While Pi is waiting in state D, if commit is received from M, then Pi commits; if abort is received from M, then Pi aborts. If no communication is received from M, or P fails while in D, Pi goes to F and blocks.

Discussion

This protocol has the serious drawback of blocking when communication failure occurs and no message arrives while Pi is in D, or if Pi is in D and fails. In order to remove that drawback the 2PAC described below is used. It is clear

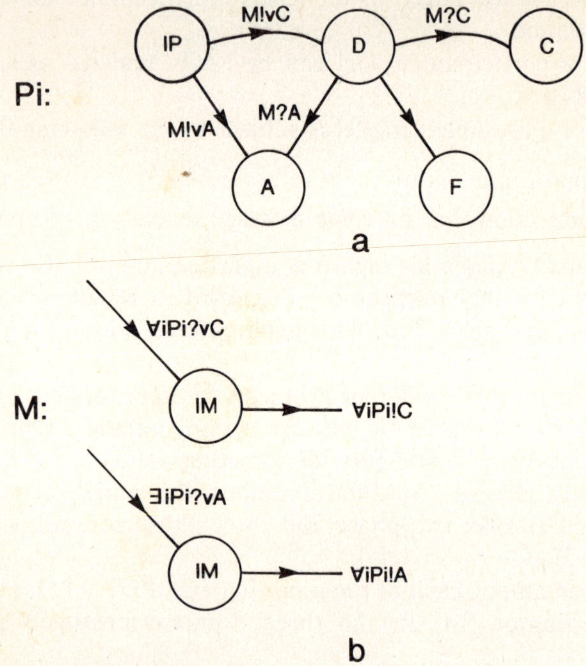

Figure 6.2 SPAC protocol

that there is no provision in SPAC as to how long Pi has to wait in D or what happens when it fails in D.

To analyze the SPAC protocol we can use Figure 6.2 and construct a compatibility matrix of states for participants Pi and Pj respectively in Sites i and j (Figure 6.3). In this matrix the ij th entry is Y (for yes) if the states can coexist; if they cannot coexist, the entry ij is N (for no).

i \ j	A	D	F	C
A	Y	Y	Y	N
D	Y	Y	Y	Y
F	Y	Y	Y	Y
C	N	Y	Y	Y

Figure 6.3 Site compatibility matrix for SPAC

The compatibility matrix shows that it is possible that some Pi can be in D state, while some others are in C state or F state. This happens when Pi receives C but the coordinator fails soon after and Pj remains in D or F. Also, it is possible that Pi received A while in D, but that the site of Pj failed while in D, and Pj did not know about the abort of Pi. Thus D and A can coexist. This protocol prevents only A and C from coexisting; hence it is a weak protocol. To improve this situation, 2PAC and 3PAC protocols have been designed.

6.6.2 Behavior of 2PAC

The two-phase protocol (2PAC) has three more features than SPAC:

1. M initiates conversation by sending requests to all Pi for vote commit/abort, thus enabling each participant to know the names of other participants so that communication among the participants can take place if the coordinator fails.
2. Time-out period is provided for replies to be heard by M from Pi or by Pi from M, thus eliminating indefinite waiting.
3. After sending vote commit each Pi in state D can go to the abort state if aborted by M or can go to F state to recover if commit is not received from M within the time-out period; it can then send a *help-me* message to other Pj.

Figure 6.4(a) illustrates the behavior of the participant Pi and Figure 6.4(b) illustrates the behavior of the coordinator M. Here we use the following additional notation:

bV: begin voting; tt: time-out; DM: doubtful state of M.

The plain English description of the behaviour is as follows:

M: At the initial state IM, M sends vote request bV to all Pi; then M waits in state DM for a specified time duration (time-out).

Pi: At the initial state IP, if bV is received from M within the time-out period, Pi sends vote commit to M and waits in state D or sends vote abort to M and aborts. If no request for vote is received by Pi from M within the time-out period, Pi aborts and sends abort to M.

M: While M is waiting in DM for reply from Pi, if vote commit is received from all Pi within time-out period, then M sends commit to all Pi. If time-out occurs before receiving vote from some Pi or vote abort is received from any Pi, then M sends abort to all Pi.

Pi: While Pi is waiting in D, if commit is received from M, then it commits; if abort is received from M, then Pi aborts. If time-out occurs and no reply is received from M, Pi goes to state F, looks at log and recovers; Pi looks at the names of participants Pj from vote request of M and sends help-me to all other Pj directly.

Pj: When Pj receives help-me from any Pi, it checks log whether vote request was received from M; if not, it aborts and informs M and Pi; if vote request has been received and Pj is waiting for reply from M, it does nothing; if Pj has sent vote commit to M and Pj has received commit from M, then Pj informs Pi accordingly; if Pj has sent vote abort to M and Pj has aborted, or Pj has received abort from M, it informs Pi accordingly.

Pi: If any other Pj has committed, then Pi commits; if any Pj has aborted, then Pi aborts; if Pi receives no reply from one or more Pj, then Pi remains blocked.

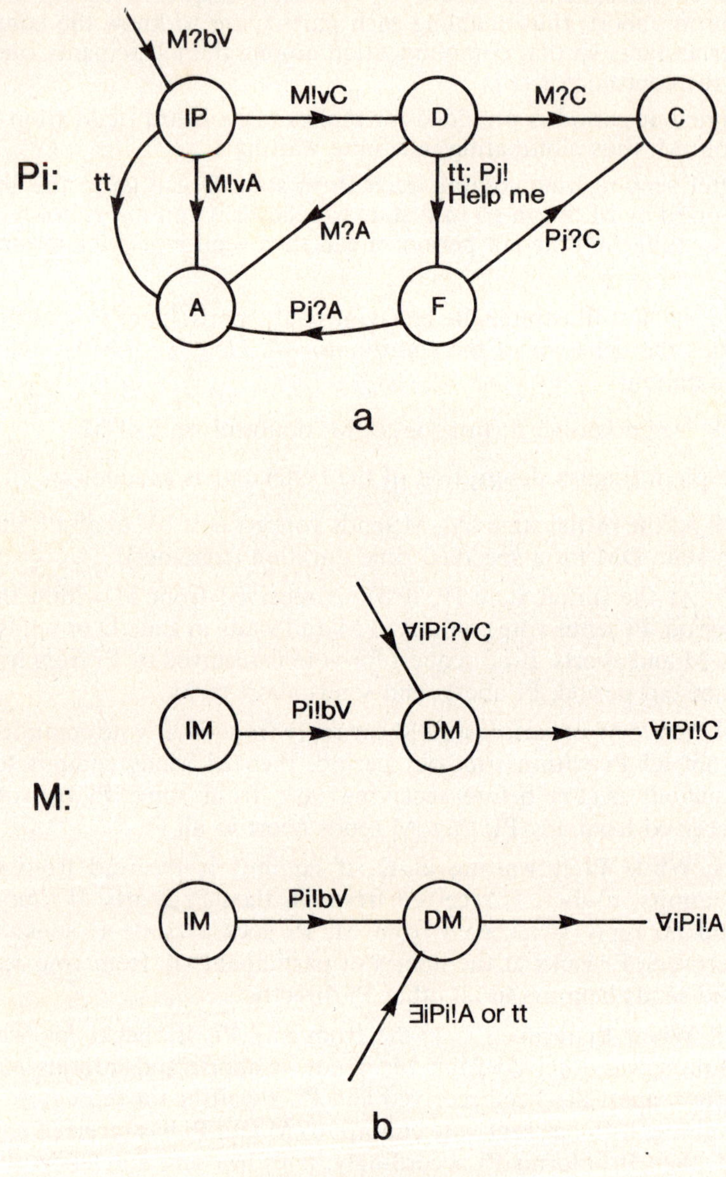

Figure 6.4 2PAC protocol

Discussion
Using Figure 6.4 we can analyze the 2PAC protocol. We can show that the participants Pi and Pj at sites i and j respectively can coexist in states A, D, F or C as dictated by the following compatibility matrix (Figure 6.5). Here the entry ij is Y (for yes) if the states can coexist; if they cannot coexist, the entry ij is N (for no).

i \ j	A	D	F	C
A	Y	Y	Y	N
D	Y	Y	N	N
F	Y	N	Y	Y
C	N	N	Y	Y

Figure 6.5 Site compatibility matrix for 2PAC

For example, one participant cannot be in state D and another in F; this is because in state D, if no A or C is received from M, the time-out would place the Pi in state F. Further, D and C cannot coexist, since nonarrival of C or A will put the Pi in state F. In the latter state F there may be some Pi which were cut off while in D. These do not know whether other Pj have committed or aborted; hence F and A, F and C or F and F may coexist. Thus it is clear that no process can enter into C while another is in D. However, some processes may become stranded in F, thus causing blocking.

If a participant in state D fails to receive C from M because of its own failure or coordinator failure, it reaches F state where, if it has not failed, it can contact other Pj. If other Pj have received commit, it commits; if others have received abort, it aborts.

It is clear that the facility to communicate with other participants may unblock Pi; but this is not definite, since all the sites might have failed. The strategy of consulting other participants to unblock and terminate when a participant has failed in its doubtful state is called a 'cooperative termination protocol'. It works with a good probability of success in practical situations.

The 2PAC is one of the most widely used protocols and rarely causes blocking. It uses 3n messages if there are no failures (as seen from Figure 6.4), sending bV, vC or vA, commit or abort.

6.6.3 Behavior of 3PAC

The three-phase protocol (3PAC) has one more extra command than 2PAC. This extra command is called the 'precommit' (PC) which is issued by the coordinator (compare Figures 6.4 and 6.6) as explained below:

Before sending C, a precommit command PC is issued by M to all Pi; these precommit messages are acknowledged by Pi. The last of the precommit messages is sent by M earlier than the first of the commit messages; also there is a time-out mechanism for receiving acknowledgment.

The use of the PC has the following consequences: After sending vote commit, each Pi in state D can go to abort state A if aborted by M; or it can go to state F if no pre-commit is received from M within time-out, and can send a help-me message to other Pj.

If pre-commit is received from M, Pi acknowledges and goes to state R (about to commit); if in state R commit is not received from M, it goes to F after time-out, sending a save-me message to other Pj. If commit is received from M while Pi is in state R, it goes to C.

Thus two types of transaction go to the F state: those which sent a help-me message (as they did not receive precommit from M while they were in D) and those which sent a save-me message (as they did not receive commit from M while they were in R).

Figure 6.6(a) illustrates the behavior of participant Pi, and Figure 6.6(b) illustrates the behavior of coordinator M in 3PAC. We use PCM to denote the state of M after it sends precommit to Pi. The plain English description of the behavior is as follows:

> M: At the initial state IM, M sends bV request for vote commit or vote abort to all Pi; then M waits in state DM for a specified time duration (time-out).
>
> Pi: At the initial state IP, if bV request is received from M within time-out period, Pi sends vote commit to M and waits in D; or Pi sends vote abort to M and aborts. If no vote request is received from M within time-out, Pi aborts and sends abort to M.
>
> M: While M is waiting in DM for reply from Pi, if vote commit is received from all Pi, M sends precommit to all Pi. If time-out occurs before receiving vote from some Pi or if vote abort is received from any Pi, then M sends abort to all Pi.
>
> Pi: While Pi is waiting in D, if precommit is received from M, Pi acknowledges to M and moves to R (about to commit); if abort is received from M, then Pi aborts. If time-out occurs but no message is received from M, Pi moves to state F, looks at log and recovers; then sends help-me to other Pj directly.
>
> M: M waits for acknowledgment in state PCM from all Pi for precommit; if time-out occurs, then M sends commit to all Pi (ignore failures of Pi).
>
> Pi: While Pi is in R, if commit is received from M then Pi commits; if time-out occurs and no reply received from M, then Pi moves to F, looks at log and recovers; Pi sends save-me to all other Pj directly.
>
> Pj: When receiving help-me from one or more Pi, Pj checks its present state; if Pj is in abort state, it sends abort to all Pi. If Pj is in F state and has earlier sent help-me or save-me to others, it informs other Pi. If Pj is in commit state, it informs other Pi.
>
> Pi: If all participants Pj have responded and no abort message received by Pi from any Pj and all are commit or save-me messages (including self), then Pi commits. If all participants have responded with abort message or

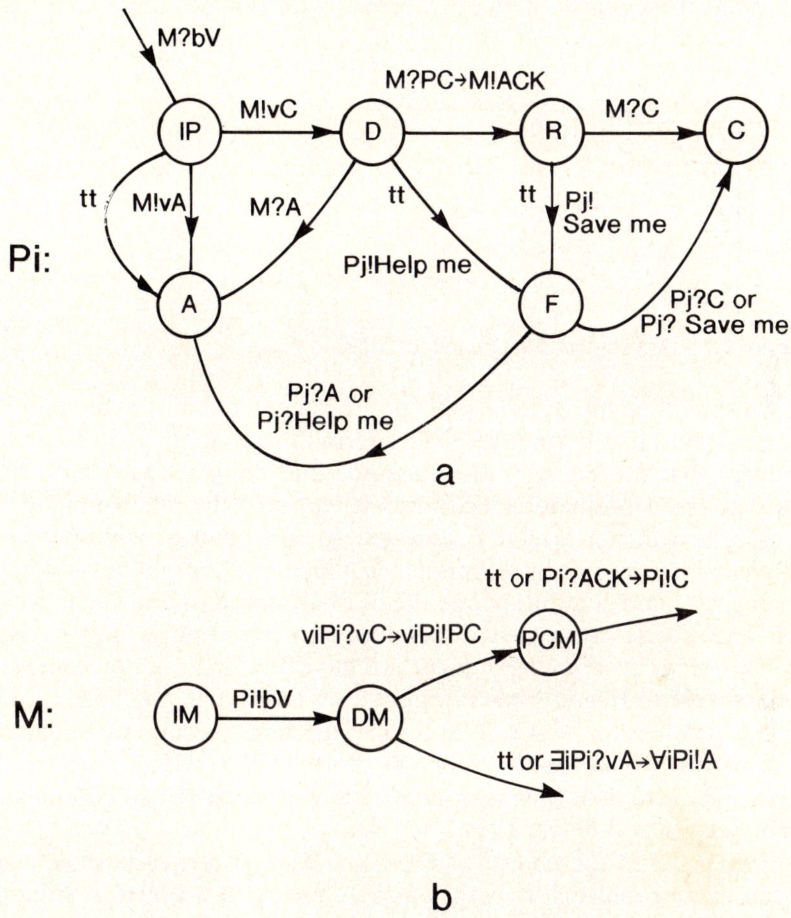

Figure 6.6 3PAC protocol

help-me message, then Pi aborts. If some participants have not responded, Pi remains blocked.

Discussion

Using Figure 6.6 we can analyze the 3PAC protocol. We see that for any two subtransactions at sites i and j the participants Pi and Pj will be respectively in states A, D, R, F or C as given by the compatibility matrix in Figure 6.7. This matrix tells the following: if the ij th entry is Y (for yes), the i th and j th sites can coexist in these states; if the ij th entry is N (for no) these states cannot coexist.

i \ j	A	D	R	F	C
A	Y	Y	N	Y	N
D	Y	Y	Y	N	N
R	N	Y	Y	Y	Y
F	Y	N	Y	Y	Y
C	N	N	Y	Y	Y

Figure 6.7 Site compatibility matrix for 3PAC

For instance, if any Pi is in D state, no Pj can enter C; this is because Pi can be in state D only if it has not received precommit or abort. If Pj has received precommit, it has moved to R. If we assume that the message is not lost, it is possible that the coordinator failed after it had sent the precommit to Pj. In such a case, Pj will not receive C and will go to F, and Pi will also go to F. Alternatively, if Pi received precommit but failed and did not acknowledge M, Pj may receive C and commit; but by then Pi has moved to F owing to time-out. Hence F and C can coexist. It is possible, however, that A and F can also coexist. This is because some Pi might not have received A or precommit, and on time-out went to F; and some Pi might have received A and gone to state A.

It is not possible for A and R to coexist, because precommit would not be sent by M if any one Pi is aborted or has aborted. Thus without precommit no Pi can enter R. Also note that as in 2PAC, pairs of states (D, F), (D, C) and (C, A) cannot coexist at different sites.

A crucial issue is the choice of time-out. This is not easy, since a wrong choice can cause problems. It is therefore necessary in a practical situation to check that exclusion criteria are satisfied where time-out is critical. For example, in the above case we must make sure that no Pi is in D while any Pi commits from F.

The above 3PAC is not resistant to network disconnection. Assuming no failures, it takes 5n messages (see Figure 6.6), sending bV, vC or vA, precommit, acknowledgment, and C or A. Also, the amount of communication involved is $O(n^2)$ for n participants when the coordinator fails. Therefore it is useful to elect a new coordinator among the participants, since it involves less communication. There are numerous algorithms for this purpose (see Raynal 1987, 1988).

6.6.4 Coordinator election

In the last section we mentioned that while in F it is necessary to seek the cooperation of other Pj participants, since the coordinator does not respond. In Figure 6.6, this happens when Pi does not receive precommit from M while in D or does not receive the C while in R. In both cases Pi cannot act unilaterally to make a decision. This is because it is possible that there is a subtransaction in state D that has not received precommit and moved to F; hence Pi must make sure that no Pj that moved from state D is in F when it wants to move to C. In order to deal with these matters more effectively it is necessary to elect a new coordinator at this stage. This coordinator then controls the commit or abort of those transactions stranded in F and performs recovery.

Several algorithms are available (see Raynal 1988) for electing a coordinator. Obviously the complexity of these algorithms depends on the nature of the interconnection graph (topology) among the participants — for example, whether it is connected by a ring or connected as in a tree, or fully interconnected (complete graph).

If the graph is arbitrary the election process is complex, since an exploration of the network is needed to visit all participants and choose a unique one among them that has connections with all other participants. For this purpose, each participant is given a unique identifier, and it is customary to assign the job of coordinator to the largest (or smallest) identifier. The depth-first search of the graph is useful for exploring the neighbor with the largest identifier. Most algorithms require $O(n^2)$ messages; the best election algorithms operate on networks which are fully connected (complete) graphs or rings with a complexity of $O(n \log n)$, for n participants (see Raynal 1987, 1988). All these algorithms use the *Selective extinction principle*, whereby each participant receives a message from one of its neighbors and may or may not acquire new information. If it does acquire new information, it sends a message to its next neighbor; otherwise, it does not communicate.

We will now illustrate how the above principle can be used to elect a coordinator among n participants connected by a unidirectional ring topology. We assume that the failure of a participant does not prevent communication among live participants; some LANs, such as the Ethernet, have this feature.

6.6.5 Election algorithm in a unidirectional ring

Let n participants be arranged in any order in a unidirectional ring. Because of the unidirectional nature, it is clear that any message can reach the sender only if it passes through all other participants. Each participant Pi has a unique identifier i, which it transmits to its left neighbor (say) Pj. Then Pj compares its identifier j with i and passes on to its left neighbor the maximum of i and j. Finally, when a participant receives its own identifier, it knows that it is the greatest identifier among live participants and has been elected as the coordinator. It then informs all the other participants of its identifier.

Example

Consider a unidirectional ring of participants:

3 2 5 6 1 4 (3)

If 6 fails, then starting the election at 3, we will pass on the message until 5 is elected. A dead participant will not respond, and so if it has the largest identifier, it will not be circulated, and if it has a smaller identifier, it will be extinct on election.

Discussion

The above algorithm requires 2(n-1) messages when the largest identifier initiates election and all numbers are arranged in a random order. The most favorable situation is when the processes are arranged in increasing identifier order and the largest identifier initiates; here we require O(n) messages. The least favorable situation is when the identifiers are arranged in decreasing order and all initiate election simultaneously; this requires $O(n^2)$ messages. On average, this algorithm needs O(n log n) messages.

6.6.6 Recovery using new coordinator

A newly elected coordinator carries out the following termination protocol:

1. It sends messages to all participants to ascertain their present states.
2. After a time-out occurs it collects all messages from live participants.
3. If any Pi is aborted or if no Pi is committed, it sends abort to all; then undo takes place at all sites.
4. If any Pi is committed, it sends precommit to those who came from D and were stranded in F. After they acknowledge, it sends commit to all in F. Before commit, the redo takes place at each site.

6.6.7 Quorum protocols for link failures

The protocols that we have described so far are not suitable when the networks break and the sites fall apart into isolated clusters. In such a case, each isolated cluster may elect its coordinator. Since in 3PAC a newly elected coordinator ignores failures of some participants and commits or aborts them, when there are isolated clusters each cluster may commit or abort independently, thus causing inconsistency. Several different types of protocols based on voting have therefore been proposed.

In these protocols, a number of coordinators are created at the beginning of each transaction. These coordinators reside at different sites, each independently executing 2PAC or 3PAC with its participants. Two integers — QC (Quorum Commit) and QA (Quorum Abort) — are specified respectively as a quorum for C or A actions. A transaction commits if at least QC coordinators vote to commit and aborts if at least QA coordinators vote to abort. Each participant counts for the required quorum when moving to the commit state from the doubtful state D. This scheme works if QC + QA is greater than the number of coordinators.

The performance of the system depends on the choice of QA and QC. Obviously, when there is one coordinator, this protocol reduces to 2PAC or 3PAC. Increasing the number of coordinators may not always be desirable, since they can slow down the commitment. The performance and practical advantages of quorum protocols are yet to be determined (Skeen 1982).

6.6.8 Crash recovery

Further studies have recently been made concerning crash recovery in distributed systems (see Radhakrishnan et al. 1988). This an important area for research.

EXERCISES

1. Describe how a stable storage can be implemented.
2. Prepare a detailed table about the technology, speed, chunk size and capacity of various types of storage media used in computers.
3. Explain these operations: flush, fetch, pin and unpin.
4. Write a program to create a log of a schedule.
5. Explain the actions of 'redo' and 'undo'. Why are they called 'idempotent'? What will happen if they are not idempotent?
6. Write a program for garbage collection and checkpointing in a log.
7. State the 'Byzantine Generals' Problem'. Why is it analogous to the distributed commitment problem?
8. What is a voting recovery model? Explain its use in understanding the distributed commitment.
9. Explain why no method can guarantee independent recovery of a failed subtransaction.
10. Program SPAC, 2PAC and 3PAC protocols using occam.
11. Study the failures that can arise in the use of time-out. How does one determine time-out in 2PAC and 3PAC in various states?
12. Program the election algorithm in a unidirectional ring.
13. Program the election algorithm for a tree of processors.
14. Program the functions of a newly elected coordinator using occam.
15. Write a program that creates a log of a distributed schedule at each site.
16. Program the quorum-based 2PAC protocol.

REFERENCES

Jones, G. 1987. *Programming in occam*. Prentice Hall, UK.

Radhakrishnan, T., Li, H.F. and Venkatesh, K. 1988. 'Concurrent and domino-free recovery'. In *Distributed Processing*, eds M.H. Barton, E.I. Dagless and G.I. Reijns, 219–35. North-Holland, Amsterdam.

Raynal, M. 1987. *Distributed Algorithms and Protocols*. Wiley, UK.

Raynal, M. 1988. *Networks and Distributed Computation*. MIT Press, USA.

Shrivastava, S.K. 1985. *Reliable Computer Systems*. Springer-Verlag, USA.

Skeen, D. 1982. 'A quorum-based commit protocol'. *Proceedings of the 6th Berkeley Workshop on Distributed Data Management and Computer Networks*, Berkeley, 69–80.

7 Operational transaction processing systems

7.1 INTRODUCTION

In this chapter we will briefly describe some currently operational transaction processing systems (both centralized and distributed) which use the concurrency control and recovery techniques described in earlier chapters. As stated in Chapter 1, the transaction service is basic to database systems, file systems and operating systems. Therefore, when describing these operational transaction processing systems we will follow that classification. Since most of the systems are proprietary, we will be able to set out only the basic principles used in each of them rather than their actual implementation.

As indicated in previous chapters, any operational transaction processing system should have facilities for concurrency control and recovery from failures. In addition, a multisite transaction processing system needs to provide facilities for the following actions:

1. transaction routing (or asynchronous transaction processing): routing the messages from one site to another to execute a transaction at another site;
2. distributed processing: executing a program at one site and invoking a program at another site;
3. data request shipping (or function shipping): executing a program at one site to perform operations on a database at another site.

The flexibility and performance of the methods used for routing, processing and shipping determine to a large extent the types of tasks which the sites can carry out. If a system has facilities for routing transactions but not for distributed processing and data request shipping, we call it a remote transaction processing system. Such a system does not involve concurrent operations on database at different sites. However, if a system has only facilities for distributed processing and data request shipping, we call it a distributed transaction processing system.

In the next section we will first describe two widely used commercial systems for remote and distributed transaction processing:

1. MSC (multiple system coupling);
2. ISC (intersystem communication).

Both these systems were developed by IBM: MSC provides for routing, while ISC provides for distributed computing and data request shipping.

We will then describe AIM (Advanced Information Manager)/SRCF (Shared Resource Control Facility) and IDCM (Integrated Data Communication Manager), developed by Fujitsu (Japan). This will be followed by a brief description of other operational systems — database systems, client-server systems and operating systems that offer transaction services.

Finally, in Section 7.6 we will introduce the language ARGUS that can provide linguistic support for distributed transaction processing. This approach may be gaining recognition and may be widely used by future designers of distributed transaction processing systems.

7.2 COUPLING OF SYSTEMS AND COMMUNICATION

A basic requirement for the design of a distributed transaction processing system is to couple the systems at different sites and provide for data communication and concurrent program execution at different sites. Although several new languages, such as Ada and occam, are now available, many commercial systems use important coupling and communication tools, such as MSC (multiple system coupling) and ISC (Intersystem communication), developed by IBM (see IBM in References), AIM (Advanced Information Manager)/SRCF (Shared Resource Control facility), and IDCM (Integrated Data Communication Manager). These tools have been found very effective for the design of remote transaction processing in IMS and distributed transaction processing using CICS (of IBM) or AIM (of Fujitsu).

7.2.1 MSC/IMS

A remote transaction processing system MSC /IMS has the following features:

1. An end user can invoke a transaction at another site from one site. That is, the end user can enter an input message to invoke a transaction; this message will be placed in the queue at the required site of entry. Then IMS will examine a catalog that indicates whether a local program is available at another site; if one is available, the message is transmitted and the results are returned to the initial site. Thus location transparency is provided, since the end user need not know where the data or programs are located.
2. A local program at one site can invoke a program at another site. The program at another site can invoke a program at yet another site, and so on, with each program using only its local data.

However, both these features allow only routing of messages to invoke separate transactions without any concurrent operations at the different sites; thus they are not subtransactions (or 'cohorts' in the terminology of CICS). As a result, atomicity is not guaranteed with the program invoked at a local site. Each local application program at a site should therefore take care of the recovery at its site; this may result in an inconsistent database.

7.2.2 ISC/CICS

This system allows two or more sites to be connected to carry out both distributed processing and data request shipping. Consequently the end user or an application program (called the 'agent') at one site can:

1. invoke a program (agent) at another site without ceasing its own execution at its site;
2. perform a database operation at another site.

The main advantage of ISC/CICS is that it provides for atomicity of execution of a transaction that can execute subtransactions (called 'cohorts') at different sites concurrently. Thus it provides for recovery of all the subtransactions as one unit.

However, since CICS does not maintain a catalog of the location of programs, it does not provide location transparency. Hence the end user should specify the site of availability of the required program.

On the other hand, CICS provides for access transparency in data request shipping. Each local site has a catalog of the databases available at remote sites; using this, the request will be transmitted to the appropriate site. Then a transaction called a 'mirror transaction' is invoked at the remote site. If it does not perform any updates, it is cancelled; otherwise, the initiating transactions and the mirror transactions are active until the commit point is reached to enable recovery and ensure consistency.

7.2.3 CICS and DB2

In a CICS environment, CICS acts as a scheduler when applications use DB2 as a database management system. That is, DB2 is subordinate to CICS; this combination acts as a database/data communication system.

There are explicit commands to commit (C) and abort (A) a transaction in CICS. Two commands called *syncpoint* and *syncpoint rollback* are respectively used for C and A actions. The user must ensure, by suitably specifying *syncpoint,* that tasks do not exclusively hold resources for an unreasonably long time. If a CICS task terminates normally, CICS commits all changes; if the task terminates abnormally, CICS backs out all changes.

In a CICS transaction processing system, there are various task and interval control commands which can be used to ensure serializability. The task control commands control concurrency using the following facilities:

1. acquiring exclusive control over a resource (X lock);
2. releasing exclusive control over a resource (Unlock X or X*).

The interval control commands provide the following facilities:

1. initiating a process at a specified time;
2. suspending or delaying a process for a specified time interval;
3. starting a process on occurrence of a specified event.

The interval control command mechanisms can be modified suitably to realize timestamp-based concurrency control. For handling recovery, CICS uses logging.

In CICS the abort and associated recovery is known as 'dynamic transaction backout (DTB)'. The log used for DTB is called a dynamic log. If a transaction completes normally, the log is released; hence the log can be reused by other transactions. This helps in saving space in logging. Also, CICS uses the backward recovery method with checkpointing if the whole transaction processing system crashes. This scheme, which is called 'activity keypointing', reduces the time for recovery. CICS also has facilities to handle media failures (such as head crash) by using backup files and logging. CICS and IMS teleprocessing networks consisting of hundreds of terminals are now in regular use.

7.2.4 AIM and RDB II

AIM, a product of Fujitsu (Japan), is a transaction processing system. In conjunction with RDB II (the database management system) it acts as a database and data communication system; 2PL is used for concurrency control and logging is used for recovery. Also, it uses timestamps for breaking deadlocks. Facilities exist for recovery from media failures by using backup files and logging. AIM systems consisting of hundreds of terminals are now in regular use. Recently, Fujitsu has developed AIM/BRIDGE that enables CICS applications to operate under AIM.

7.3 DATABASE SYSTEMS

7.3.1 System R

System R was developed by IBM and has the following key features:

1. It achieves serializability by using two-phase and multigranular locking on a single copy. Also, it provides for lock escalation, the locks being held until commitment or abort of each transaction.
2. It achieves recovery through a two-phase commit protocol using logging and shadowing.

7.3.2 System R*

System R* is a distributed version of system R and was developed by IBM. Each site and each transaction are given unique identifiers. A home site is identified for each transaction. Distributed deadlock is detected by constructing a wait-for graph; deadlock is broken by aborting the transaction which has done the least amount of work.

7.3.3 SQL/DS and DB2

These systems are also IBM products and use techniques similar to R for concurrency control and recovery (see Date and White 1989).

7.3.4 ORACLE

This system is a product of Oracle Corporation. For concurrency control ORACLE uses 2PL and allows additional concurrency through a two-version scheme. For instance, if a transaction 1 wants to do R action on x that is currently under W action by 2, then 1 can read a prevalue without waiting for the release of X lock by 2. However, if 1 wants to read the new value, it has to wait for a X lock on x.

7.3.5 INGRES

INGRES is a product of Relational Technology Inc., and its design was greatly influenced by the UNIX operating system. It provides for complete location transparency. Concurrency control is based on 2PL. The locks are predeclared before execution in centralized schedules in order to avoid deadlocks. Recovery is effected through a two-phase commit protocol (see Malamud 1989). Distributed INGRES uses centralized deadlock detection employing wait-for graphs.

7.3.6 SDD-1

This is a product of Computer Corporation of America (1980). Concurrency control is achieved through the use of timestamps, and recovery is supported through the use of a two-phase commit protocol. The Thomas write-ignore rule is used here.

7.3.7 DDM

This system is also a product of Computer Corporation of America. Concurrency control is based on 2PL with multiversions. Deadlocks are possible and are detected periodically and resolved.

7.3.8 POREL

This system was developed by the University of Stuttgart. It uses 2PL for serializability. To avoid deadlocks, locks are preclaimed. There is a total ordering of sites, and lock requests are not granted unless locks have been granted at preceding sites.

7.3.9 SIRIUS-DELTA

This system was developed by INRIA in France. It uses 2PL with a deadlock prevention strategy.

7.3.10 DDTS

This system was developed by Honeywell Corporation. It uses 2PL and deadlock prevention. Also, it uses a two-phase commitment strategy for recovery and a write-all approach for multiple copies. It supports automatic enforcement of semantic integrity constraints that are user-specified.

7.3.11 RDB II

This system was developed by Fujitsu. It uses 2PL for serializability and logging for recovery.

7.4 CLIENT-SERVER FILE SERVICES

7.4.1 XDFS File Server

This system was developed by Xerox Corporation (Mitchell 1982, 1985; Svobodova 1984). It supports database-oriented applications. For concurrency control 2PL is used; abort and explicit end are used to break deadlocks. XDFS allows three types of locks: read, write, intention write.

The intention write lock allows a transaction to modify its own copy of the file. This intention lock is a soft-write lock which allows other users to read other copies of the files when the lock is on. Before commit, the intention write lock is to be promoted to write lock in order to have exclusive access. Locks are time-limited; this enables one to break deadlocks. When deadlocks are broken in this way, the users are informed. The intention write lock supports atomic transactions by using shadow page and intention log; it also allows multiple files in multiple servers.

7.4.2 Cambridge University File Server

This system was developed at Cambridge University. It uses X lock and S lock, but no deadlock detection algorithms are used. Time-outs are used to break deadlocks. Atomic transactions are supported in single file only. Shadow page and log are used for recovery (see Needham and Herbert 1982).

7.4.3 Swallow

This system was developed by the Massachusetts Institute of Technology. It uses multiple files on multiple servers. The multiple-version timestamping technique is used for concurrency control. Atomic transactions are supported by creating tentative versions. Write-data requests cause a tentative version of the whole file to be created; this is ignored when a transaction aborts.

7.5 DISTRIBUTED OPERATING SYSTEMS

7.5.1 LOCUS

This system is a distributed operating system developed by the University of California at Los Angeles (UCLA). It is essentially a distributed version of UNIX (see Popek and Walker 1985). Operations can be carried out on files at three different sites; a shadow copy is used during transactions. The synchronization of concurrent access to files is done at the synchronization site. There is provision for file locking. Furthermore, LOCUS provides failure transparency. Even if there is a crash, the files will remain in a consistent state.

7.5.2 ACCENT

This system is a distributed operating system developed at Carnegie-Mellon University. It is a communication-oriented operating system (see Rashid and Robertson 1981).

7.5.3 MACH

This system is a distributed system kernel developed at Carnegie-Mellon University, and is an extension of ACCENT. It is suitable for distributed systems and can emulate UNIX. It includes a remote procedure call interface language called Matchmaker that enables distributed programs to be built in any language — for example, C, Ada, Lisp.

7.5.4 CAMELOT (Carnegie-Mellon Low Overhead Transaction)

This distributed operating system was also developed at Carnegie-Mellon University (see Spector 1987). It uses locking and hybrid atomicity. Type-specific locks can also be used (see Schwarz and Spector 1984). Thus semantic concurrency techniques can be implemented through the use of CAMELOT.

A time-out mechanism is used to break deadlocks. Later versions intend using wait-for graphs for deadlock detection. CAMELOT uses the logging procedure rather than the shadow page for recovery. Commit protocols are used for distributed commitment.

7.5.5 Amoeba FUSS

This system was developed by the Vrije University and CWI, both of Amsterdam (see Mullender and Tanenbaum 1985; Tanenbaum and van Renesse 1985). It appears to users as a collection of processes and information objects maintained by servers. Both stable and volatile storages are used. Locks are used for large transactions and optimistic concurrency control for small problems. A multiversion approach based on optimistic concurrency control is used.

Two types of locks are employed, one on version and the other on pages; they resemble hierarchical locks.

7.5.6 APOLLO DOMAIN

This system was developed by Apollo Computer Incorporated (Leach et al. 1983; Levine 1987). Timestamp technique is used here for concurrency control. Provision for locks such as S, X and intention locks exists. There is no waiting for locks, and they are accepted or rejected immediately. When a remote object is locked, the request goes to the database at its home computer, and its timestamp is returned and its out-of-date pages are cleared from its local cache. Before a remote object is unlocked, the modified pages are sent back to its home computer.

7.6 ARGUS: A LANGUAGE SUPPORT SYSTEM

ARGUS was developed to support distributed transaction processing systems. To do so, it organizes and maintains programs that reside at various sites and communicate. ARGUS was developed at the Massachusetts Institute of Technology by Liskov (Liskov et al. 1981; Liskov 1982; Liskov and Scheifler 1983). Its language is based on CLU, an object-oriented language. It allows the user to define abstract data types as in Modula 2. Abstract objects composed of data values and of procedures that operate on the latter may be created dynamically. When programs execute operations on these objects, the data can be accessed and updated concurrently.

A basic atomic activity is called an action. An action is like a transaction: it may complete and commit or abort. Atomic objects are encapsulated within atomic abstract data types. In ARGUS, CLU is extended to provide for atomicity properties based on stable storage. Each ARGUS program manipulates a collection of objects, some of which are in stable storage and some in volatile storage. When the objects are declared stable, they are updated atomically and remain until the process terminates. If a process crashes, the system aborts incomplete transactions, restarts and brings all the stable objects to a consistent state. Thus recovery facilities are available.

An application program consists of a number of actions that make use of modules called *guardians.* A guardian is a basic construct. It provides a controlled access to a resource or a set of resources, and it contains processes which are sequential programs and data objects. While an action is similar to a transaction, a guardian is similar to a server. The processes in a guardian manipulate data objects and can communicate with one another through shared objects.

Several guardians cooperate to realize a distributed system. Each guardian is like a node which supports one or more processes sharing memory; different guardians commmunicate through remote procedure calls, which are handled through interguardian interfaces called 'handlers'. Handlers are essentially subactions (subtransactions), and the calling program in a guardian is suspended until a handler returns the result.

When a number of handler calls are made to the same guardian, the operations can become interleaved. Therefore, synchronization and mutual exclusion are required to preserve consistency, and are achieved by using locks on data objects. Very complex locking schemes can be devised. Also, many versions of a data object can be created for a client; the temporary versions remain transparent to other clients.

A two-phase or three-phase commit protocol can be used to commit actions and maintain interguardian consistency. Thus ARGUS is a very useful language for implementing distributed programs as a client–server model with facilities for concurrency control, recovery and atomicity of actions with different granularities.

We can realize all the functions of a distributed transaction processing system using ARGUS, and thus it provides a powerful linguistic approach to distributed transaction processing. This linguistic approach may gain wider acceptance in view of its simplicity, generality and clean semantics.

EXERCISES

1. Read about the ISC/CICS system. Explain why it is a popular commercial system.
2. What are the basic differences between the MSC/IMS and ISC/CICS systems?
3. Read the original papers of Liskov (and of Liskov and others) on ARGUS in order to understand their likely impact on the design of future distributed transaction processing systems.
4. Try to simulate a guardian, using Modula 2.
5. Use Ada for simulating a subset of ARGUS.
6. Use the References below to determine what is the most popular concurrency control scheme used commercially.
7. Use the References below to determine what is the most popular recovery scheme used in commercial systems.
8. Compare the magnitudes of the different time-outs provided by various commercial systems for deadlock elimination. Try to explain how the magnitudes were arrived at.
9. If you have the facility to use INGRES and ORACLE, compare and contrast the concurrency control and recovery schemes used.
10. How are timestamps provided in SDD-1?
11. Read about the LOCUS operating system. How does it provide for failure transparency?
12. Read about the type-specific locks in CAMELOT. Where are these locks applicable?
13. Read about the Amoeba system. To achieve concurrency control Amoeba uses both optimistic and locking techniques. Comment on each of these schemes from the performance point of view.
14. The APOLLO DOMAIN system uses both timestamps and locks for

concurrency control. Why did the designers provide for both these techniques?

15. Read about ACCENT. How does it provide for communication?
16. If you have facilities to use DB2, examine its locking schemes.

REFERENCES

Computer Corporation of America. 1980. Introduction to a system for distributed databases (SDD-1), *ACM Transactions on Database Systems* 5, 1–68.

Date, C.J. and White, C.J. 1989. *A Guide to DB2.* Addison-Wesley, USA.

IBM Corporation. IMS/VS Version 1 System Administration Guide (IMS/MSC). IBM Form No. SH20–9178.

IBM Corporation. CICS/VS System/Application Design Guide (CICS/ISC). IBM Form No. SC33–0068.

IBM Corporation. IMS/VS Version 1 Programming Guide for Remote SNA Systems. IBM Form No. SH20–9054.

Leach, P.J., Levine, P.H., Douros, B.P., Hamilton, J.A., Nelson, D.L. and Stumpf, B.L. 1983. 'The architecture of an integrated local area network'. *IEEE Journal of Selected Areas in Communication,* SAC-1 (5), 842–56.

Levine, P.H. 1987. 'The Apollo DOMAIN distributed file system'. In *Distributed Operating Systems,* eds Y. Paker, J. Banatre and M. Bozyigit, 241–60 Springer-Verlag, USA.

Liskov, B. 1982. 'On linguistic support for distributed programs'. *IEEE Trans. Software Engineering* 8(3), 203–10.

Liskov, B. and Scheifler, R.W. 'Guardians and actions: linguistic support for robust distributed programs'. *ACM Transactions on Programming Languages and Systems* 5(3), 381–404.

Liskov, B., Atkinson, R., Bloom, T., Moss, E., Craig Schaffert, J., Scheifler, R., Snyder, A., 1981. 'CLU Reference Manual'. In Lecture notes in Computer Science 114, Springer-Verlag, USA.

Malamud, C. 1989. *INGRES.* Van Nostrand Reinhold, USA.

Mitchell, J.G. 1982. *File Servers in Local Area Networks.* Xerox, Palo Alto, Calif.

Mitchell, J.G. 1985. 'File servers, local area networks: an advanced course'. In *Lecture Notes in Computer Science* 184, 221–59. Springer-Verlag, USA.

Mullender, S.J. and Tanenbaum, A.S. 1985. 'A distributed file server based on optimistic concurrency control'. *ACM Op. Syst. Rev.* 19, 51–62.

Needham, R.M. and Herbert, A.J. 1982. *The Cambridge Distributed Computing System.* Addison-Wesley, UK.

Popek, G. and Walker, B. 1985. *The LOCUS Distributed System Architecture.* MIT Press, USA.

Rashid, R. and Robertson, G. 1981. 'Accent: a communication-oriented network operating system kernel'. *ACM Op. Syst. Rev.* 15, 64–75.

Schwarz, P.M. and Spector, A.Z. 1984. 'Synchronizing shared abstract types'.

ACM Transactions on Computer Systems 2(3), 223–50.

Spector, A.Z. 1987. 'Distributed transaction processing and the Camelot system'. In *Distributed Operating Systems,* eds Y. Paker, J. Banatre and M. Bozyigit 331–54. Springer-Verlag, USA.

Svobodova, L. 1984. 'The servers for network-based distributed systems, *ACM Computing Surveys* 16(4), 353–98.

Tanenbaum, A.S. and van Renesse, R. 1985. 'Distributed operating system'. *ACM Computing Surveys* 17, 419–70.

8 Microcomputer platform for transaction processing

8.1 INTRODUCTION

The development of VLSI (very large scale integrated circuit technology), accompanied by the development of the microprocessor, has had a tremendous impact on the price-to-performance ratio of computers over the last decade. Together with these developments, the advances in storage and communication technology have created a revolution in the production of micros (personal computers and intelligent workstations) and associated software systems. The main advantages of these systems over a centralized mainframe system are reduced hardware–software costs, faster response time, flexibility and scalability, and a variety of graphics facilities. Consequently, micros are shedding their 'personal identity' and acquiring a widespread 'business identity'. This new role in business began with their ability to link and communicate with mainframes, minicomputers and other micros, as explained in the next section.

8.2 MICRO-MINI-MAINFRAME LINKS

Initially the communication between a micro and the mainframe or mini was supported by terminal emulation. Soon, however, facilities appeared for transferring data files between a mainframe/mini and a micro (called 'file transfer') for further processing. The transfer of files from mainframe/mini to micro is called 'downloading', while the transfer of files from micro to mainframe/mini for inclusion in corporate databases is called 'uploading'. Access to database management systems from a micro thus became possible, as did several different actions such as extracting information from a mainframe database and downloading it into a micro.

Although the facility for moving data from one environment to another has become available, a program in the micro environment cannot run in the mainframe environment, and conversely. Hence it becomes necessary to introduce what is called a 'seamless link', which can run programs in both the mainframe and micros when these are connected by a LAN. (In the terminology of distributed systems the purpose of this link is to achieve access and location transparency in a heterogeneous distributed network of machines.) Such a link will permit the design of application programs that can use the best features of both the mainframe and micro environments: the micro providing a rich, dynamic interface with graphic facilities and the mainframe permitting the storage of a large database and complex input/output intensive operations. IBM's recent Advanced Program-to-Program Communications Protocol (APPC) establishes such a link.

Furthermore, IBM OS/2 (extended edition v. 1.2) uses APPC to implement remote data services; this allows one OS/2 machine to request data from the database manager on another OS/2 machine in the LAN. Also the APPC provides communication between OS/2 machines and mainframe machines, and thus seamless communication is now a reality. It is this aspect which makes the micros attractive as a platform for distributed transaction processing using the client–server architecture.

8.3 CLIENT-SERVER ARCHITECTURE

In Chapter 1 we briefly described the basic principles of client–server organization and its use in transaction services. The client–server organization splits up the functions of a DBMS into a front end (client) where data is manipulated and displayed and a backend (server) where data is stored and accessed. The clients are generally micros, while the server is either a micro or a multiuser machine, such as a database machine, a minicomputer or a mainframe. The server stores the global data and performs common processing, while the clients perform local processing. The clients are connected to the server by a LAN. The application programs run on the clients and when they require data, the request is shipped to the server. The latter executes the request against the database and the results are shipped back to the client. Thus, as mentioned above, the processing is split between the clients and the server. In the context of transaction processing the server acts as a scheduler and manages the concurrent requests from different clients. It also provides the required recovery and security facilities.

The client–server architecture has been made possible by the development of PC-based operating systems such as OS/2. It has the following specific advantages over an ordinary file-server in a centralized mainframe environment:

1. Flexibility/scalability: It is possible to add or remove servers and clients according to processing needs.
2. Resilience: When a software or hardware failure occurs in one client, another client can be used to continue processing.
3. Performance Improvement: Since the centralized functions are performed by the server and local functions are performed by the client, improved performance is possible.

8.4 CLIENT-SERVER TRANSACTION PROCESSING SYSTEMS

The client–server architecture is useful for the design of both centralized and distributed transaction processing systems. The clients are transactions or actions, while the servers are the transaction managers, schedulers and data managers. As a result, the tasks of maintaining consistency, exclusivity and concurrency and providing recovery from failures are carried out by the server. Different forms of concurrency control and recovery facilities are offered in different commercial client–server systems (Gold-Bernstein 1990).

There are a number of commercial client–server systems using SQL. They are available from Sybase Inc., Gupta Technologies, Relational Technology Inc. and Oracle Corporation (see Dale 1990). A number of client system software are available: IBM's OS/2, UNIX and DEC's VMS. The OS/2 extended edition (EE) includes the OS/2 EE Database Manager, which can access DB2 data. Thus a client in OS/2 EE environment can access data in the server if DB2 is running on the server.

8.4.1 Sybase SQL Server

This system is a relational database server that implements the client–server organization. It communicates with client applications in a server/requester mode. All requests to the SQL server are made using a dialect of SQL called TRANSACT SQL, which is compatible with both IBM DB2 and ANSI SQL standard.

The SQL server consists of two parts: the server and the link-level function, and the procedure call library which runs on the client workstation. Client workstations run on OS/2 or DOS. The server can carry out the parsing, compiling and optimizing of SQL statements as well as query execution and transaction management.

The Sybase server can be classified as a single-server multiclient multithread system (Figure 8.1). Since an application makes a call to one server only, the server performs a complex scheduling when several clients send requests simultaneously. The Sybase system can be extended to a multiserver system, but transparency and distributed query capability are not supported.

This system uses page-level locks. It supports multiple levels of locking in which the least restrictive lock is automatically placed by the system. S and X locks are used as in 2PL. Provision is available for deadlock detection and resolution.

In addition, the Sybase server provides for automatic recovery and uses checkpoints for improving performance. Facilities also exist for mirroring the transaction log as well as the database.

8.4.2 Gupta SQLBase server

This server supports location transparency via its routers, which provide name

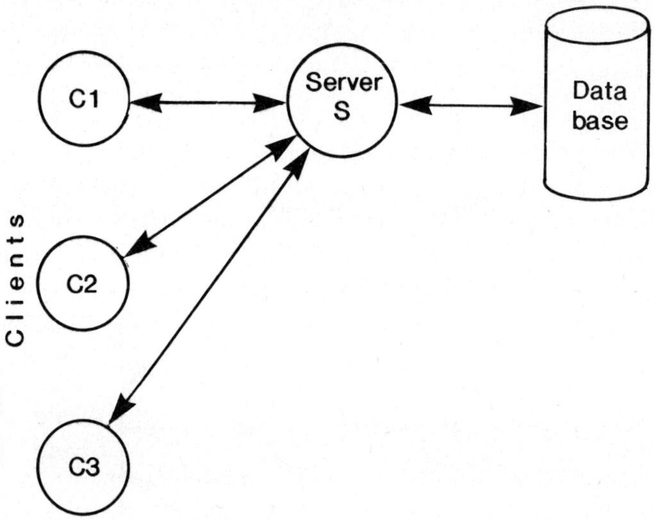

Figure 8.1 Sybase system

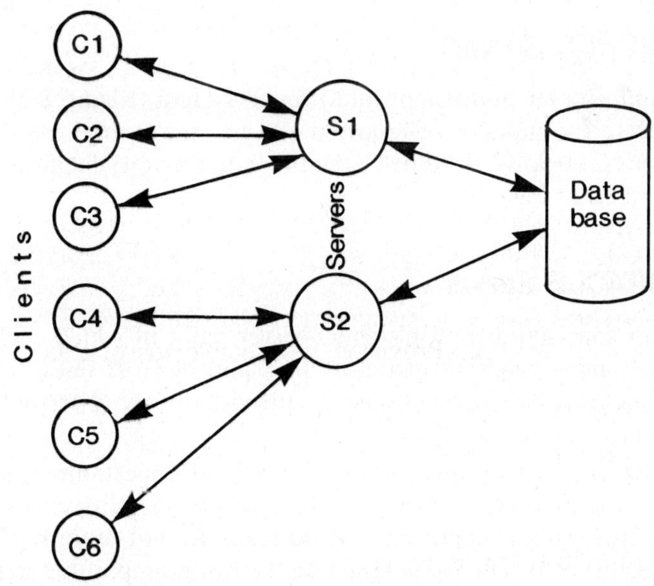

Figure 8.2 Ingres system

services and resolution across database servers and clients on the LAN. It uses granular locking consistent with IBM's DB2. Programmers can choose different granular locks and perform lock escalation. Facilities are available for deadlock detection and deadlock abort by time-outs. Furthermore, this server provides for automatic transaction rollback and recovery using logging.

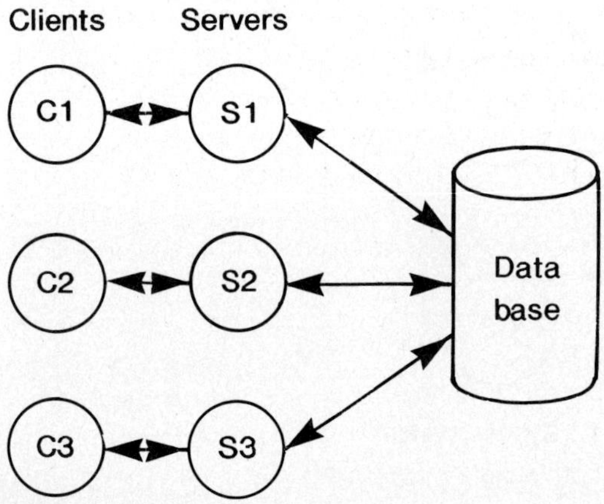

Figure 8.3 Oracle system

8.4.3 INGRES Server

This is a multiserver multiclient multithread system (Figure 8.2). A choice can be made as to the number of required servers and each client can choose any server it needs. Locking, deadlock detection and recovery facilities are similar to those described in Section 7.3.5.

8.4.4 ORACLE Server

This system consists of multiple-client-server pairs in which each server has a single client and a single thread control (Figure 8.3). It does not support distributed updates by transactions; it provides only distributed read-only transactions.

The ORACLE server uses a combination of timestamps and locking for concurrency control. This locking is called 'row-level multiversioning', which, it is claimed, maximizes concurrency. Read locks are not used; read-only transactions see a consistent set of data based on the timestamp of the transaction. This server provides local deadlock detection on a single server and a time-out mechanism for distributed deadlocks. Recovery is effected by using a form of logical log and backup.

8.5 FUTURE TRENDS

Distributed transaction processing over several servers running on hosts across the globe is now a reality. As database interoperable client programs become available, the performance of transaction processing will improve. In the coming years significant developments are expected in the following directions (see Gawlik, Haynie and Reuter (1987)):

1. provision of a distributed architecture that facilitates full portability of applications across heterogeneous software–hardware platforms;
2. robust transaction processing across a heterogeneous environment, including support for servers providing such functionalities as data storage and retrieval, electronic and voice mail, and faxes;
3. development of enterprise-wide network computing that integrates personal computers with corporate minis and mainframes.

EXERCISES

1. Compare the functionalities of the following: cohorts in CICS, coroutines in Modula 2, handlers in ARGUS and the client–server model.
2. Compare the guardian–handler model of ARGUS with the client–server model.
3. Read about Ada rendezvous. Compare its function with MSC of IBM. How can client–server software systems be realized by using Ada?
4. What are the schemes used for locking and deadlock detection in Sybase SQL server, Gupta SQLBase Server and Oracle Server?

REFERENCES

Dale, R. 1990. 'Client–server database: architecture of the Future'. *Database Programming and Design* 3, 29–37.

Gawlik, D., Haynie, M. and Reuter, M. 1987. 'High Perfomance Transaction Systems', *Lecture Notes in Computer Science*, Vol. 359, Springer-Verlag, USA.

Gold-Bernstein, B. 1990. 'Does client–server equal distributed database?'. *Database Programming and Design* 3, 52–62.

Appendix

Contact addresses for further information on products:

DBASE
Ashton-Tate 10150 West Jefferson Boulevard, Culver City, California 90230.

DB2, SQL/DS, CICS, R, R*
IBM Corporation, Programming Publishing, PO Box 50020, San Jose, California 95150.

INGRES
Relational Technology, Inc., 1080 Marina Village Parkway, PO Box 4006, Alameda, California 94501.

ORACLE
Oracle Corporation, 20 Davis Drive, Belmont, California 94002.

RDB II and AIM
Fujitsu Australia Limited, 475 Victoria Ave., Chatswood, NSW 2067.

SDD
Computer Corporation of America, 575 Technology Square, Cambridge, Massachusetts 02139.

Sybase
Sybase, 2910 Seventh Street, Berkeley, California 94710.

Index